UELL S. AN

SUCCESS CYBERNETICS

This ebook was created with StreetLib Write
https://writeapp.io

Table of contents

A WORD FROM THE AUTHOR

This book will shock you. It will make you roaring mad. It will absolutely delight you. It will make you laugh so hard you'll hold your sides. It will intrigue you. It will get you so excited that you jump up and down. It will give you so much horsepower that steam will shoot out of your ears. It will open your eyes. You'll see a brand new world. You'll find a strange machine hidden in your head. And you'll learn how to use that machine to help you get the things you want.

Two things this book won't do: It won't bore you, and it won't make you sad. After you read it, you'll be done with those forever.

It's about a new science, but in a way, it's about me. Training people is my business, and this new science enables me to do it. You'll find me scattered everywhere through these pages, because I have to tell you what's happened to me and what's happened to the people I've trained and how I got to be the way I am and how they got to be the way they are—in order for you to see exactly how to use this new science to help you get the things you want. It can do that and more. It can help you be smarter, healthier, more vigorous, more skillful. It can help you be stronger, more self-reliant, more creative. It can help you communicate better, persuade better, lead better. It can help you overcome adversity, attract opportunity, achieve happiness.

If you're a man, it's going to be the best news you've ever heard. If you're a woman, you may not like it. You'd better read it anyway. Because when it hits the market, there are suddenly going to be a lot of men around, and you'd better get used to how they're going to behave. Once they get here, you'll like the book. You'll realize you've been missing something all along.

Don't let the word cybernetics throw you. It's just a word, and by the time you get through with this book, it won't be any more complicated than cat. The important thing to understand right now is that it's a method for becoming sane—very sane. Clear-eyed sane. Crystal-clear sane. It's a method for seeing exactly what's in the world and how to put the pieces together to get the things you want.

I don't have to tell you that there are all kinds of people. All kinds is the kind that I've trained. I've trained presidents of corporations, scrubwomen, and waiters. I've trained actors and politicians, housewives and artists. I've trained mechanics and longshoremen, sailors and soldiers. I've trained lawyers and bankers, actresses and models. I've trained clerks and typists and secretaries and stenographers. I've trained cops and convicts, cowboys and lumberjacks. I've trained tool makers and architects, salesmen and engineers. I've trained bootblacks and ditch-diggers and news vendors and caretakers. I've trained cab drivers and bellhops and bartenders and belly dancers. I've trained pilots and stewardesses, government workers and club women. I've trained doctors and dentists, teachers and students. I've trained scientists and philosophers, writers and musicians. I've trained blind men and deaf men and men without legs.

That's a pretty fair cross section. It entitles me to say I know something about people. What I know about them is this: They all can be better. They all can be saner, more effective, and much happier— and that's just what they become with Success Cybernetics.

You won't find this a treatise or an argument for a philosophy. You're going to be in my head and in the heads of the people I've trained. You're going to attend seminars and lectures, training programs and bull sessions. Sometimes you're going to be me, sometimes somebody else. You're going to sit in offices and bars and houses and conference rooms. You're going to ride airplanes and automobiles, bulldozers and trucks. You're going to see séances and magic, fraud and illusion. You're going to laugh yourself sick at the things people do. You're going to work in a logging camp, be a deckhand on a freighter. You're going to pilot an airplane and get stuck on a wall. You're going to shuffle cards and tell your own fortune. You're going to get drunk and be struck by a thought. You're going to think your way into the inside of trees. You're going to have a diamond in your head that grows hour by hour. You're going to watch a naked dancer jump over a table. You're going to turn people into magnets and put a horse in an office. You're going to fish and shoot ducks and set off explosions. You're going to be hypnotized and wake up clear-eyed and grinning. You're going to wake up sounder and saner than ever before. You're going to find a world full of joy, drama, and laughter. You're going to get yourself excited. You're going to stay excited. And you'll never be un-excited again.

INTRODUCTION

Here's a wonderful new system of self-development based upon the most recent discoveries of the brain sciences and their close relationship to the computer sciences.

In this book, U. S. Andersen shows you how your brain and nervous system are under the automatic control of your "Mental Computer"—and gives you scores of "computer instruction" techniques for programming this mental computer to automatically increase your skills and performance in any area you choose!

Just as a computer can be programmed, you, too, can rapidly program a "guidance system" and a "power mechanism" into your brain and nervous system—and quickly combine the two into an automatic data processing unit that instantly emits spontaneous success responses to all outside problems.

Cramming his book full of true case histories from his own experience in training people, U. S. Andersen gives you a unique approach to solving all your problems . . . handling people more easily . . . and building automatic success habits into your life through mental programming.

Within these pages you'll discover:

- How to program your mental computer to unleash your greatest potential—under all circumstances and in any situation—and quickly become a winner!
- How to create a power mechanism that turns on your energies and enthusiasm full blast. How to like yourself—enjoy yourself—while blasting full speed ahead to your targets!
- How to program the Success Mechanism into your nervous system so that you respond to signals in the same manner as a guided missile. You'll be astonished at the speed, power and control you'll develop!
- How to use programming techniques to constantly improve your skills and abilities, based on a breathtaking, new discovery about how

the brain functions!

- How to "compute" ideas that are productive and useful and put money into your pocket—and how to cast off worthless ideas!
- How to run your mental data cards through your psychic "scanner" and find quick solutions to unsolvable problems!
- How to "keypunch" your mental data cards to attract opportunity into your mental computer. Throw luck out the window once and for all. Become a magnet for enterprises that are destined for success!
- How to operate your mental computer to gain lasting happiness—how to use it to make others happy—how to not only succeed, but how to have fun doing it!
- . . . plus much, much more!

Yes, just as machine "cybernetics" is revolutionizing the technological world, so brain "cybernetics" is revolutionizing the world of man's performance. . . because it synchronizes your goals with the automatic responses which will achieve them for you.

Machine cybernetics already has taken man into outer space. Human cybernetics seems certain to uncover the vast potentials of his inner world—unlocking immense powers of the mind!

·1· HOW TO USE THE NEW SCIENCE OF SUCCESS CYBERNETICS

WHEN YOU SET the thermostat on the wall of your room at seventy degrees and the temperature in the room falls below seventy, your furnace comes on. That's cybernetics—the science of automatic control. It's given us the automatic pilot, the fire control mechanism, the guidance system in missiles, the automated assembly line, and the electronic computer. It puts a brain in machines, a brain that responds automatically to signals, quickly and efficiently, performing hundreds of accurate calculations in a split second, and it's taught us how to train the human brain and nervous system to the same kind of performance.

HOW TO PREACH SERMONS AND WIN FOOTBALL GAMES

Success Cybernetics is automatic control that hits a selected target. If the automatic control misses the selected target, that's failure cybernetics.

There was this preacher who never could remember the names in his sermon, so he'd pin them inside his coat and refer to them as he preached. One Sunday, he started out by saying, "And the Lord created the first man, and his name was —Adam. Then the Lord created the first woman, and her name was—Eve. Then Adam and Eve had a son, and his name was—Robert Hall. Oops!"

There are computers which occasionally function like that, only they never say, "Oops!" A guy with a bank balance of $2.98 gets a statement that shows he's got $298,000.00 in the bank. But it's pretty tough to get that money out. Somebody is almost certain to wake up to the fact that the computer made a mistake, and the machine is then fixed. But there are people who keep acting their whole lives long as if Cain were Robert Hall or they've got three hundred thousand on deposit when they've got only three. But now they can be fixed too, in just the same way as the computer is fixed. With Success Cybernetics.

Success Cybernetics synchronizes goals with the automatic responses which will achieve those goals. If you aim at a target and hit it, your goal and responses are synchronized, and you're using Success Cybernetics. If you aim at a target and miss it, your goal and responses are unsynchronized, and you're using failure cybernetics. Everybody uses one or the other. I've had experience with both. I remember my experience with failure cybernetics well. I played on a Stanford football team that lost eight straight games.

Were our goals and responses synchronized? Judge for yourself.

Just prior to the last game of the season, we were going back to New York City to play Dartmouth, when one of the boys on the team came up to the coach and said, "Coach, this is the last game of the season. After this, we can break training, can't we?" The coach looked at him with big, sad eyes. "What are you going to do now?" he asked. "Take dope?"

HOW TO BUILD TOWERS AND TURN ON THE COFFEE

There are success responses and there are failure responses, and no athlete ever became a winner by doing his training in night clubs. There was a sports writer on the San Francisco Chronicle who must have been a cybernetician himself. He wrote a column that was headed, "Stanford Team Six Inches from Success." His subhead read, "That Six Inches Is Between Their Ears."

It's with the automatic responses that exist in the six inch span between our ears that Success Cybernetics is concerned. A computer can be built so complex and sophisticated that it can guide a missile to Mars and take pictures after it gets there, but if they put the wrong responses into that computer, it couldn't turn on your coffee. The human brain is like that. No telling what it's capable of. Nobody's using more than a fraction of its potential. Don't take my word. They'll tell you that at every brain research laboratory in the country. But people train responses into the brain when they're five years old, like crying to get candy, then wind up frustrated and surprised when that response doesn't produce money when they're thirty. That brain can make all the money its owner asks it to. It just has to be trained with success responses. It's like the computer that sent the missile to Mars, but which most people use to turn on the coffee.

How many storage cells are there in the largest computer ever made? Forty thousand. How many storage cells in the human brain? Ten billion—two hundred thousand times the capacity of the largest computer ever built. That's the kind of fabulous machine you and I carry around between our ears, and Success Cybernetics is concerned with training the responses into it that will enable the use of its full capacity. The cat's now out of the bag. The brain builds towers as easily as it turns on the coffee. How you use it is up to you.

HOW TO TYPEWRITE AND PLAY THE PIANO

You see, over at IBM or Rocket-dyne or General Information Systems, when they want a computer to perform a certain job, a group of people sit around the room and design the attitudes and habits that will enable the computer to accomplish its goal. These People are called programmers, and the attitudes and habits they design are called a program. They install the program in the memory of the computer, and when they press a button, they get a success-response. If they don't get a success-response, they don't throw away the computer or say it's stupid or hasn't any talent or is a natural-born loser. No, indeed. They know there's nothing wrong with the machine except its attitudes and habits, and they simply pull them out of the computer and redesign them until they get a success-response. In short, the machine functions only as well as its habits and attitudes, and now Success Cybernetics has proven that people are just the same way.

For example, when you first learn how to typewrite, you have to think, "Which finger hits which key?" and your typing is slow and full of mistakes. If you accept that as your standard and adopt the attitude that you're a bad typist, you set that program into your nervous system and remain a bad typist as long as that program operates. But if you set up an attitude to become a good typist, that programs your nervous system so that your subsequent typing trains you into success habits. Then a day arrives when you can look at a sentence on a piece of paper or think of a sentence in your mind, and your fingers automatically transcribe that sentence onto the paper in the typewriter, responding to signals accurately and efficiently like the thermostat on the wall, the guidance system in a missile, or the program in a computer. The same thing happens when we learn how to play a piano, drive an automobile, fly an airplane, drive a golf ball. We set attitudes and habits into the nervous system and they determine the success of our efforts. Maybe it takes some off the frosting off the heavenly cake to regard the human body as a complex machine, but the moment we begin to realize it is, we are well on the way to getting its best performance. Mystics will still argue for a little man in the skull, and there he may dwell for all anyone knows, but his hand isn't on the helm, there's an automatic pilot, and the best he can do is to see that pilot is properly programmed to reach its goal. The brain and the nervous system comprise a computer-like machine and must be treated as such to achieve successful performance.

HOW TO PLAY CHESS WITH A LEARNING MACHINE

You say a machine can't learn? Are you in for a surprise! It started in the laboratories of IBM. One day, a bunch of computer scientists were gassing about what computers could do, and one smart aleck chirped, "Wouldn't it be something if we could teach this machine to learn?" That was a knee slapped. When they stopped holding their stomachs and started drying their eyes, the smart aleck continued, "Wait a minute. What causes learning? It's just an attitude, isn't it? And can't we set an attitude into a computer? All we have to do is design a circuit that says, 'Periodically, I'm going to go over the things I've done and throw out the things that didn't work and keep the things that did work and try some things that look like they might work.' Now that shouldn't be so hard to do." In an instant, the big joke became theory, and they set to work to build a learning machine.

When it was finished, they stored in its memory the standard moves of a game of chess. Then they called in ten chess players. Two of them were rank amateurs, two highly skilled professionals, the rest scaled between. They were told, "Boys, play the machine." The boys played the machine. They all beat the machine. Then they were told, "Play it again, and again, and again." And the third time around the computer beat the two amateurs, and the thirtieth time around it had beaten everybody but the two professionals, and here was a machine designed to learn and to keep on learning and to constantly improve its skills and abilities. Who can say as much for people?

It's no great secret that IBM keeps this computer under wraps. It would throw so many vice-presidents out of work that we'd be up to our hips in private washroom keys. Is there any choice between a machine that keeps learning and one that has already decided to stop? IBM ran a few learning machines off the assembly line. The first one scared hell out of them. They decided to ask it a question to which nobody knew the answer. They asked it, "Is there a God?" The little slip of paper came out and said, "There is now!" Don't panic—that's apocryphal.

HOW TO DO IT YOURSELF, SOMETIMES IN AN INSTANT

Mainly, the learning machine woke up the psychologists, who had been slumbering peacefully for years. But since the machine had no id or childhood traumas and would not lie on a couch and free associate, they were at a loss as how to deal with it. Nevertheless, something had to be done. The machine could replace people, and they were people themselves. So they took their hats in their hands and humbly consulted the computer scientists as to whether this learning technique could be applied to humans. "Sure," they were told, "it's only an attitude." The silt hit the fan.

What of the great god Freud and his mysteries? What of the labyrinthine depths of the subconscious mind? It was nonsense to think that something so simple could work with the complex Freudian mind. A dignified exit was in progress when a computer scientist remarked gently, "You fellows ought to have the machine's attitude. It throws out the things that don't work and tries the things that look like they might work." A couple of guys at the rear overheard that remark. It started them thinking. They decided to do something about it, and the cybernetics of the mind was born.

Over at Columbia University they took a bunch of bad spellers and put them in a class and told them they were good spellers. Everybody began to spell better. They took a bunch of kids who couldn't do math and told them they were good at it. Everybody improved at math.

They took some people who were lousy public speakers and told them they were good speakers. No more lousy speakers. Amazing. A person's attitude determined what he could learn, just like the machine. But nobody believed it except the people who saw it. Why should they? Everybody is addicted to his own pet complexity. If you don't believe that, have an attorney draw up some papers saying, "The cat caught the rat." You'll get fifteen pages which nobody understands.

So the Freudians continued to pour out their jargon—id, ego, super-ego, ad infinitum. The kid who was a bad speller had suffered a trauma when he misspelled a word and the class all laughed, The cyberneticians were only curing the trauma with support psychotherapy, and without a license to practice to boot. Let them try out their nonsense on some psychotics, then they'd see. The cyberneticians obliged. They went to a funny-farm and told a few inmates, "You're sane." The inmates became sane. Ten thousand tomes on psychology became obsolete overnight, and a grinding of teeth sounded in scent-laden offices from Los Angeles to New York. No sense probing the past when the issue was clear. Attitude determines human performance. If the performance is poor, just change the attitude. That doesn't take five years at twenty-five dollars a week. You can do it yourself, sometimes in an instant.

HOW TO GET BLACK EYES AND BECOME A BAD SALESMAN

The only thing difficult is that attitudes become habits, and the only problem with changing them is that we use them to think. That's the trouble with us humans. We think that we're thinking when we're making elaborate rationalizations to justify our responses, which are often bizarre and produce continual defeat.

Here's a kid five years old who goes out in the street and gets in a fist fight and comes up with a black eye and runs home crying. Next week another fight, another black eye. The week after that, he comes up with a bloody nose. It gradually dawns on him that it might be a good idea to stay off the street. So he stays away from the other kids. He keeps his mouth shut if they talk to him. He sits in the corner at parties. No black eyes. The attitude works fine. And so he keeps on using it day after day, month after month, year after year. Just like learning how to typewrite, just like learning how to play a piano, just like learning how to drive a car, he builds a habit into his nervous system—an automatic response.

Then this kid gets to be thirty years old, and he takes a job as a salesman. The first day out, he raises his hand to knock on a door and suddenly feels sick to his stomach. It must be the flu, he rationalizes, and goes home to sleep it off. Next day, he doesn't make it out of the car, because reading in the paper that there's a financial recession, he rationalizes: What's the use in calling on anybody, they won't have any money. That gives him time to examine his product carefully, and he rationalizes a lot of flaws in it, so eventually he doesn't leave the house at all. Why should he? Nobody would buy the product anyway. And all the time he believes that he's thinking.

Eventually his sales-manager calls him in and asks him how he expects to sell anything when he never sees anybody, and this kid, grown to thirty but still using attitudes and responses that kept him from getting a black eye when he was five, recites a tale of woe and hardship likely to bring tears to anyone's eyes but a sales-manager's, perfectly logical, perfectly reasonable, seemingly factual, and completely hogwash. It is the same kind of logical garbage that drowns us with words in newspapers, books, and magazines, and gives people the illusion that they're thinking when they're only reacting and often most poorly. Just "the cat chased the rat," blown up into fifteen pages of logical obscurity. Reason is a smokescreen. People don't think, they react. And they react the way they've been trained to react. And when they react poorly they explain it with reasons. Ipso facto, we get the ego and id and the Oedipus complex and power drives and deprivation complexes and penis envy, which make mighty fine fiction if you're allergic to fact.

HOW TO DANCE AROUND A CAMPFIRE WITHOUT BRINGING RAIN

People are what their experience has conditioned them to be. If experience has conditioned them to failure responses, they must be reconditioned to success responses in order to achieve goals. This is not done by investigating the past. Who cares what caused it? What changes it is what matters. And changing it is done in the present.

Let's face it. Short of physical disability, which is the province of physical medicine, the only reason people wind up on the psychiatrist's couch or in a mental institution is because they're trying to reach goals with failure responses. That produces frustration. Frustration unglues the brain and nervous system. It can be laid to the will of God or the Oedipus complex or astrology or just plain bad luck, but that doesn't cure it. The only thing that cures it are success-responses. And success responses can be trained into the brain and nervous system in the very same way that failure responses were trained into it. Pavlov proved it. It's being done every day with rats, dogs, horses, and people. Why is it ignored? For my money, it's for the same reason that an Indian dances around the fire to bring rain. No self-respecting rat would continue such efforts in the face of centuries of frustration. He has no imagination.

That the Indian kids himself is clear to most people. What isn't clear to most people is that they too kid themselves anytime they justify continuing a habit that produces failure. Either they become frustrated, or if they rationalize the failure, deluded. In either case, they're nonfunctional, just complex machines programmed for failure. Yet today anyone can change failure habits to success habits. That's Success Cybernetics.

The nervous system is a habit robot. It makes automatic responses to signals the same way as the thermostat on your wall. If it doesn't turn on the furnace, it needs better habits.

HOW TO TALK TO A BRAIN

Cyberneticians are tenacious guys. When they found out you couldn't always make a good speller out of a bad speller by telling him he was a good speller, they looked into the matter further, making continual comparisons between the nervous system and the functioning of a computer. The problem was how to get success experience into the nervous system when failure experience had become a habit. A guy with a nervous system trained to failure was on a treadmill. He continued to produce more failure experience and ingrained his failure habits even further. If he was young enough, you might get him to change his habits by telling him he was different, but for most people habits were so deeply ingrained that they couldn't be changed by words or will power. The only thing that could change them was new experience. It was the old ploy about leading a horse to water but not being able to make him drink.

Then somebody got to thinking about machine language and the fact that it was only electricity. At the input terminals of the computer, words and numbers are converted to electrical current which circulates through the machine, is modified by the attitudes and responses of the machine, then is delivered to the output terminal where it once again is converted into words or numbers. "Hey!" he cried, "that's the same way the nervous system works! At the input terminals of the senses, sights and sounds are converted into electrical current. Electrical current circulates through the nervous system and is modified by attitudes and responses, then is delivered to the output terminals of the lips, tongue, voice box, hands, fingers, and feet, where it is converted into actions." This was interesting, sure enough.

HOW TO READ A NEW KIND OF STOCK MARKET GRAPH

Then the cyberneticians got real cute. They decided to investigate what went on in the brain when it was having experience. They got some people together, attached electrodes to their heads, led the electrodes to an encephalograph machine so they could record the brain waves, then had a lot of odd events transpire in the room. A woman screamed, somebody fired a gun, a dog ran across the room. Then everyone clustered around the brain wave graphs to see how the brain had reacted. What they saw looked like a stock market graph.

" I've got an idea," somebody hollered. "What we're looking at on that paper was caused because a portion of the brain was tickled by electricity, right? Light from a dog was converted to electricity at the retina, passed over the optic nerve and tickled a tiny portion of the brain, and the person saw a dog. The dog was in his head, even though it was caused by a dog outside his head, true? Now what would happen if that person imagined a dog?"

Everyone began talking at once, but the upshot was that nobody could account for the imagined dog on any other basis than that the same tiny portion of the brain was tickled by the same kind of electricity. Presto! They whipped blindfolds over the eyes of the people who had electrodes on their heads and asked them to imagine a gunshot, a woman's scream, and a dog running across the room. Then they recorded the brain waves of the imagined experience and compared it to the brain waves of the real experience. The two brain waves were absolutely identical!

They sat down weakly and considered this revolutionary fact: The nervous system didn't know the difference between a real and an imagined experience! Therefore it followed that imaginary experience was just as much a conditioner of attitudes, responses, and habits as real experience! Therefore it appeared that a person could condition himself to success responses by using his imagination to create success experience!

HOW TO SHOOT GOLF, PLAY CHESS, AND MAKE BASKETBALL SHOTS

They put this theory to test at the University of Chicago. They called in some kids from the undergraduate school, divided them into three groups, had them throw basketballs at a basket, then scored their ability to make goals. Then they took the first group and told them, "We want you kids to come out to the gym for one hour a day and practice throwing the basketball through the basket." They took the second group and told them, "We want you kids to forget about basketball. Don't touch a basketball. Don't even think about it." They took the third group and told them, "We want you kids to get by yourselves for one hour each day and imagine yourself successfully throwing the basketball through the basket."

At the end of thirty days they gave the three groups another test. The kids who had actually practiced one hour a day showed an increase in performance of twenty-four percent. The kids who hadn't practiced at all showed no increase in performance. And the kids who had practiced one hour a day only in their imaginations showed an increase in performance of twenty-three percent! There it was. The nervous system didn't know the difference between real experience and imagined experience. Successful performance in the imagination could create success habits.

Here's a conversation with Johnny Wooden, head coach of the national champion U.C.L.A. basketball team. Question: "Johnny, do you ever have your boys mentally rehearse their shots?" Answer: "It's my first rule. Unless a kid can clearly visualize the basketball going through the basket, there's no chance he can throw it in when he has to."

Artur Schnabel rehearsed piano playing in his head; Capablanca rehearsed chess playing in his head; Ben Hogan rehearsed golf shots in his head; every successful artist, athlete, businessman, salesman, whether he's aware of it or not, constantly rehearses successful performance in his head. That's what builds into him the habitual attitudes and responses that cause him to perform successfully in actual situations. And every failure, whether he's aware of it or not, is constantly rehearsing failure performance in his head. That's what builds into him the habitual attitudes and responses that cause him to perform unsuccessfully in actual situations. And I'm not talking about positive thinking. All the positive thinking in the world won't make the basketball go through the hoop if you throw it out the window. I'm talking about conditioning success responses into the brain and nervous system through mental rehearsal.

HOW TO USE SOME STUFF YOU DON'T REALLY NEED

The story is told of a positive thinker who fell out of a fifteenth story window. Every time he passed a floor, people on that floor could hear him say, "So far, so good." Same as the Indian dancing around the campfire to bring rain, right? Maybe it keeps him stupidly happy, but he's in for a surprise. It won't rain, and the ground is moving up fast.

The trouble with positive thinking is that most people think it's magic. They think you can move the world with thought. They sit in their rooms and try getting things done by being optimistic. So what happens? Nothing. Just the Indian endlessly dancing around the campfire.

The only thing positive thinking can move is you! And the way it moves you is the way it conditions your responses. If you think you're going to move the world by being optimistic, you naturally do nothing. You don't even throw the basketball out the window. You let it sit on the floor and try to wish it through the net. The guy in the funny-farm who thinks he's Napoleon is a positive thinker for sure. The only difference between him and the Indian is that he's in and the Indian is out. In view of their results, both are somewhat over-optimistic, proving that attitude is not everything. Right action and realistic goals are just as important. Since the Indian and the pseudo-Napoleon have neither, their attitudes produce only illusion.

Goals, attitudes, and actions can be called a man's motivation.

Some people have trouble with that word. I remember coming back to Detroit with the Detroit Lions after we'd won a surprise victory over the Chicago Bears, and walking into the old Savarine Hotel to be greeted by the old janitor who was all smiles. "You won!" he exulted. "How did you do it?" I answered, "Because we had motivation." That old man scratched his head and looked puzzled. "Motivation?" he asked. "What position do he play?"

You can be assured it's an important position. But psychologists persist in looking for motives in motivation, rather than regarding it as the sum total of a man's habits. They tell us some people are motivated by love. I once heard of a man who wanted to learn a little something about love. He bought a big book called *How to Hug*. He didn't learn much. It turned out to be Volume 6 of the Encyclopedia Britannica. Some good signal response might have saved him a few bucks. What difference does it make why people do things? They do them out of habit, that's all we have to know, and the habits are either success habits or failure habits, and if they're failure habits they can be changed to success habits by creating success experience in the mind.

HOW TO MAKE A BIG SCORE FAST

A number of years ago I ran my first seminar. Thirty salesmen and five sales-managers were in the group. They were being told about success habits and failure habits, and during a coffee break one of the sales-managers came up to me, chuckling. "You know," he said, "I've got a guy working for me that's a living example of what you've been talking about, though I never understood him before. When he came to work for me, I thought I'd found a gem. He was personable, intelligent, well-educated, and fine looking. I trained him for three months and gave him the best territory in the company. He should have made $30,000 a year. He worked there a year and made $7,000. The head office threw a fit and told me to fire him. I just couldn't bring myself to do it, so I gave him the worst territory in the company. I figured he'd quit and I'd be saved the embarrassment of firing him. He worked in that bad territory a year. He made $7,000. Boy, I thought, this guy's really caught fire. I brought him back in and gave him the best territory.

He worked there a year. You know what he made? $7,000!"

Here was a guy whose nervous system obviously was conditioned to an income of seven thousand dollars a year. When that sum was reached, rationalization set in. He was like a powerful car capable of going one hundred fifty miles per hour, but he was running around with a governor on his engine that kept him from going over thirty. Failure habits take many forms, and one of the most pernicious is putting a low ceiling on performance.

Those early training programs were fun because when we pulled off a miracle we got excited; later it became matter-of-fact. That guy who never made more than seven thousand a year is now making more than thirty thousand a year because his sales-manager put him through Success Cybernetics and conditioned his nervous system for achievement. And that sales-manager doesn't harangue his salesmen or scare them or beguile them with prizes. He trains them in success habits, and he runs the top division in the country.

HOW TO PLAY MUSIC YOU'D LIKE TO PERFORM TO

So how does Success Cybernetics train people to achieve success? First, it has them set goals. Then it has them list the actions that will achieve those goals. Then it has them list the attitudes that will allow them to take those actions. Actions are a guidance mechanism. Attitudes are a power mechanism. Together they make up a success mechanism, just as is programmed into a missile or the memory unit of a computer. Cybernetics Success Training installs the success mechanism into the nervous system by practicing it until it becomes habit.

First, the success mechanism is carried about on a card, and the person conscientiously performs the actions and adopts the attitudes each day. Second, he rehearses the actions in his mind until he can clearly visualize them. Third, he rehearses the attitudes in his mind until he can clearly feel them. Fourth, he repeats the elements of his success mechanism to himself at night before falling asleep, thus giving each of the elements the suggestive power of auto-hypnosis. And fifth, and most important of all, he creates only success experience in his mind.

Simple, isn't it? Conditioning is always simple. Pavlov conditioned his dogs to salivate when a bell was rung. No food was present, but they salivated anyway. Automatic response is the hallmark of the nervous system, and it can be trained any way we choose.

Why do I say that the most important element of Cybernetics Success Training is to play only success experience in your mind? Because if you allow failure experience to transpire in your mind, it conditions your nervous system for failure. Sometimes I have people imagine they've got two record cabinets in their heads. One group of records carries success experience. The other group carries failure experience. If they find themselves playing failure experience on the imagination's turntable, they simply switch records. The nervous system responds according to what it has experienced.

HOW TO HOLD ONTO YOUR HEAD

Pause to reflect on the number of people who are trying to get themselves back on the beam by reviewing failure experience. This is called psycho-analysis. They go over and over the same failure experiences—defeat, guilt, sadness, loneliness, and nausea. So what happens? They condition their nervous systems for more failure. If finally they can be talked into accepting their failure, they are discharged as cured. That's like curing a broken leg by cutting it off. Not that that isn't sometimes tried. They'd amputate our heads if the cyberneticians would let them. That's a sure way to eliminate worry.

So how do you use Success Cybernetics? First, you make up your mind that you can condition yourself into any attitude, response, or habit you desire. Don't worry about that. You'll be firmly convinced by the time you finish this book. Secondly, you create for yourself a personal success mechanism consisting of the goals you want to achieve and the attitude-habits and the action-habits that will achieve them. Effective attitudes are derived from an expansive self-concept. An expansive self-concept attacks. A limiting self-concept retreats. We'll go into details about this in later chapters. Finally, you train the success mechanism into your nervous system by daily practice, both mentally and physically.

Meantime, remember these four mental conditioning laws: 1. You are what you concentrate on. 2. What you concentrate on seems real. 3. What you concentrate on grows. 4. You always find what you concentrate on.

In these four laws lies the power of cybernetics to condition the nervous system to success.

·2· HOW TO FIND AND DEVELOP YOUR GREATEST POTENTIAL

PEOPLE DON'T BELIEVE possible what hasn't happened to them. This little axiom accounts for all mediocrity. A guy once stood on a street-corner and tried to sell twenty dollar bills for a dollar. Nobody would buy them, and he wound up in jail. Everyone is always gushing because so-and-so has such talent. Mozart wrote sonatas when he was eight years old. His father was a musician. The world calls Mozart a musical genius. But this maestro of the keyboard would never have learned how to play chopsticks if he'd been born in darkest Africa and had never seen a piano. A man is the product of how he reacts to his environment. Sure, heredity counts for something. If you've got two heads, you have to wear two hats.

HOW TO GET A BIG PRESENT WITH A BLUE RIBBON

Ever hear of anyone climbing a mountain who didn't want to? Then why should you believe that people become excellent by accident? People become excellent by first believing that excellence is possible to them, then doing something about becoming excellent. Some people sit at the foot of the mountain and try to wish themselves up to the top. Others keep looking at the top of the mountain and figuring out reasons why the thing is too high. Some postpone the ascent until they get around to it or are sure they won't fail. Still others keep their eyes on the ground at their feet. This allows them to find worms.

Notice how a man gets to the top of the mountain. He first sees it is there. He secondly sees it is possible to climb. Third, he decides to get to the top. And fourth, he starts climbing. This simple sequence of events accounts for the development of all skills and abilities.

Not long ago I went to a benefit show with a friend. During the performance, a guy juggled fifteen plates in the air. It looked like an invasion of flying saucers. Afterwards, I asked, "Wasn't it remarkable how well he juggled those plates?" My friend answered laconically, "What was remarkable was not how well he did it, but that he could do it at all."

That set me to thinking. Here's a kid who learns how to juggle two plates.

Whatever possesses him to think he can handle fifteen? Then it came to me. He tries to handle one more. Before he can become a fifteen-juggler he has to become a three-juggler, then a four-juggler, and so on. And now he's become a fifteen-juggler, by a process of juggling one more plate. A man climbs a mountain by taking one more step. And people rise from mediocrity to excellence by the same step by-step process.

Ah, the agonies of the poor souls who wish they had talent. They act as if excellence were a package under the Christmas tree, and Santa Claus a fink for leaving them out. Everybody got the same present, with a blue ribbon too—a billion dollar computer between his ears. All anyone has to do is program it for excellence. It's got capacity to spare.

HOW TO DISCOVER AMERICA, OR ANYTHING ELSE

I ran a seminar for middle-management executives. One walked around for two days wringing his hands. "If I could just discover my talent," he moaned, "then I could really take off." I kept telling him, "One doesn't discover a talent, one decides on it." But he had me tuned out. He liked the problem better than the solution. Finally, it bugged me. If he insisted on a search, I'd give him one.

I wrote something on a piece of paper, put it in an attaché case, locked the case, hid it, handed the key to the no-talent executive. "Somewhere in this room there is an attaché case," I told him. "In it is the secret of your hidden talent. You have the key that unlocks the case.

Find it, and the answer is yours."

He spent a happy half-hour hunting around the room while everybody else paid attention to the seminar. Finally he found the attaché case, opened it and read the paper. Not a peep out of him. He looked as if he'd been hit over the head. After the seminar he didn't even say goodbye. Today, he's a vice-president.

Sure, it was corny. But sometimes you have to be. Nobody hears what they don't pay attention to. So I got his attention. That was enough. What was on the slip of paper? Only this sentence: "Columbus discovered America because he decided it was there."

One day I tried to teach my son how to ride a bicycle. He was eager and enthusiastic. Then he fell off. He wasn't hurt, but he sat on the curb and cried. I asked him why he was crying. He wailed, "Because I can't ride a bicycle." I sat down on the curb and cried with him. It suddenly hit me that grown-up boys have the same problem. They try to juggle fifteen plates, and when they can't, they think it's a law.

I finally told him nobody was born able to ride a bicycle. People learned. All you had to do was decide that you wanted to. The rest was training. So he pushed it around. He put one foot on a pedal and used it as a scooter. At last he was able to stay aboard it. Finally he could start me shuddering as he went flashing by, hollering, "Look, dad. No hands!"

HOW TO GET GOOD BY NOT DOING NOTHING

Talent, ability, skill—why beg the question? The answer is training. People excel because their nervous systems are trained to excellent responses. They didn't get that way by accident. They trained themselves.

I was born in the sawmill district of Portland, Oregon. People worked in the mills or on the log-booms in the Willamette and Columbia Rivers, and they worked twelve hours a day, when they worked. One summer vacation, while I was going to Stanford University, I got a job in the loading yard of one of those mills, unloading flat cars of two inch thick, twelve-inch wide, twenty-foot long, soaking-wet planks of rough lumber. I took the job because it was piece work. We got paid for each car we unloaded. I was a big strong guy, and I figured I'd make some money with my muscles. At ten A.M. on the first day, I quit.

I'd had it. I was beat. I ached all over. I told my partner, a little sinewy Irishman half my size that I couldn't work any longer because it hurt.

He chewed tobacco. He always had a wad of it in his mouth, and it puffed out one cheek so he looked like half a chipmunk. He let fly a stream of tobacco juice that peeled the paint from the siding. Then he growled, "You have to keep doing it when it hurts in order to be able to do it."

I cleared the sweat from my eyes and peered at this runt. There he stood, fresh as a daisy. It was unbelievable. "Get back up on that flat car," he ordered. He shamed me into it.

For two weeks he grinned while I suffered. The more he grinned, the madder I got. Then and there, I made a decision. I'd get so good at this thing I'd wear out that runt. I fumbled and stumbled and puffed and strained and ached. The weeks went by. I didn't ache any more. I started to get good. I never did wear out that runt, but the last month of that summer each of us made more money than the superintendent of the mill.

How do you find your greatest potential? Just like Columbus, you decide that it's there. How do you develop your greatest potential? Just like Andersen stumbling around on top of that flat car, you train yourself for better performance.

HOW TO TAKE OUT THE GARBAGE BEFORE IT'S TOO LATE

They asked me to address the Building Material Dealers Convention in Palm Springs. Before my talk a guy came up to me and started blowing the whistle of doom. "Things are bad," he groaned. "Southern California is overbuilt. The whole industry will have to retrench. There'll be a lot of failures this year. What are you here for?" I told him I was going to talk about data processing. He wanted to know what that was. I told him it was like when you had garbage in the house, you had to take the garbage outside. He looked somewhat puzzled. I hope the speech clarified it for him.

I called the speech GIGO, for Garbage In, Garbage Out. I pointed out that garbage was something you couldn't use, and what everybody in the room couldn't use was the idea that things were bad and the industry would have to retrench. Data processing was the science of sending useful information through a computing machine to get answers about how to take action. And the best piece of useful information for everybody to put in his think-tank right now was that every building in America would have to be duplicated within forty years.

They gave me a standing ovation. Nobody wants to be told that it can't be done, he wants to be told that it can.

A man finds his greatest potential by deciding that he has it, and he develops it by training. What he comes up with in the end may look like a blinding talent, but it's really a self-creation. That genius is one percent inspiration and ninety-nine percent perspiration is an a old saw but true. If you found it hidden in an attaché case, maybe you'd listen.

How do they find a computer's potential? By deciding that they want that computer to do something better. How do they develop that computer's potential? By training its responses to do a better job. The same thing applies to your human computer. You carry a data processing machine between your ears. Give it instructions for growth, and it will produce more talent than Midas had gold.

Oh, I know, you want to be sure. You're at the foot of the mountain, and you'll climb it as soon as you find the best way up. I hope you live long enough. Mountains are climbed by people who start, not by people who want to be sure. Look at a library. It's got all the knowledge in the world, but it gathers dust unless somebody moves it off the shelves.

HOW TO FIND OIL BY NOT EVEN LOOKING

Now I'm not arguing against common sense, except I'd like to point out that it's rather uncommon. A guy who can't carry a tune isn't going to aim for a career as an opera singer. No question about it, some people try. They wind up giving their concerts for Ward 39. This is called overlooking the obvious.

In the oil business you run into guys called doodle-buggers. They find oil like a witch. They walk across the ground with a magic wand, and when it points down, oil is supposed to be there. They make their money by saying no, which puts the percentages in their favor, because most wells are dry. We hired one for the fun of it. He walked over the lease, and sure enough, he said no. Afterwards, he spent a week trying to get the oil out of his shoes. The ground was soaked with it and became a big field. He couldn't see it because he had his eyes on his wand. He overlooked the obvious.

Beliefs that exclude the obvious induce their possessors into running up blind alleys. What's the answer? To generate beliefs that are based on the obvious. Most of us need to enter more fully into human competition. That shakes us up and brings out our best talents. I'm trying to tell you your potentiality is great. There's no telling what you are capable of. How high you go is mostly a matter of where you set your sights. Columbus aimed at America. Now explorers aim at Mars. In a few years, the universe. Then where? You can be assured that it will be higher.

When I was up at Stanford University I used to occupy myself every Saturday afternoon in the spring throwing a sixteen pound iron ball as far as I could throw it. Only one guy in the world could throw it farther. Now with that same performance I couldn't place in a college track meet. They throw it fifteen feet farther. They set their sights higher.

If you look at human evolution you see it's a continual process of the impossible made possible. Individual evolution is no different. There's a magic transition between "I can't" and "I can." Genius doesn't descend like a thunderbolt from heaven. It isn't picked up as knowledge from books. It steals over the man who sees his own possibilities. It arrives in reality for the man who develops them.

HOW TO GET THINGS DONE WITHOUT EVEN WORKING

So now we're after two things: To find our greatest potential by deciding that we have it, and to train that potential until it's fully developed.

Somebody said that the world is made up of two kinds of people —people who divide people into two kinds of people and people who don't. Okay, I'm with the former. I see a world full of deciders and undeciders. God save the undeciders. He'd better. They can't save themselves.

They hired an efficiency expert at one of the companies I worked with. He wanted to fire an executive who made too many mistakes. Somebody got around to checking the number of decisions that executive made. More than the rest of the executives combined. Nine out of ten of his decisions were right. They fired the efficiency expert and kept the executive.

A torpedo hits a target by making mistakes, then correcting them. It keeps getting off course and coming back on. It's a top flight decider because it knows where it's going and can correct its mistakes. Now just suppose it didn't know where it was going or refused to decide for fear of making a mistake. Where would that torpedo wind up? On the bottom, spent and exhausted. The same thing applies to undeciders.

They ran a management team into industry to find out what top executives had in common. It wasn't blue eyes. It was the ability to make decisions. Short, tall, fat, skinny, they all had it. Somebody got the bright idea to ask them how they acquired it. The unanimous answer: We just began making them. When you start doing anything you start training the nervous system. It gets better and better at automatic response. There's no strain for the torpedo at making its countless decisions. It makes them automatically because it's trained to decide.

HOW TO BECOME AN ORACLE

Sometimes I'm consulted like the Oracle at Delphi. Incense is lighted, the prayer rug rolled out. The inevitable problem: What should I do? I gather into my chest the gasses of heaven. Eyes spitting fire, I thunder, "Decide!" People usually think that this answer is code, and set about deciphering it. Now and again some simple soul gets the drift. He makes a decision. His problem is solved.

There must be a million reasons for indecision. What's the use going over them? They'd make a whole book and would no doubt sound reasonable. The fact is indecision's no good. It has to be gotten rid of. You don't get rid of something by finding out why it's there. You get rid of it by replacing it. An undecider becomes a decider by making decisions.

I recall attending a lecture one time by a guy whose name I can't remember, but they ought to make him a saint. The whole affair was a symposium on the development of human potentialities, and everybody was getting up and saying what's wrong with people. To understand the words that were coming over that microphone you'd have to have a dictionary. But you didn't need a dictionary to know it was nonsense.

Garbage is garbage even if you call it perfume. I picked up the idea we were in a hell of a mess because of what our parents did to us, then I went to sleep. I woke up when the guy who ought to be a saint came on. He said, "In order to change, you've got to change."

The eggheads on the platform didn't crack a smile, but I sure whooped it up in my ringside seat. When a guy cuts through ten thousand words with one simple sentence, it's not only funny, it deserves plenty of applause. I gave him my best. It was the only sensible thing I'd heard in two days.

Who cares why something is lousy or mixed-up or no good? The point is to fix it. If you called a plumber and he came into the house and said, "You've got a broken pipe there. That'll be ten dollars," you'd hit the ceiling. And the plumber would go out of business. But erudite imbeciles survive by telling us what's wrong with us. Maybe we're masochists. One thing is for certain. As long as we don't make them fix us, they won't. They've got a good thing going.

So how do you make a decision? You decide!

HOW TO SHOCK YOURSELF INTO WORKING

Then there are the have-to-be-surers. They cry plaintively, "But what if I'm wrong?" A guy like that used to play end for the St. John's Bachelors in Portland. He could never decide which way the play was going, so he just stood there. One day somebody brought a chair for him. Interestingly, he began to sit in it. It was a great crowd pleaser and the only time I ever saw an undecider contribute a thing. The Bachelors had just eleven men and they needed him on the field to conform to the rules. But they finally began to charge him admission. That's how all undeciders wind up—paying admission to their own performances.

So the oracle responds to "But what if I'm wrong?" with a thunderous shout, "Then you'll know it!" And once more the code book is consulted. Only those who see the obvious see the truth. You make the right decision by making any decision. That allows you to correct your mistakes.

There's absolutely no way to escape making decisions, and there's nobody to make them except you, yourself. By all means feed data into your computer, but you have to demand the decision or it'll never come out. Endless rumination produces more rumination, because whatever we keep doing builds up a habit. When you make a habit of making decisions, you'll begin making them easily and accurately as well.

There's an acute mental disorder that hits undeciders. People spin their mental motors, but nothing conies out. It's called schizophrenia. It enabled the psychologists to get back at the computer. One day a computer began spinning wildly. Its tapes were all racing, but no answers came out. An industrial psychologist happened to wander in. Somebody asked him, "If this thing were a person what would you do with it?" The psychologist peered at the computer and diagnosed schizophrenia. "We'd give it an electric shock," he said. They shot the juice to the computer. It began producing answers.

If you're an undecider there are other ways of applying shock than being strapped to a table and having electrodes set in your head. Just make a decision. That will shock your nervous system into producing some answers.

HOW TO SELL YOURSELF TO SOMEBODY WHO'LL BUY YOU

There appears to be no limit to human potentials. Training consistently develops better performance. When Frankie Albert came to Stanford, he was a left-handed passer. Critics also noticed he had two left feet. His first football season was a comedy at which Stanford fans cried. The very next season, he became an All-American. It seemed like a miracle to everyone but Frankie. He had manufactured the miracle out on the practice field, running and throwing until his arms and legs ached. Somebody asked Frankie how he managed to do it. He said, "I just sold myself on the fact that I could." They ought to give him an honorary doctorate for that statement. It's really the secret of all great performance.

I was once hired to hypo the production of a sales force. Before the first meeting, the sales-manager growled, "Don't go highbrow with these boys. Keep it simple." He hadn't counted on how simple I'd be. I got up and said, "Before you call on a customer, assume that you'll sell him." Then I sat down. The rest of the meeting was pregnant with silence. Afterwards, the sales-manager refused to pay my fee. Later, he paid it happily, when sales increased. They all remembered what I said, and everybody tried it, and everybody accomplishes what he assumes he can do. I was pleased with the results, of course. Thirty dollars a word is a good speaking fee.

My dentist is a champion rifle and pistol shot. He likes to hunt elk and moose. One day he was out in the wilds of Idaho with a tenderfoot. This guy shot up a box of cartridges, but the elk remained standing. Finally he asked in exasperation, "Why do I keep missing?" The dentist replied, "You don't raise your sights."

I chipped a bicuspid when he told me this story. There's nothing so bull-headed as a guy who keeps missing. He fires all his ammo and thinks the target moved. He can't believe that he's shooting where he's aiming and that if he wants to shoot higher he has to raise his sights.

HOW TO TAKE A POSITION WITHOUT BEING MOVED OUT

So Success Cybernetics says that you find and develop your greatest potential by deciding that you have it, raising your sights, then training yourself to develop better performance.

What's a good technique for deciding you've got greater potential? I like the one used by Lee Artoe, a Chicago Bear tackle. I once saw him stop fifteen running plays when he was out on his feet. His machinery kept working because he was programmed for success. Afterwards, he told me how he did it. He said, "When I take my position, I make up my mind that nothing or nobody is going to move me out of it." How's that for decision?

When you take the position that you're going to be good, let nothing or nobody move you out of it. Your friends will keep pointing out that you have plenty of faults, that you can count on. Just tune them out. If you sit down to chat with a well-meaning friend, and he starts out at once with, "The trouble with you, Harry—" put cotton in your ears. Pull the box out in front of him, and start stuffing your ears with cotton. He might take the hint, and even if he doesn't, you won't hear what he says. He's mouthing the suggestions that turn action to apathy. That's ten times more dangerous than the hydrogen bomb.

I once went to a doctor who said I was going to get sicker. If I'd had time, I'd have sued him for malpractice. As it was, I gave him a roasting. Then I went to a doctor who said I'd get better. I got better at once. When the pill-dozers realize that the human machine functions according to its instructions, they'll throw out their pills and start telling people they're getting better. In that enlightened age, it will be a capital offense to tell anyone he's going to get sicker. You can kill a man by telling him he's going to die. Witch doctors do it all the time, and some of them are loose on the streets of America.

HOW TO TURN A QUICK TRICK

No question about it, one rotten apple can spoil a whole barrel. Either you get rid of that apple or coat the others with veneer. I've seen both techniques used. When a guy is so negative that he brings everyone else down, some managers still keep him and try to help him solve his problem. That's a noble human motive, but what usually happens is they don't solve his problem, and the whole organization goes to pot. There are two techniques for handling a situation like this. One is a quick trick, the other a slow one. The quick trick is to fire the first guy who gets down on himself and the world. The slow trick is to make everybody else so thick-skinned they can't be infected. Tough minds prefer the first, tender minds the second. The second is humanitarian, but it takes more time. Every apple in the barrel has to be coated, trained to tune out the negative, to pay no attention to "I cant's" and "What's the use's." But sometimes it's the only solution. The bad apple might be the boss's son.

This situation is common in families. There's a prophet of doom, and he gets the floor. Everybody hides and plays everything safe. They're stuck with the bad apple and pick up his infection. Some of these families can be saved by the thick-skinned technique. They tune out the bad apple, become immune to his infection by not admitting his microbes. In the Navy, this is called the silent treatment. When the prophet of doom finds nobody listening, he sometimes becomes anxious to do some listening himself. With his mouth shut for a change, he's able to learn, and often becomes positive.

For my money, everybody needs training in the thick-skinned technique. With the world so anxious to tell you it can't be done, what else can save you but some kind of armor? Build your inner belief and surround it with steel. It deserves such protection. It's your most precious possession.

When people have trouble raising their sights, it's simply because they're trained to shoot low. But when they're shown that they can be trained to shoot higher, they'll usually respond by giving it a try. Everybody likes to play games. Learning to shoot higher is a game played in the mind. In order to shoot higher, you have to pretend.

There is a story about an ugly princess who wanted a handsome prince. In order to win him, she had the court magician make a beautiful mask for her. The deception worked fine, and she married the prince. One day she fell, and the bump broke the mask. She expected the prince to look at her with horror. When he didn't, she ran to a mirror. Her face was now beautiful. The same kind of magic is worked by pretense.

When we examine this magic we see it's not magic at all, but the scientific law of our nervous systems at work. Whatever we continually pretend becomes habit. If I'm a coward but pretend to be brave, I eventually make bravery a habit. Then I'm brave automatically.

OPERATION PRETENSE

So we find and develop our greatest potential by pretending we have one and that we can develop it. Thus we are able to set our sights higher, to train ourselves to be better. Operation Pretense is carried out within the framework of the four mental conditioning laws set forth in the last chapter. Let's take the first one: We are what we concentrate on.

If I concentrate on failure, I get feelings of failure. If I concentrate on success, I get feelings of success. Which feeling is likely to produce my best effort? Feelings of success, isn't that true? So I pretend I'm successful, and I do this by concentrating. Eventually I make success feelings a habit. By a mental act that originates in pretense, I achieve my best effort. A man is what he practices. He practices what he concentrates on. When he concentrates on success, he practices success. That trains his nervous system to produce success for him.

The libraries are full of books about how to discover yourself. It's made us a nation of self-seekers. To my knowledge, nobody has yet found the self by looking for it. The reason is simple. The self isn't there. It has to be created. It's created by what a person concentrates on. When he concentrates on something that he wants to become, he trains himself to become it by an act of pretense.

You might think this is a sin the way some people react. Outraged, they protest, "I want to be myself!" They ought to be happy to give that self up. They all have the same symptom. They are infected by failure.

I remember a bizarre dream. This guy had a can opener and was opening up a human being from eyebrows to pelvis. When he pulled back the edges and peered inside, he recoiled with a start. Nothing was there. That's what people find who search for the self. Nothing. The self isn't found, it's created.

Take the second mental conditioning law: What we concentrate on grows. Everybody has had experience with this one. You're on your way home from work and a cop gives you a traffic ticket and a tongue lashing to boot. When you finally get home, you kick the dog and get in a fight with your wife. Concentration on trouble makes trouble grow, because that's what you're looking for. A guy in a poker game loses a few hands and gets scared of losing more. More disciplined players watch him with a smile. They know that scared money never wins. A guy who's trying not to think of white elephants, thinks of white elephants. If you try not to think of failure, you think of failure. That's why scared money never wins. To produce success, you have to think of success.

HOW TO BECOME A WINNER INSTEAD OF A LOSER

The third mental conditioning law is a real cutie: What we concentrate on becomes real. By misusing this one you can wind up in the funny-farm believing you're Napoleon. We come to believe anything we concentrate on, no matter how bizarre or fantastic. A guy can start out as a conman promising heaven, but if he continues to promise it, he winds up a believer. That's the history of conmen. They wind up fanatics. Don't kid yourself that they become sincere through some moral revelation. It's a law of the mind that what we concentrate on becomes real. You can start playing around with astrology with your tongue in your cheek, but if you persist in concentrating on it, you'll wind up believing it. Use this law to induce beliefs that produce fruitful action. Concentrate on achievement, success, energy, confidence, skill, joy, persistence. These allow your best effort. If you concentrate on being Napoleon, you have a severe handicap. Your troops were killed off two centuries ago.

The fourth mental conditioning law is a great teacher: We always find what we concentrate on. The outcome of our efforts always tells us what we are concentrating on. I know a successful executive who divides people into winners and losers. That's all he wants to know about them, and he makes a practice of hiring winners. He even carries his theory onto the golf course, pairing himself with people who win. He could make a nice living just playing golf.

People who win are people who think victory. People who lose are people who think defeat. It's hard to convince a loser that he looks for defeat. Reasoned justification makes up a whole literature. Don't waste your time on it. It's just prolonged weeping, which is always embarrassing in grown-up men. Losers all think the world should be changed. It never occurs to them that they might change themselves. But they can, simply by concentrating on winning. That sets up success habits. We always find what we concentrate on.

To find and develop our greatest potential, we discipline our minds with four mental laws. We concentrate on growing, achieving, winning, confidence, persistence, determination, and success. We find our greatest potential by setting our sights higher. We develop our potential by thinking success.

We'll discuss these four mental laws in greater detail in subsequent chapters. Meantime, it's important to understand that they always work whether you consciously use them or not. The greatest danger in your life lies in dwelling on failure. The greatest reward lies in thinking success.

·3· HOW TO SET YOUR SELF-CONCEPT TO SWITCH ON SUCCESS

THERE'S A THING that happens in the brain of some animals when they're first born. It's called imprinting. The initial experience is indelibly recorded in the nervous system. It causes a newborn duck to follow the first thing that moves.

In the laboratory, they put a new-born duck with a chicken. The duck followed the chicken. It thought the chicken was its mother. Since its mother was a chicken, it thought it was a chicken too.

There was a pen for ducks and a pen for chickens. The duck went into the pen with the chickens. All the chickens knew the duck was not a chicken, and they practically pecked it to pieces. But that didn't make the duck think it was a duck. It just couldn't understand why everybody was mad.

They put the duck into the pen with the ducks. Nobody pecked it, but that duck wasn't happy. It flew about the pen looking for a way to get back to the chickens. It didn't like hanging around with those odd looking ducks.

This may give you the idea why it's important what we think we are. The world is full of ducks who think they are chickens.

WITHOUT SCALPEL, OR SUTURES, OR BUCKETS OF BLOOD

If you think you're a leader you act like a leader because that's your self-concept. If you think you're a pea-picker you act like a pea picker because that's your self-concept. People sometimes deny that anything so obvious could have any importance. In cases like that, it's necessary to illustrate. I hypnotized an insurance salesman and told him he was a bear. He growled and lumbered around the room looking for honey. I asked him the premium on ten thousand straight life. He growled and kept looking for honey. I held the rate book in front of him and asked him again. He tried to eat the rate book. Everybody agreed that his self-concept had changed. Fortunately, he was able to regain the idea of being an insurance salesman, though his boss tells me he's still prone to hibernate.

In the memory unit of an electronic computer there is stored a program of instructions which governs the machine's behavior. If the machine could think of itself, that program of instructions would be its self-concept. The memory unit of the human being picks up a program of instructions from experience. Since the human being can think of himself, that program of instructions makes up his self-concept. If it tells him to act like a chicken, he does. It doesn't make him become one. It just makes him act like it.

The importance of the self-concept is twofold. First, if people are acting like chickens, they must start acting like humans before they can function as humans. Second, if people are acting like failures, they must start acting like successes before they can function successfully. This means that the self-concept can be out of touch with reality and you can wind up in the pen with the chickens. It also means that if you accept yourself as you are that's just where you'll stay forevermore. Remember the guy I wanted to saint? "In order to change, you've got to change." That kind of work begins with the self-concept.

Maxwell Maltz performed plastic surgery on ugly faces. Most of these people had been playing ugly roles. Afterwards, they looked in the mirror and saw they were beautiful. They began playing beautiful roles. Their self-concepts had been changed by a surgeon's knife. The same thing can be done with Success Cybernetics, without scalpel, or sutures, or buckets of blood.

HOW TO COME IN OUT OF THE RAIN

Each of us plays a part and plays it to the hilt. One could say we're totally involved in our roles. I heard of an actor who once played Macbeth. He really threw himself into the part. When he left the theatre at night, he prowled the city looking for kings to murder. It took several months in Bellevue to straighten him out. That's a pretty good description of the way the self-concept functions. What a person thinks he is not ordinarily a matter of what he has decided to be. It's a matter of what life has hypnotized him into being. He can wind up in the breadline or become President, depending on whether or not his self-concept is functional. If the self-concept is non-functional, he has to be dehypnotized and trained to think of himself differently. If the self-concept is functional, leave well-enough alone.

The most noticeable thing about the self-concept, whether it's functional or not, is that nobody wants to part with it. There's a kid in the funny papers who carries around a blue blanket. If somebody tries to take it from him, he goes into a panic. That's the way people are about their self-concepts. No matter how dirty and moth-eaten it is, they hang on with a death-grip. They stay in the pen with the chickens or wind up in Bellevue or continually make seven thousand a year when they could be making thirty. Like Popeye the Sailor, they keep shouting shrilly, "I am what I am and that's all that I am." They don't even eat spinach when they have to be strong.

When you see how easily the self-concept can be changed by hypnosis, it's difficult to understand why it's so hard to change when people are awake. The reason is simple on close observation. We think with our self-concepts, and they're continually finding plenty of reasons why we shouldn't change. In order for a person to change his self-concept, he has to change his thinking. You can't get a guy to come in out of the rain if he doesn't think it's raining. If he catches pneumonia, he'll think he caught it from you.

HOW TO KICK A KIGMIE

At first glance we seem faced with a dilemma: A person can't think outside his self-concept, so how can he change it? There's a time when he can. The self-concept only functions when we're with others. When we're alone, it relaxes its grip. Check Tolstoy on this. He said, "I've never observed a man who thought he was alone who didn't appear insane." Either his self-concept is missing or the guy thinks he's nuts.

Why does the self-concept only function when we're with others? Because the reactions of others gave it birth in the first place. People are a mirror in which we see our reflection. If you looked in the bathroom mirror every morning and an ape stared back at you, you'd get to think you were an ape. Reflections from others hypnotize us into beliefs about ourselves. The minute we're with others we begin to think and behave the way people have hypnotized us into thinking and behaving. Put a bunch of chickens into a pen, and the first wild skirmish establishes the pecking order. One chicken pecks all the others. Another pecks all but one. One miserable chicken gets pecked by everyone and has no one to peck. This pecking order never changes. Chickens are hypnotized into it by their first skirmish. Despite our pride in the knobs on our brainstem, our nervous systems are essentially no different than a chicken's. Our first skirmish with life hypnotizes us as well. The only way we can break out of it is by using our imagination. That's something chickens don't have. If they did, they'd seldom wind up in the pot.

When a man is alone, he can imagine that he's different. If he does this repeatedly, over and over, he'll change his self-concept. This will enable him to change his behavior with people. He'll move up in the pecking order. When he moves up in the pecking order, he moves toward success.

Cybernetics training made one man a president by elevating his self-concept so he could move up the pecking order. But it broke up his marriage. His wife had gotten used to pecking him at home. When he reversed the order, she fled for Reno in tears. He was glad to be rid of her. That's what happens when you move up in the pecking order. You're glad to be rid of the people who've been pecking you. When you stay down in the order, you love to be pecked. Remember Capp's Kigmies? They loved to be kicked. That's the lowest spot in the pecking order. Some people have self-concepts so low that they couldn't even kick a Kigmie.

HOW TO PECK THE HEAD ROOSTER

I once took a salesman, the lowest producer in an office, and got him enthused with the idea that he could be best. We worked on his self-concept until he began pecking the head rooster. He didn't become the top producer, but production skyrocketed as everyone scrambled frantically to stay ahead in the pecking order. My boy wound up next to the top, and they won't keep him there. He's still pecking the head rooster. And everyone's sales are moving up month after month. Now I've even got a fight talk called, "How to Peck the Head Rooster." It starts a sales crew scrambling, and they sure begin to produce. The sales manager becomes a referee instead of a ramrod, but he loves the figures he sees on the board.

People full of fight have healthy self-concepts. They can get better. Apathetic people have unhealthy self-concepts. They don't think they can. Anybody who sells a philosophy that takes the fight out of people is selling mediocrity. You have to fight in order to get better.

I meet many people whose self-concepts are high, but I don't necessarily like them. They're usually people who try to peck me. It's easy to like someone who lets you peck him. Getting along with people who try to peck you is the secret of building a winning team, whether it's business or baseball. People who try to peck you also try to peck others. They're out to win. I have a friend who's built an international business on one simple premise. He just hires people he doesn't like. They're all fighters, and they've moved his business to the top. I know another man who only hires the people he likes. If anyone starts pecking, he gets rid of him at once. He owns and operates a football team that finishes last year after year. The people he gets rid of win championships elsewhere. But he doesn't get the drift. When you get rid of fighters, you wind up with losers. Leo Durocher wasn't far wrong when he said, "Nice guys finish last." Anyone out to improve, steps on somebody's toes. That often makes him unpopular with the owner of the toes.

HOW NOT TO GET ULCERS

It's easy to see that a man who continually loses has a low self-concept. But it's equally true that people who continually win can develop over-inflated self-concepts. This is called being fat-headed. Then somebody comes along and pushes them over because they're only half-trying. A healthy self-concept demands victory and success, but it doesn't quibble about paying the price. It impels action, always doing its best, and it views every task as a challenge.

There's a constant inner crisis in the person determined to excel. It's the same kind of atmosphere generated in a football locker room before the team takes the field. They know they can win but they know they'll have to play their best, perhaps better than their best, and that's just what they do. As they go from crisis to crisis, they constantly improve. The same thing applies to the man with a healthy self-concept. He constantly improves because he drives himself to be better.

Lately we've been deluged with hogwash about how people who drive themselves wind up with stomach ulcers. The hardest working man I know has this answer: "I don't get ulcers. I give them." That ought to provide the answer as to who gets the ulcers. It's the people who get pecked, not the people who do the pecking. Selye even demonstrated this in experiments with rats. He gave them every disease known to man, and he did it by taking the fight out of them. They just sat there and shivered and developed stomach ulcers. People low on the pecking order do the same thing. You get rid of a stomach ulcer by showing some fight.

I know a guy who makes a nice living teaching frustrated executives how to punch pillows. They make believe that the pillow is the boss or the wife or whomever they happen to be mad at. It has a good effect in keeping blood pressure down, but it doesn't do a thing to change the pecking order. It just makes them put up with it. They'd get a better effect by punching the boss or the wife. It has the same soothing reaction on the liver, and you wind up with a new boss and a more docile wife.

THE USES OF ENEMIES

Look at the action on a grade school playground. There's a din to wake up the dead. Where people are full of fight, people are alive. When you take the fight out of them, they're vegetables. You get all that action on a grade school playground because the pecking order is still fluctuating and self-concepts aren't set. Try sitting around a board of directors meeting. It's like a tomb. People quietly assume their places in the pecking order and only open their mouths to say what's expected of them. Self-concepts are set, the pecking order established. If you can get them fighting with each other, you resurrect them from the dead, and their company too. Such was the miracle of Lazarus.

When the fight's gone from a man, he is said to be depressed. If the depression doesn't lift, he's in melancholia. That's about as low as a self-concept can get. There's one step lower. That's suicide. Which gets rid of any self-concept at all.

The surest way to bring a man out of depression or melancholia or save him from suicide is to get him mad. When he gets mad, he starts to fight. When he starts to fight, he becomes alive. His self-concept goes higher. Life is directly proportional to willingness to fight. When you get a man fighting, you give him more life. That's why enemies are more valuable than friends. Friends kill you with kindness. Enemies start you to fighting. I feel so strongly about this that if I knew some friend were coming to my house for the conscious purpose of doing me some good, I'd run for my life. I know of few human events more insidious or dangerous.

So the basic ingredient of a healthy self-concept is the willingness to fight. That by itself certainly won't produce success, but put together with a guidance mechanism, it's infallible. I know an actor with a healthy self-concept. He fights all the time, but mostly in bars. He produces plenty of action, but he has a lousy guidance mechanism. He's not just a little failure though. He's a great big resounding one. A healthy self-concept produces plenty of power. That power is channeled to success or channeled to failure by the guidance mechanism that makes up a man's habits. Power and guidance, that's a success mechanism. We'll design one in the next chapter. Meantime, we're developing the power that will allow us to use it.

BRAINWATCHERS WHO DON'T WATCH

I've heard that a New York publisher once offered a reward of one million dollars for anyone who could design a test that would show whether or not a man had motivation. That's a pretty big order when they can't design a test that shows anything. A battery of testers came into one company, gave everybody a test, then advised the president to fire his best salesman. It was a hell of a joke, but very expensive. Bill Veeck hired some testers to pick a baseball team for him. Then his scouts picked a team by using their eyes. The two teams played each other. The score was approximately ninety to nothing, the brain watchers' team was so bad. The testers stoically went back to administering their tests. It's amazing that people can overlook the obvious and get paid for it. Seems everyone would know that one look is better than ten thousand words.

I know a sales-manager whose company makes him give a test to every man he wants. If the man doesn't pass the test, he can't be hired. The sales-manager gets the men he wants by taking their tests himself. They get very good scores because he knows all the answers. He runs the top office in the country, and the testers think it's because of their test. By such enforced necessities do false philosophies flourish.

You might as well stick a man with a pin as give him a motivation test. If he hollers, "Ouch," or sits there and takes it, get rid of him. If he punches you in the nose, put him to work. All you're after is to find people with fight. The rest can be learned. Now we've realized that fight can be learned too, by putting it into the self-concept.

Let's go back to the poor spellers. It turned out they were poor spellers because they thought they couldn't spell. That was their self-concept. When they changed their self-concept to "I'm a good speller," they began to spell better. The same thing applies to the willingness to fight. The man who won't fight has a self-concept that says, "I'm not a fighter." Often this is made manifest by an insane desire to have everybody like him. The way he goes about this is to let everyone walk over him. He winds up in the lowest spot in the pecking order because his self-concept puts him there. He never gets any better because he can't fight to improve.

FIGHT FOR IT!

I've taken some of these nice guys who wouldn't hurt a fly and made raging tigers out of them by giving them one order: "Fight for it!" They make the waiter take back their meals because the peas were put on the plate the wrong way. They edge in front of people in the grocery store line. They make their kids shut up and their wives too. You've never seen such a furor. They actually have to be held back once they learn they can fight. Some of them get fired from their jobs, but they always wind up with a better one and in a higher place in the pecking order. There's nothing so satisfying as bringing a dead man to life.

You set your self-concept to switch on success by training yourself to fight. You implement it by setting your sights high and training yourself to think "I'll prove I can do it" about every task that you tackle. That's all there is to a self-concept. The rest depends on building a guidance mechanism for the power that is being generated.

Let's take the first step in training the self-concept to fight. As with all reconditioning of our reflexes, we have to begin our work in the mind. A man can't fight because he automatically doesn't. Therefore he can't gain experience of fighting successfully. But he can create synthetic experience with his imagination. So he starts out by mentally rehearsing fighting in his mind. It's an enjoyable game. He takes a sock at all the people he hates, and there is absolutely no danger of their hitting him back.

In point of fact, this is how it usually starts out, with some kind of imagined physical violence. This poor guy has been inhibiting his fighting instinct so long that when he first lets it loose, it is murderous. All the more reason for playing the game in the mind. If he actually knocked off his boss, he couldn't change his self-concept. Ten thousand volts would put an end to the experiment.

HOW TO MOVE UP IN THE PECKING ORDER

As time goes by, mental rehearsal for fighting becomes increasingly subtle. One begins rehearsing his pecking by socially approved means, standing up for his rights, refusing to be a doormat, refusing to be a scapegoat, insisting on a hearing, standing up to authority, driving ahead to improve his performance. One day, he actually surprises himself by acting this way. His self-concept is changing because he's experienced successful fighting in his head. That changes the connections of the nerve cells and. neurons. A new self-concept is forming.

Now he carries around a card that reminds him to implement his mental rehearsal with action. The card says, "Fight for it!" It reminds him of how he's supposed to behave, so he fights for it. Notice what happens. The reflection that comes to him from the mirror of people also begins to change. He sees they respect him, that some even fear him. The image that started in his mind now has been projected into the world. He's becoming a fighter.

Then he does something else. He starts saying, "Fight for it!" as he falls asleep. This pops the suggestion into the subconscious in the same manner as if given by a hypnotist, because each of us passes through the hypnotic state as he's falling asleep. Within a few weeks or months, this non-fighter becomes a fighter by the simple expedient of taking charge of his mind. He changes his self-concept by creating inner experience that forms it anew.

Of course, it's important that he fight about things that are important. If he fights with the plumber when he should be fighting for customers, his motive power is wasted. He has to choose a worthwhile arena. The best arena is professional performance. Perform better there and you make more money. This also wins the approval of the wife and kiddies.

There's always somebody higher on the pecking order to use as a target. If you're a salesman, he's some guy selling more. If you're an executive, he's got the next job up the ladder. Don't walk around on tiptoe, come out and say it. Tell him you're planning to beat him out of his job.

I'll always remember a guy who came into my office looking for work. When I interviewed him, I asked about his ambition. "My first goal is to get your job," he said. I hired him, and today he's running the company. I have no regrets. People who get to the top got there by fighting. They respect fight in others. When they see someone walking around on tiptoe, they either think he's spineless or planning a midnight attack. They like a man who says where he's going and backs it up with action. Such men make a company grow. This is fine with the men at the top. They usually have a piece of the action.

HOW TO CUT IT AND TRY IT AND SEE IF IT WORKS

Some people talk big but don't back it with action. They're often accepted at face value, but their non-action catches up with them. I recall a professional football coach who recruited a tackle away from being a bartender. The way he got to thinking this bartender would make a good tackle was by hearing him tell about all the guys he beat up each week. It made him sound like a combination of Jack Dempsey and Attila the Hun, just the right thing to turn loose on unsuspecting opponents. When the bartender showed up at training camp, he quit after two hours and slunk back to his bar. He had the words, but he didn't have the action. It was a serious disappointment for the coach. But he learned a lesson.

We condition ourselves to fight by mentally rehearsing ourselves fighting, then we turn this mental experience into action by using autosuggestion. First, the card with the instruction to fight, then the suggestion made to one's self when falling asleep. The end result is we begin to act like fighters. When we begin to act like fighters, we begin to get better.

It's difficult to assess the damage done the human psyche by people who keep spreading the word that life is sunshine and flowers. Anyone who believes this must think he's in the wrong world. Such fantasy does the greatest disservice to the people who harbor it. They can't handle their problems, so they expect them to be handled by Heaven. Life didn't evolve from amoeba to man in a nice easy manner. It fought its way up, breathing vapors of fire. The fight isn't over. It's only beginning. A healthy self-concept looks at the world with unclouded eyes.

Science lifted man into space by this simple theorem: "Cut it and try it, and if it works, use it." In one single century scientific theory has produced more human progress than all preceding efforts. It's time for us to realize that any other theory of action is either a shell game or the babbling of idiots. I'm talking about theories of human conduct that present the world as it isn't. We do one thing in church, and another in the office—that gives us split personalities. This is called being a solid citizen.

A HANDY TOOL TO SLIP IN YOUR KIT

When a man starts changing his self-concept, he has to pare his ideas down to the bone. Only one is worth keeping: If it works, use it; if it doesn't, then change it. Let the preachers point out ideal ideals. Then you'll have them on tap when you find an ideal world. Most people have trouble surrendering false values because they've been told such values are good. Despite error and anguish and defeat and frustration, they keep right on using them. This is torturing yourself and pretending it feels good.

Here's a guy raised in a society that's trained him to monogamy. He takes up residence in the South Seas where everyone has five wives. He takes only one, and the whole tribe ostracizes him. Notice his reaction: He's right and they're wrong. It just never occurs to him that by changing his value he could make it more workable. Besides that, he'd have four more wives.

I'm aware that some people think it's not ideal to fight. Naturally, they're losers. Their aim may be to make losers of winners or to win some award for their failure to fight. One thing is certain, they seldom produce. But they enjoy the fruits of the people who do. Picture Michelangelo struggling to paint the ceiling of the Sistine Chapel, Pasteur burning lights through the long night, Einstein wrestling with the equations that set off nuclear physics, Henry Ford over the forge that launched the first Model T. Whatever they created, they created because they fought for it. How's that for a useful tool to slip in your kit?

" What's the use fighting?" cry the non-achievers. Fortunately, there's always been somebody ready, willing, and able. Without him, we'd be in a hell of a fix. I'm telling you to set your sights on goals that are useful. I'm telling you to go after them with actions and attitudes that have plenty of fight. That's scientific method; it's good because it works.

THE USES OF PEOPLE BUILT INTO OUR HEADS

An effective self-concept generates fight, but it doesn't kick dogs and slap babies. Andrew Carnegie is reputed to be the toughest man who ever sat behind a desk. But the railroads he built are still with us today, and the foundation he created still advances human welfare. Meantime, most of the people who think you shouldn't fight have trouble supporting themselves.

I'm not saying that a society shouldn't provide for its members. Why have a society at all unless it gives such protection? I'm simply saying a society functions better when its members are fighters. That makes them achievers. Achievement makes a society great. Goldwater hung himself from the Presidential tree by stoutly maintaining, all evidence to the contrary, that opportunity and training were equally available to all people and that people who weren't successful were just plain lazy. I recall the cartoon that shot him down in flames. There was this charwoman scrubbing the office floor, and Goldwater was saying, "What's the matter with you, anyway? Where's your ambition? Why don't you go out and inherit a department store?" I guess you could say his self-concept was high, but his world view a little distorted.

It may have occurred to you that a self-concept consists mainly of attitudes, and that if your attitudes are right your self-concept is straight. This is basically true, but is often misleading because a man's attitudes are seldom what he says they are. They're much more likely to be what he sees. Psychologists call this the phenomenon of projection. Here's an example: A guy drove into the gas station in a small town. He said to the attendant, "I'm thinking of moving here.

What kind of people do they have in this town?" The gas station attendant looked the guy over. "What kind of people did they have in the last town where you lived?" The guy answered, "Everybody there was surly and a sorehead." Said the gas station attendant, "That's the same kind of people you'll find in this town."

Recall our fourth mental law? We always find what we concentrate on. The gas station attendant must have known about it. It accounts for projection. We find the same people and same circumstances wherever we go. They're built into our heads. You can learn a lot about yourself by paying attention to what you see. What you see is your self-concept and contains your real attitudes, no matter what you think they actually are.

HOW TO POWER YOUR SELF-CONCEPT

Now we're skating on thin ice, because the greatest sin in self development is looking into yourself. Stay away from introspection as if it were poison. Introspection is self-criticism and plays failure experience on the imagination's turntable. Stay strictly with what works and what doesn't work. Throw out the things that don't work, keep the things that do work, and try the things that look like they might work. What you see tells you what you are. To change what you see, change your self-concept. That's all the self-analysis anyone needs. That's all he can handle, if he wants to grow and achieve. I know a guy who built a birdhouse and named it *Insight.* He'd spent five years in psychoanalysis. He loves it when people ask him why he calls the birdhouse, *Insight.* "Simple," he says. "*Insight* is for the birds."

So we set the self-concept to switch on success by programming it to fight for the things that we want. We set our sights on higher performance, because when we move toward higher performance our abilities grow. We train ourselves into a fighting self-concept by disciplining our minds with four mental laws. Let's restate them now in the light of the self-concept. 1. The self-concept is formed by what we concentrate on. 2. Concentration makes the self-concept seem real. 3. The self-concept grows toward the image of our concentration. 4. What we find in the world reflects our self-concept.

Cybernetics training produces mental discipline, the ability to think something useful instead of something useless or dangerous. You can think a new self-concept into existence by a process of visualizing yourself playing this new role. You speed up the process by autosuggestion. You reinforce this synthetic experience by taking the actions that ingrain it into your nervous system. Soon, things that seemed impossible are done automatically. We build our first great success habit when we build a healthy self-concept, and it becomes a faithful executive vice-president when we've trained it into our nervous system.

HOW TO START YOURSELF A WAR

The self-concept governs energy, power, force. It's the motive power for action. When you set your self-concept to "Fight for it!" you switch on success. It's equally important to build a guidance mechanism for this power mechanism to work through. In the next chapter, we'll discuss how to design a guidance mechanism and combine it with a power mechanism to produce an automatic success mechanism. Then we'll lay out a program for training the success mechanism into the nervous system. Right now, just to get an idea of the power unleashed by a fighting self-concept, try carrying a card that says, "Fight for it!" I promise you more action than you've had in years. Everyone will say, "I wonder what's happened to Joe? He seems so excited." Sure, he's excited. He's got something to fight for.

I was on the roster of speakers at a recent convention. A crusty old guy who turned out to be the president got up and gave everybody hell. Someone called him General. I asked if he'd been in World War II. "In it?" was the horrified reply. "My Gawd, he started it!" Get out there and start yourself a war! You too can be a general.

·4· HOW TO DESIGN YOUR OWN AUTOMATIC SUCCESS MECHANISM

THE WORD COUNTDOWN is well understood at Cape Kennedy, Florida. All through the long night preceding a rocket launching, hundred of engineers, scientists, and mathematicians busy themselves over the complicated apparatus that will launch and guide the missile. What are they doing? Why, they're checking its success mechanism, checking to be sure that every attitude, response, skill, and ability has been properly installed in the rocket, checking to be sure that all these attitudes, responses, skills, and abilities have been properly coordinated to make a success of the rocket's mission. The period of time which they have to do this is the countdown. And when the countdown is finished, when the zero hour arrives, when the moment for action has come and the success mechanism has been checked and all systems are go, they blast off at the target!

The earth has been orbited by such a procedure. A missile has landed on the moon. Mars has been surveyed millions of miles away. And all because the success mechanism has proved such a remarkable device for getting the job done. Thirty men lost their lives trying to fly the Atlantic. Not one single life has been lost in the exploration of outer space. Why has a job a thousand times more difficult proved hundreds of times more simple? Because today's procedure puts the emphasis on the success-mechanism, while yesterday's procedure put the emphasis on starting the trip.

HOW TO GET AS HIGH AS A ROCKET

Success is a matter of a proper success mechanism. That's been proven in rocketry, the computer sciences, in every working, producing machine conceived by the mind of man. And the startling development, the revolutionary discovery which science has given us is that the brain of man is itself a machine which can function no better than the success mechanism with which it is programmed.

What goes into a success mechanism? Basically, attitudes. Attitudes that produce the actions that get the right results. How high will a rocket go? Why, just as high as its success mechanism will propel it. Its attitudes determine its altitude. How high will you go? Just as high as your success mechanism will propel you. Your attitudes determine your altitude. What will an electronic computer accomplish? Anything that its success mechanism allows it to accomplish. Its attitudes determine its aptitude. What will you accomplish? Anything your success mechanism allows you to accomplish. Your attitudes determine your aptitude.

Here is the program for combining guidance mechanism and power mechanism into an automatic success mechanism, a program tried, tested, and proven in my work as a training consultant and by the thousands of men and women who have gone through Success Cybernetics training programs. 1. Set goals for yourself. 2. List the daily actions that will carry you to your goals. 3. List the attitudes that will help you take these daily actions. 4. Train these actions and attitudes into your nervous system until they become automatic.

HOW TO DRILL AN OIL WELL TO LEARN MORE ABOUT IT

Every great accomplishment, every invention, every discovery and advance of mankind has been made because somebody started out to do it. They can't even build a rocket, take even the first step in designing its success mechanism, unless they know what they want that rocket to do. You can't build a house unless you know what it's for. You can't build a house unless you know what you want it to be. And you can't take control of your own destiny, mold yourself into anything at all, unless you know what you want to be, where you want to go.

Goal setting—the first step on the journey of achievement.

I remember coming back to Potter's Motel, a slat-sided, paint peeling wayside stop in Comanche, Oklahoma, at 4 A.M. in the dark morning, dog-tired, dirty, disappointed because I'd just drilled a dry hole on the rolling farmlands west of town, and this old oil driller I'm with, a guy whose rig had spent three days and nights reaming out water and mud, water and mud, but no oil, not a drop, not a smell, a guy with caved-in cheeks and a mouth like a blade, who usually only opened it to say "Yup" and "Nope," came into my motel room and we had a drink together, and I cried in mine while he watched.

Oh, was I feeling sorry for myself! I'd put in my time, my effort, my money, and now this. All gone. All lost. Fate had singled me out of all the human beings on earth as the one guy to have his fingers stepped on. And I didn't like it. It hurt. Deep in my little cocoon of self-pity— poor little old me.

Then this guy, who must have had several drinks by then, this old guy who had never finished grade school and whose hands were as hard and thick as rocks, put his drink down on the table and asked me a question. "Why did you drill that well?"

I thought he was crazy. "To find oil!" I screamed.

" Oh," he said, "I guess that's why you're disappointed. I thought you drilled it to see if oil was there. And I thought you drilled it to learn more about it, so you could maybe find it the next time."

HOW TO DRILL SEVEN DRY HOLES IN ONLY THREE YEARS

I couldn't get it out of my mind. It went round and round in my head that night in my dreams. Sure, I'd drilled that well to find oil, that had been my goal. But wasn't there a bigger goal after all—the growth of my own ability and skill? That's what eventually could find the oil, if I had the guts and the perseverance and the discipline to improve my knowledge and skills and attitudes. And three years and seven dry holes later, when oil gushed up out of the casing and covered the floor of a rig in the eastern hills of Kentucky, and I slipped in it and bellowed with glee and slapped the tool-pusher on the back, I remembered that night in Comanche, Oklahoma when an old driller had set me on the path to building a success mechanism that could get the job done.

Goals are for growing. No growth is possible without goals. Millions of people walk blindfolded through life, groping in the dark, moving this way and that, never more than a few feet, because they don't know where they're going. They're waiting for an inspiration, a bright star in the sky, a voice from the beyond, for the wind to change. And they never grow because they have no direction. Goals are not just for achieving. They're signposts to guide us to development of our potential. They're signposts to guide us to development of that person we ought to be, which we ought to be because we can be. A man in the wilderness enroute home stops only for a moment when he finds a trail mark blazed on a tree, only for a moment to be satisfied he's on the right path. If he sat down there full of congratulations and self satisfaction and lost all thought of the next blazed tree and the next and the next, he'd never get home. Goals are signposts. When you take your satisfaction from your own personal growth, you've arrived at that position of un-shakable inner peace and perseverance that no obstacle or detour can disturb.

HOW TO FIND DIAMONDS IN THE FUNNIEST PLACES

I worked one summer on a cattle ranch in eastern Oregon. My job was to clean out the stalls each morning. I got the job because I'd answered an ad that said, "Cowboy Wanted." The ad wasn't entirely misleading. They gave a boy a shovel, and the cows provided the material to fill it.

It was a chastening experience. Piece work. I could never get ahead of the cows. I'd get those stalls spanking clean by five in the afternoon, then they'd bring back the cows, and the next morning, all over again. I finally went to the foreman, a grizzled cowpuncher with a face like mahogany, and told him I wanted a promotion. He said he thought I deserved it, and he'd give me one the next morning, and all that night in my dreams I rode the range on a fiery pinto, and the next morning, for my promotion, he handed me a bigger shovel.

Now I like a joke as well as anyone, but I thought that was going too far. I considered using the shovel to shorten the height of the foreman, but was restrained by a remark he made. He said, "Go back to work. You might find you've gotten a promotion after all."

So I did. Much to my surprise, I was finished by three in the afternoon. The bigger shovel did it. And then I realized that even in this job, the lowest on the face of the earth, ideas could make the job easier, efficiency measures could be taken, that if I thought long enough and tinkered long enough I might be able to get this job done so quickly they'd have to make a cowboy out of me to keep me from standing around. Within a week I had every Rube Goldberg contraption in the barn you could think of. I even developed a phobia about having anything spilled on the floor. And I was out of the barn with the work done by ten in the morning, and they finally had to put me to work rising with the bunkhouse gang. From stable boy to cowhand in one easy lesson, and I never forgot it. I got what I wanted not by quitting what I was doing but by starting to grow and to learn right where I was.

Too many of us are always looking over the fence at pastures we think are greener. Too many of us are always quitting this and starting that, moving from here and moving to there, hoping for that one big break, that one wonderful opportunity that will make our fortune. Russell Conwell told the true story of a man who sold his farm and went all over the world prospecting for diamonds, never found them, and died disillusioned. And that farm of his, the one he sold, turned out to be the biggest diamond mine in the world. Maeterlinck wrote a story about a man who searched all over the world for the bluebird of happiness, never finding it, finally returning home to find it in his own backyard.

Where do you start on the ladder of achievement and success? Where do you set your goals? Right where you are now. Right where you are now is the best of all possible places to start, and the only place you can start. You start where you are now by turning your attention to how you can do your job better, how you can do it more efficiently, how you can improve your product, service, ideas, or relationships; how you can improve your skills, talents, and abilities.

HOW TO RECEIVE A DAMFOOL MEDAL

During World War II, I was gunnery officer on a destroyer escort. For those of you who don't know what a destroyer escort is, I will give you an idea. It is a roller coaster at sea. You go down the big drop of each wave and up the next one. The standard decor of each face is green. Lunch is never served—it's mopped up.

As part of my job, I was in charge of the torpedoes, and because I was a recent civilian unaccustomed to these things and so was my crew, we occasionally made a mistake. One day we launched a torpedo over the side without setting a goal in it, and here was this gadget, 750 pounds of TNT, circling idly around in the sea, and nobody knew where it was going. Up to then, we'd been keeping a pretty tight formation, but almost instantly thirty-five ships turned and took off for the horizons in all directions. We didn't hear of some of them for days.

Nobody got hit by that torpedo, and it finally spent its energy and wound up on the bottom. But the next day, when we dropped anchor in Bermuda, our practice maneuvers port, I realized I'd achieved overnight fame as the man who, single-handedly, had routed the United States Fleet.

The admiral called me into his office to receive my dam-fool medal. He was an old salt, up through the ranks, and his presentation address was an awesome shade of purple. When he ran out of breath, he sat there and glowered, and then he said something I'll never forget. He said, "Son, if you never learn another thing in this man's navy, remember this. Never fire until you know where you're shooting, or the ship you sink may be your own."

There it was, the same formula they refined and used to hit the moon with, to reach Mars with. Check your success mechanism. Be sure your goals are set. And that's the fundamental project of every individual and organization in America today. When definite goals are not set, a project winds up like the common pin —pointed in one direction and headed in another.

Goals are the bare bones of success, the framework that fleshes out talent and ability. No man can aspire too high, set goals too high, as long as he sets up at the same time the thing to be accomplished today. A journey of a thousand miles begins with a single step. The ladder that leads to achievement has a rung one foot above the ground, right where you are. Know what you want, decide what you want, decide on the steps to accomplish it, take that first step today, and nothing can stop you from climbing toward the stars.

HOW TO FIGURE YOUR FORTUNE ON A CHINESE ABACUS

Because I'm a writer, every once in a while someone will come up to me and say, "I've got a great idea for a story. You write it, and I'll split the profits with you." And I scream, "Wait! I've got a great idea myself. You write it, and I'll split the profits with you!"

Here's a guy trying to sell me some work he doesn't want to do. Not only doesn't he want to do it, he can't. He doesn't know the importance of training.

When I first started to write, I saved my unpublished manuscripts. First, I bought a three room house to save them. Then I bought a six room house to save them. Then I bought a ten room house to save them. Finally I burned them and moved into an apartment. But when I burned them I performed a ritual. I counted each page I threw into the fire. Seven thousand two hundred and twelve. Seven thousand two hundred and twelve hours racking my brains and guts and heart, training myself to write. And now some guy wants to trade me his idea, an idea that came to him in a flash, for my seven thousand hours.

Well, you might say, his idea could be great. And I say no, a plain flat no. Great ideas come to people who have trained themselves to perceive them. If it was a great idea, he wouldn't be bringing it to me, he'd be doing it himself, because he'd know how. People who haven't trained themselves, who don't know how, can't see what's there. They can't differentiate a good idea from a bad one. Look at the abacus. What is it? A bunch of beads on wires. But to a Chinese merchant the position of those beads represents two thousand nine hundred and fifty dollars, the sum total of a year's effort at buying and selling merchandise, and if you ask him to figure it again, he moves his fingers so rapidly over those beads you'd swear he was playing a piano. And what he sees in that abacus, things you and I can't see, he sees because he's trained.

Oh, the merchants of luck and fortune and charms and easy street have made beggars of us all. The key to accomplishment is training. The trained eye sees things that are absolutely undiscernibly to the untrained eye, and great ideas are had by people who are trained, and great deeds are wrought by people who are trained, not by luck or chance or magic as the merchants of gullibility would have us believe.

HOW TO RUN FAST WHEN YOU CAN'T EVEN WALK

The startling effectiveness of Success Cybernetics is due to the fact that it awakens a renewed interest in training. It exposes a man's potentiality to himself, shows him what he is capable of being, reveals the powers and aptitudes that are dormant in his own mind and nervous system and motivates him toward their development. He begins to see that almost the entire functioning of his brain and nervous system is reflexive, that they cannot possibly function and better than they have been trained to function. He begins to see that the fundamental process of training is repetition, iteration, doing the thing over and over, whether it goes on in the mind or in the physical world, until he builds into himself a finely honed network of automatic responses that will get the job done, until he builds into himself a true success mechanism.

How does a man train himself to high performance and accomplishment? First, he sets goals. Then he decides on the abilities, skills, and attitudes necessary to accomplish those goals. Then he practices, every day, day after day, mentally as well as physically, conditioning his mind and body to the smooth, easy, flowing performance that separates the pro from the amateur. He works. Isn't that an ugly word? Doesn't that make you want to vomit? But it's the truth. There is no magic key to easy street. The key is training. And that's work.

I remember a young fellow badly burned about the legs, and the doctors said he would never walk again, but his father said he might be able to—if he practiced, if he trained. So he did. He practiced stretching. He practiced exercising. Finally, he practiced standing. One day he practiced a few tottering steps. Then he trained, trained hard, and at last he was able to walk. But by now he'd got the habit, so he kept on training. And one bright day, Glenn Cunningham won the Olympic Championship in the 1,500 meter run, the fastest human being on the face of the earth, on legs that once wouldn't hold him.

HOW TO PLAY GOLF ON ONLY ONE LEG

How do you train to improve your performance? You practice, day after day. You practice the things that will enable you to perform better at the job you hold now, and you practice the things that will enable you to handle a bigger job, and you do this when it hurts.

Bob Morgan, Hollywood's top stunt man, was run over by a train during the filming of *How The West Was Won.* He was badly mangled and lost a leg. The doctors didn't believe he'd live. He did. Then they didn't believe he'd walk—he did. Then they didn't believe he'd play golf. He did. Then they didn't believe he could hold a job. He does. He's in charge of all stunts at a major motion picture studio, and he shoots golf in the seventies. How did he do it? Here are his own words: "I just kept doing the things that hurt."

He trained. He thrust against pain. He kept doing the things that hurt, and pretty soon they didn't hurt any longer, and pretty soon he became good at them, and then they became easy.

That's the mark of a man who's bound for greatness, because he's tempering his mind and body and skills by pushing himself toward higher performance even when it hurts. What we don't use, we lose. But what we use when it hurts grows. And when we've grown, the thing that used to hurt seems easy. That's the magic in training, in practicing day after day, in pushing yourself toward higher performance even when it hurts.

Einstein couldn't pass algebra. Glenn Cunningham couldn't walk. Helen Keller couldn't talk or hear or see. Franklin Roosevelt was paralyzed from the waist down. How were they able to accomplish their great performances? By training, by thrusting against pain. And what they put to work in their lives, you and I can put to work in ours. Start training today, pushing yourself forward in the pain and fear areas, breaking through performance barriers, until you become good, until you become great.

HOW TO GET PROMOTED BY BOTCHING IT UP

Back in the years when I was in the advertising business, we hired a bright young boy off the street. We hired him because we liked the way his mind worked and because we liked his attitude. The first job we gave him was to draw up a presentation for an account we had our eye on. He said he could do it, and he worked on it a week, then brought it in and threw it on the desk, and we went through it. It was lousy.

I shouted at him, "I thought you knew how to draw up a presentation!"

He grinned and answered, "How did I know I couldn't? I'd never tried."

So we gave him a promotion. Why? Because he didn't go strictly by the book.

Because he was willing to use his imagination. Because he was willing to tackle something new. Because his attitude was that he could do anything until proven wrong. And today he's running his own advertising agency, and his copy is a continual exploration of the frontiers of communication.

What a limiting legacy Sigmund Freud left us when he told us that we are what our past has made us. Millions of people are walking around today with the idea that they can't do a thing about their lives because the past has trapped them where they are. They discount the greatest power of their own minds, imagination, which can sever the hold of the past anytime they are willing to discipline it toward growth.

Two men are born in the slums. One winds up in the breadline, and we say, "No wonder. His past made him what he is." But the other winds up as president of a great corporation. How do we account for him with a psychology of the past? How do we account for him with a psychology that makes memory the most important function of the human mind? We can't. We need a new human dynamics which places primary importance on imagination. We need a psychology of the future. Because here was a man who created a future in his mind, and harnessed his imagination to it, and rehearsed in his mind the steps by which he would achieve that future, and that had the effect of creating synthetic experience which gradually replaced the memory of his past. And so he was enabled to develop the skills, attitudes, abilities necessary to achieve that future. Here was a man who used his mind as it was meant to be used, with imagination, aimed at the future, severing his connection with the past, growing his whole life long.

HOW TO BECOME A MANAGER WHEN YOU CAN'T EVEN SPELL

I have a friend, Tommy, who was in the oil business and decided to leave it and go into another field. He was sitting with a friend of his in an office in Houston one day when the phone rang and a national sales-manager was on the other end of the line announcing that he was looking for a western sales-manager for Vanadium Products. "I've got the man for you right here in this office," Tommy's friend said, and handed Tommy the phone.

" What do you know about vanadium?" asked the sales-manager.

" Hell," said Tommy, "I can't even spell it."

The sales-manager chuckled. "We don't want you to spell it, we want you to sell it. Do you think you can?"

" If you can make it, I can sell it," answered Tommy.

" You're hired," the sales-manager said.

That's probably the shortest job interview in history, but look what it accomplished. Tommy showed himself to be without pretense, willing to tackle something new, and he showed he believed in himself.

Contrast that with the hundreds of other applicants that sales manager must have interviewed. "What do you know about vanadium?" "Well, it makes steel more flexible." "How would you go about selling it?" "Well, over at so and so, we used to do it this way."

We used to do it this way! Nobody is interested in the way they used to do it! What everybody is interested in is a new way, a better way to do it. Nobody buys memory. Yet everybody is willing to pay, and pay high, for imagination.

The lie now has been pinpointed. Man is not restricted to what his past has made him. He is not limited to the resources of his memory. He is capable of becoming whatever he can imagine. Imagination has brought us every great invention, discovery, has produced all progress throughout all human history. And when a man has begun to harness his imagination to the tasks before him, he has opened wide the doors to his personal growth.

HOW TO REMEMBER A GIRL YOU MADE LOVE TO

And something interesting about memory. We remember what we imagine. We're always hearing that so and so has a good memory. Check the facts, and you'll find that man has a good imagination. He has the power of making images and associations in his mind so that they combine into experience, and this experience is stored in his nervous system so that he can recall it. Success Cybernetics has trained thousands of people to better memories—for names, faces, facts, and data, by teaching them how to use their imaginations, the image making power of the mind, so that this synthetic experience can be stored in memory.

And how is experience stored in memory? By associating it with some want, desire, or pleasurable anticipation. An old man was asked if he could remember the first girl he'd ever made love to. "Well," he said, "I forget the name and the face, but I ain't never forgot the feeling!"

It's what we concentrate on that we remember. In fact, it's what we concentrate on that we become. It's what we concentrate on that determines the direction of our growth, or even if we will grow at all. Nobody grows who concentrates on the past. But growth is produced in everyone who has his face and mind and heart turned toward the future.

It's only been recently that the concentration mechanism has been isolated in the brain of man. They found it over in the Brain Research Laboratories of U.C.L.A. They call it the Reticular Formation. It's located at the top of the brainstem and in the lower thalamus, a group of cells with wire taps to every organ and muscle of the body, a group of cells which appear to have the same function and organization as the master program unit of an electronic computer. This group of cells determines what we pay attention to, how we respond to the incoming data from any particular event. It's an attention-focusing mechanism.

Here's how it works. You're reading the newspaper, see? You're right in the middle of the story about how Sandy Koufax pitched a no hitter, arid your wife asks you to take out the trash. Do you hear her? You bet your life you don't. That old Reticular Formation is really operating, focusing your attention on what's important to you, Sandy striking out the side, keeping out what isn't important to you, the trash that's supposed to be taken out. And notice the survival value. While you're enjoying Sandy's final strikeout, your wife takes out the trash.

HOW TO PLAY SIXTY MINUTES WITHOUT GETTING KILLED

Back in the days when I played football, sixty-minute men were commonplace. If anybody tried to confine us to a defensive or offensive platoon, we'd think he was trying to make sissies out of us. I remember going sixty minutes against the Chicago Bears at Wrigley Field without drawing a deep breath, without noticing a single shock or pain, and when the game was over coming off the field hardly able to walk, I had so many sore muscles. Why didn't I notice these when the game was on? Because I was concentrating on the game.

Concentration can block out pain, guilt, fear, resentment, anger. The use of it has even made its way into dentists' offices. Now they put earphones on a kid and play music for him, and he doesn't feel any pain because he's concentrating on the music. The mind is aware only of the things that are being concentrated on.

And what is concentration? Why, it's pictures in the mind, isn't it? It's images in the mind that demand attention, isn't that true? And what are images in the mind but imagination? So what is concentration but the disciplined use of imagination?

Learning to concentrate is simply learning to discipline the imagination. Instead of the imagination flying off this way or that, engaging in fantasy, chewing over the past, it's put to work in the service of attaining objectives, it's put to work in the service of achieving goals. Mental rehearsal! Performing in the mind, building up synthetic experience that enables better performance, better attitudes, more confidence, more skill. People are put on the track of continued growth and increasing effectiveness by learning how to discipline their imaginations through concentration, by learning how to build synthetic experience through mental rehearsal.

B. C. Morrison was my partner in the oil business. He fought Stanley Ketchel. He lost, but he fought him, and that's something. He discovered oil fields. He built refineries. He put together an oil royalty company. He had the first concessions in Venezuela. And he once told me, "Everything I've ever done has been important to me. It taught me how to concentrate. That's why I've lived three lifetimes in one." And he died in the middle of a wildcat venture at the age of seventy-five, still pushing outward his own frontiers by the power of concentration.

The powers of mind are memory, concentration, and imagination —and concentration disciplines the other two. The greatest of these is imagination, because it severs the hold of the past and turns our faces toward the future.

HOW TO GET GOLD BY TURNING A HANDLE

And that brings us to the most important ingredient of the success mechanism: Believe in yourself, in your potential, in what you are capable of becoming.

When I was a kid in Portland, Oregon, my hero was old man Heller. He used to march in the parades in his Civil War uniform and carry his musket. He could do tricks with it, and he had a white beard and flowing white hair and was as straight as the musket he carried, and in the basement of his house he had a gold machine. He used to tell me about it, and one day when he was gone, I sneaked into his basement and turned the handle, but all that came out was dirt. I didn't know it was really just an assay machine, and I thought he hadn't perfected it yet or I didn't have the touch, but I knew one thing: Nobody could talk old man Heller out of his belief that he was capable of getting gold. And you know what? He got it! It didn't come out of the machine. It came out of a mine in northern California, which Heller himself staked and mined and hit mother lode at the ripe young age of eighty-five! He became a rich man because he believed in himself.

And now I've lived long enough and learned enough to know that anyone who believes in himself has already discovered the richest mother lode there is, whether he ever finds gold or not, because he's unlocked the door to happiness.

A lot of people tell us what happiness is. Some of them tell us it's contentment. Borden says that works with cows, they give better milk that way. But contented human beings are seldom happy, they're just stagnating, and they don't like it, and they don't even give milk. So what is happiness? I know people who only look happy when they're cheating somebody out of money. But I doubt that's really happiness. That same man is usually pretty miserable because nobody wants to be around him. So what is happiness?

Here's a definition I'd like you to toy with. It's worked for me, and it's worked for the people I've trained. Here it is: "Happiness is the movement toward meaningful goals with the sense of being able to achieve them."

Simple, isn't it? It requires only two things: Goals that will make you grow, and belief in yourself. It's simple because it's true, and it's true because it works!

THE IMPORTANCE OF "I CAN"

So now we can throw all the soft soap out the window. Things like security, power, position, prestige, status, money—carrots on a stick, which we can chase forever and never catch. Happiness is the movement toward meaningful goals with the sense of being able to achieve them. Just set your sights high, get out into action, and believe in yourself. Happiness is what we're all after. And we don't have to postpone it. We don't have to put if off until our ship comes in. We can have it right now, this instant. All we have to do is begin our growth toward meaningful goals and believe in our ability to achieve them.

How does a man come to believe in himself? By believing that the divine spark is within him. By believing that he is part and parcel of the growth and evolution of the universe. By believing that he can accomplish anything that he is willing to dedicate himself to and train himself to be.

I played professional football with Whizzer White, an All-American, a Rhodes Scholar, now associate justice of the Supreme Court, and one day on a train trip from New York to Detroit, as we glided through a winter countryside covered with snow, I asked him how he'd accomplished so much. Whizzer, who was never given to making speeches, looked me in the eye and said simply, "I always think I can."

How do you think? Do you always think, "I can"? Or do you always think, "I can't"? Do you believe in yourself or have you lost faith in yourself? Believing in yourself is just this simple: You must always think, "I can." You must always think, "I can," no matter how the situation looks, no matter how the odds seem stacked against you, no matter what the past has been. Today, this moment, is a fresh start. Today, this moment, you can think, "I can," and when you do you'll believe in yourself, when you do you'll be happy.

COUNTDOWN

The countdown period at Cape Kennedy is an important time. The mission depends on the rocket's success mechanism, and everyone examines it carefully to be sure it is right, that all systems are go.

The countdown period in every individual's life is also important. Each person's mission depends on his success mechanism, and he must build it and check it to be sure it is right.

Sit down right now and construct your success mechanism. Start with your guidance mechanism and write down the daily actions that will allow you to reach your long-term goals. Then construct your power mechanism out of the attitudes, "Fight for it!" "It can be done." "I'll prove I can do it." "It's an exciting game." "I like me." Guidance mechanism plus power mechanism make up your success mechanism. A success mechanism consists of things to be done now. You do these things every day. That builds success habits. List the actions of your guidance mechanism on one side of a card. List the attitudes of your power mechanism on the other. This success mechanism will carry you to your target. In the next chapter, we'll lay out a program for training the success mechanism into your nervous system so that it functions easily, accurately, and automatically.

·5· HOW TO TRAIN THE SUCCESS MECHANISM INTO YOUR NERVOUS SYSTEM

CYBERNETICS REVEALS THAT each of us has in his employ a habit robot capable of carrying out intricate and complex tasks without our having to think about them. This habit robot is the human nervous system. Picture if you will the president of a big corporation sitting at his desk smoking a cigar and pleasurably contemplating his afternoon golf game, while over in the corner a computing machine takes all the actions necessary to making another million. The president is the thinking self. The computing machine is the human nervous system. That should round out the picture for you.

Somebody has to train the computer to do its job, but after it's trained, it functions automatically. Somebody also has to train the nervous system to do its job, but after it's trained, it also functions automatically. The Cybernetics Success—Training Program conditions the nervous system to automatically take the actions that produce success.

A NEW WAY TO SELL NEEDLES

I got into selling when I was eight years old. I saw an ad in Popular Mechanics Magazine that said, "Sell these needles and win a Red Racer Bicycle." All you needed was $12.95. I sent in the coupon, and when the postman came to the door with the package, my dad bailed me out and promptly gave me a lecture about squandering his money. I looked at it differently. There was something about those needles I thought was a winner. The eye of each needle was gold, and I'd heard somewhere that gold was a magnet. That gold eye would pull a thread right through it, and all over St. Johns were thousands of old ladies who couldn't see to thread a needle. A magnetic eye was the answer to their problem.

You get the pitch? I stood on the front porch, a young kid who could see like an eagle, and jammed that thread through the eye of the needle and said the gold was a magnet and the thread never missed.

I sold out in one day. I won four Red Racer bicycles in one month. I won the state sales contest. And get this: All over St. Johns, old ladies were jamming threads through the eyes of those needles, never missing!

I thought I'd got a leg up on my fortune. Even my dad was impressed. Then the sales-manager came around to present my contest award. He seemed somewhat surprised that I was only eight. He asked me how I was selling all those needles. I told him. Then my dad peeled him off the ceiling with a spatula. The gist of his subsequent raving was that the gold eye was just an ornament, and the only thing magnetic about it was what I'd dreamed up in my mind.

I couldn't believe it. How come all those old ladies were able to thread the needles? I decided to go out and tell them the truth and see for myself. And you know what? Those I told were never able to get the thread through the eye of the needle again! It took me thirty years to figure out why, and when I did, it opened up a whole new world.

HOW TO WALK WIRES, PLAY PIANOS, THREAD NEEDLES

Have you ever heard of purpose tremor? Purpose tremor is the shaking or oscillating that affects some people because their nervous systems produce too much feedback and they over-correct their mistakes. When you and I reach to pick up a pencil, it seems like a smooth movement, but our nervous systems are making hundreds of tiny corrections at each instant to guide our hands to the pencil. That's the way a torpedo runs to a target, correcting each of its mistakes through feedback, smoothly and efficiently.

Now what would happen if you lost confidence in your built-in guidance mechanism when you reached to pick up a pencil? Why, you'd be watching for a mistake, wouldn't you? And when it came, you'd consciously correct it, isn't that right? And when you consciously corrected it, you'd over-correct it, isn't that true? And then your hand would go into oscillation. You'd have purpose tremor. And all because you'd lost confidence in your built-in guidance mechanism.

I was eight years old when I sold those needles, and my sales pitch was a con, even though I didn't know it, and afterwards I was ashamed. But I'm not ashamed anymore. Because now I know I wasn't selling needles, I was selling confidence, the most precious commodity in the world. I sold those old ladies a renewed confidence in their built-in guidance mechanism, and as long as they believed in it, they could put the thread through the eye of the needle. And now I've lived long enough to know that anyone who has confidence in his built-in guidance mechanism will always thread the needle of life, no matter how high his goals are, no matter how large the tasks he sets for himself.

You want to be good. Not just one of the crowd—get-by people, but one of the top flight, high grade experts. And you can. You not only can but you will, if you train that guidance mechanism of yours to propel you to the top. First, understand what you do. Then understand how it's done. Then train, train, train, until you move at a target with the ease and speed of a guided missile in space.

Have you ever watched an aerialist walk a tight wire, high in the air? He doesn't think where to put his feet. If he did, he'd fall off. He trusts his built-in guidance mechanism, and he trusts it because he's trained it. Have you ever seen a great pianist give a concert? He doesn't think which finger hits which key. If he did, he couldn't play chopsticks. He trusts his built-in guidance mechanism, and he trusts it because he's trained it. Whenever you see any great professional work, you're watching a man with a highly trained built-in guidance mechanism, which he trusts because he's trained.

THE SECRET OF HARRY THE HUSTLER

Too many of us try to think our way into skillful performance. Too many step by step manuals are published telling us what to do every split second. So what happens? We overemphasize, over-correct, develop purpose tremor, go into oscillation. We lose that smooth, easy, flowing performance that separates the pro from the amateur. The pro trusts his built-in guidance mechanism because he's trained it. The amateur never does. He never trusts and he never trains.

There used to be a guy at a Los Angeles country club who everybody referred to as Harry the Hustler. He could shoot golf in the seventies, and he never took a lesson in his life. But he sure could sell them. He used them to soften up his opponents. When he picked out a pigeon, he'd begin by telling him how great he could be, then send him to the pro to take lessons. Right in the middle of those lessons, Harry would take the pigeon out on the course for a hundred dollars a side. Picture this guy who just had the lessons. His golf game is a long-drawn mumble, "Keep the right elbow down, keep the head still, eye on the ball, take the club back slow, swing from the inside out, finish with the hands high." Very monotonous. And one thing missing. He forgets to hit the ball. What did Harry do? He hit the ball. He let his guidance mechanism do the thinking for him. The result: He was two hundred dollars richer. The only thing the other guy got was a fit of the shakes, which even lengthy watering at the nineteenth hole couldn't dampen.

If the executive with the cigar kept getting up every five seconds to stop the computer and check its results, what would happen? He'd wind up with the shakes too, wouldn't he? And the computer would never get its job done. Successful performance is unthinking performance because it's been trained into the nervous system. Harry the Hustler made a good living by getting people to think while they were hitting a golf ball. I once asked him what he thought of when he hit one. "Nothing'," he answered. He knew his onions.

HOW TO COMMAND THE RED SEA TO PART

A number of years ago, I wrote a book, *Three Magic Words.* It was pre-cybernetics, but it still talked about developing success habits. It sold thousands of copies all over the world and helped a lot of people, but it didn't help those who missed the idea of action.

One day I got a call from a guy who said, "I read your book and picked up the point that when we think big, we do big."

" I guess you could say that's one of its points," I conceded.

" It doesn't work!" he hollered. "I've been trying to make money with it for weeks. I've been sitting here in my room, thinking big.

Nothing's happened."

" What were you expecting to happen?" I asked gently.

" What else? Somebody should send me a check in the mails. Or call me up and offer me a job."

" Now you just sit there quietly," I said. "I'm going to send over a man with a nice big net. He's going to put you in it and take you to a place where all wishes conies true. Will that be all right?"

He suggested I might have been born illegitimately, then he hung up. But maybe he got the message. The power of thought is that it can move you, not the world. The usefulness of thought is that it trains you, not someone else. If you train yourself to sit there, that's just what you do. You can train yourself to command the Red Sea to part. That won't make it part, but it will train you to command it to.

CHECKPOINT FOR SUCCESS

Here's a great checkpoint for everything that goes on in your head: Are the things you're thinking training you to take right action? If not, what do you do? Why, you change the things you're thinking, don't you? You concentrate on images that train you to right action. Mental rehearsal for success is simply this: Using your imagination in every conceivable situation to build up a backlog of synthetic experience that will allow you to function skillfully in every real situation that arises. Skull practice. Using the head. Disciplining the imagination in the service of building better attitudes, skills, and abilities. Thousands of people have improved their skills in this manner, fifteen minutes in a car, fifteen minutes in a waiting room; before, all that time wasted, now spent building better skills and attitudes through mental rehearsal.

The most fantastic thing about man is his imagination. Imagination has brought us every great invention, discovery, prompted all research, created every work of art. But it's only now that we've realized that imagination is also the key to attitude, motivation, and personal performance. You want to develop better attitudes, more drive, better skills? You want to achieve more, earn more? Then use your imagination. Set high, challenging goals. Harness your imagination to them. Rehearse their achievement in your mind. You'll be startled at the heights to which a disciplined imagination can carry you. The entire effectiveness of Success Cybernetics is due to the disciplined use of imagination. Thousands of people are achieving more, earning more, performing better today because they've taken charge of their own minds, taken charge of their imaginations.

When you paint success pictures in your mind, you initiate an inner process whereby your attitudes, hopes, aspirations, and enthusiasm are elevated in response to an image of a more promising future. Every person who aspires must first sell himself hope, the promise of a better life, and he does this by creating it in his mind. The whole essence of Cybernetics Success—Training is taking charge of the imagination. Paint only success pictures there. Start your inner process working toward the goal of a better life, and you will be motivated to achieve it. The fundamental law of Success Cybernetics is that a man is motivated to do and be that which occupies his consciousness. Keep this in the forefront of every situation that confronts you. Keep those mental pictures focused on success, and you will inevitably train yourself to create that success in reality.

WHAT OLD ARCHIMEDES DISCOVERED

Sometimes in a seminar I'll have somebody get up and try to lift himself by his bootstraps. Since I seldom have people in a seminar who are totally daffy, I usually have to use a little persuasion. There's nothing so fascinating as watching a dignified executive trying to lift himself from the floor by tugging at his ankles. I've had several get totally winded, but I've never had a single one even get lighter. Curious thing, you have to talk them into trying it, but once they get started they act as if it's possible. They get to tugging away for all they're worth. When they don't make it, they behave as if it's my fault. I've had some of them get pretty hot about it.

The reason I pull this corny bit is to illustrate that you can't get a thing done by going about it the wrong way. Effort won't do it. Energy won't do it. Will power won't do it. Persistence won't do it. Confidence won't do it. Courage won't do it. Positive thinking won't do it. By the time I run through enough of the things that won't do it, everybody is anxious to find out what will. So I ask them, "What will do it?"

Usually several of the bright ones chirp up and say, "Going about it the right way." But I don't let them off the hook that easy. "What's the right way?" I persist. Everybody stares at me with attentive, blank faces. By this time they're beginning to think it's possible to lift yourself off the ground. I'm sure they figure I've picked up a secret from Harry Houdini.

I've still got my red-faced executive there, the guy who couldn't lift himself off the ground by his bootstraps, so I throw a loop of rope over his shoulders and tighten it under his armpits while I tell them about old Archimedes. He tried to lift himself by his bootstraps too and wore himself to a frazzle. Finally, he decided there must be a better way. What he came up with was the lever. Then I lead the rope through a pulley on the ceiling, hand the end to the executive and say, "Pull!" He pulls himself off the floor.

As he dangles there, you might think he's suddenly discovered he's a bird, his astonishment is so profound. Everybody else seems equally entranced, so I hit them with the snapper. "You *can* lift yourself by your own effort. It was proven four centuries ago. All you need is a lever!"

OPERATION BOOTSTRAP

I encourage the executive to fly back to earth, get him seated again and accustomed to the ground, then I launch Operation Bootstrap. Operation Bootstrap is in honor of old Archimedes. It's a reminder that we can get a big job done by using a lever. The lever in this case is Success Cybernetics. When you try to accomplish something by going about it the wrong way, it's like trying to lift yourself from the ground by your bootstraps. When you try to move higher by using a lever, you're bound to move higher when you learn how to use it.

The whole point of Operation Bootstrap is that you can't be successful when you're afraid of failure. Just like Archimedes' law of the lever, the law of the mind is that in any conflict between the will and the imagination, the imagination always wins. You see this illustrated practically every Sunday on national TV. Some guy comes up to the eighteenth green needing a four foot putt to win twenty thousand dollars. On the practice green he made four hundred in a row. You'd think he'd be a cinch, wouldn't you? He isn't. Chances are he blows it a mile. Not that he doesn't want it the worst way. He wants it so bad he can taste it. His will power is working fine. What isn't working so good is his imagination. What if he misses it? Twenty thousand dollars down the drain. People will think he doesn't have any guts, that he choked when the blue chips were down. Somebody is sure to laugh. His wife will raise hell. Even the kids will be after him for blowing their summer camp money. Now you tell me what that man is concentrating on. When he gets behind the ball to look at the line to the cup, he actually sees a line that drifts off to New Jersey. When he gets up and hits it, you'd think he was aiming for Europe. That is, if he hits it at all. I've seen some of them stand there so long you could cast them in bronze. That's what fear does to you. It makes you do the thing you're afraid of. It makes you concentrate on what you don't want, and what we concentrate on becomes real.

What I'm getting at is that to accomplish a job you have to think of accomplishing it. If you think of not accomplishing it, you won't. It's got nothing to do with will power or courage, just imagination. Small wonder that the principal tenet of Success Cybernetics is learning how to discipline the imagination. If it's not disciplined, it's like a live grenade in your head. The first little jar, and you're blown to pieces. But if it's disciplined, it's like Archimedes' lever. All you have to do is find a place to stand. You can move the world.

HOW TO BECOME A SVENGALI

At this point in a seminar, somebody will ask me, "What about hypnosis?" What he wants is to learn how to do it. He's heard of Svengali and Trilby, and there's this girl he knows. . . . Well, what he wants to do with it is up to him. Let the ladies look out for themselves. I show him how to do it.

The famous state of hypnosis is the state of concentration. Nearly everybody goes through it several times a day. Concentration is paying attention to pictures in the mind. It makes those pictures seem real. That's all there is to hypnosis. The last time you were all wrapped up in a movie, you were hypnotized. They could have shot off a bomb outside the theatre and you wouldn't have flinched because you wouldn't have heard it. Remember the bruises I picked up on the football field? I never even felt them. I was hypnotized by a football game.

Usually the guy planning to make a Trilby out of some unsuspecting female doesn't immediately see how to put this to use. He should take a lesson from Madison Avenue. They hypnotize millions every day by getting them to concentrate on something that leads up to soap. There's this dove that flies into Mrs. Gurney's kitchen. Mighty mysterious. Now they've got you concentrating. They take you inside the kitchen and bang! They hit you with the soap. It's a wonder we don't all walk around babbling the name of that soap. Such is the power of suggestion.

In the seminar, we all play a game. I have everybody clasp his hands together in front of him. Then I ask everyone to imagine that his hands are welded together. If he tries to take them apart, they'll only squeeze tighter together. To urge them into this feeling, I say, "Try to take them apart. See? They squeeze tighter together." Then I stand there and shout at the top of my lungs, "Pull your hands apart! Pull your hands apart!" You know something? Not one of those idiots can pull his hands apart. There's nothing so interesting as a two hundred pound executive whose orders rule an empire sitting there fuming and sweating trying to get his hands apart. You can see his knuckles whiten, the sweat break out on his forehead. It's the old bootstrap deal, applied to the mind. No one can do anything when he's imagining the opposite. By the sweating and straining that goes on in the room, you might think these guys will show up at the office with their hands clasped in front of them. But they get them apart. I just say, "Imagine you can pull your hands apart." They pull their hands apart.

WHAT MAKES THINGS IMPOSSIBLE

If anyone needs any further illustration that imagination rules conduct, I figure he ought to learn Braille. You can have the strength of Hercules, but you can't lift a pencil if you imagine you can't. You can have the intelligence of Einstein, but you can't add two and two if you imagine you can't. You can have the literary talent of Tolstoy, but you can't write a sentence if you imagine you can't. And what's more important, you can have a burning desire to be rich, but you can't make five hundred a month if you imagine you can't. So much for burning desire.

A man is what he imagines, acts as he imagines, sees what he imagines, thinks as he imagines, performs as he imagines. I'm no Bishop Berkeley. I'm not trying to say there's no world. I'm saying that the portion we see of it is colored by what we imagine. In fact, the only portion we see is that which our imagination allows us to perceive. Take three guys standing on a street corner. One is an advertising man, the other a real estate man, the third an automobile man. You think they see the same thing? Not on your life. The advertising man sees the billboard, wonders how much it cost to put up that poster, whether or not he has a chance to get that account. The real estate man sees a vacant lot, wonders what the asking price is, whether or not he could promote an office building on it. The automobile man sees the cars going down the street, notices that there are plenty of Fords, wonders whether Ford might not beat out Chevy this year. Ask them to tell you what was on that corner. You might think they were on corners a hundred miles apart. What they saw was all there, and a whale of a lot more. The mind only perceives what the mind concentrates on.

WHO'S DRIVING?

Let's get to something that's even more important. I'm standing on that same corner with a guy, and I think I'm a failure, and he thinks he's a success. Let's suppose we each see the billboard, the vacant lot, and the cars. What I notice about the billboard is that everybody is always trying to sell you something, but what can you expect, the world is full of people trying to take advantage of you. What he notices about the billboard is that the gadget advertised would save him time and trouble and look nice in his home. What I notice about the vacant lot is that there's no building on it, which probably indicates things are overbuilt and we're going to have a depression, serves people right for continually chasing after money. What he notices about the vacant lot is that there is no drugstore in the area and a drugstore would do very nicely. He makes a mental note to call his real estate broker. What I notice about the cars is that the people driving new ones are all money grubbers, I can tell just by looking at them, you couldn't get me to drive a new car, I'd rather drive an old one, that shows I've got values. What he notices about the cars is that the Continental looks just great, just imagine driving that beauty up in front of the club, and going cross country it must purr at a hundred, he decides that he'll get one.

We're two data processing machines standing on a corner. The exact same data are fed into each. But one is programmed for failure, the other for success. Each finds what it looks for. That's simply science.

It may be dawning on you that you'd better take control of your mental machine or it may run you off a cliff. They peeled a guy out of a wreck on the Hollywood Freeway. He was sitting on the right side of the front seat and nobody was behind the steering wheel. He said he thought someone else was driving. They booked him for drunk driving, and he wound up in jail. Yet millions of people sit on the wrong side of the mental front seats and act as if someone else is driving. They don't get booked for drunk driving, but there ought to be a law. They're a menace to everyone, especially themselves.

Cybernetics Success-Training says that a man must decide where he's going and the habits that will get him there, then train these habits into his nervous system until they function automatically. That makes him a good driver of both cars and himself. And the fundamental technique of Success Cybernetics is to discipline the mind to think only success. That trains the nervous system to function successfully.

So now you've designed for yourself a fighting self-concept to give you the power mechanism to really take off, and you've constructed a guidance mechanism to zero you in on your target. All that remains is to train this success mechanism into your nervous system. Once it's programmed into your human computer, you can sit at your mental desk and smoke a cigar. The computer will take care of hitting the target. The only effort is training. The rest is automatic.

HOW NOT TO HAVE HOLES IN YOUR POCKETS

I had a big strapping guy tell me he felt like an idiot carrying around a card that told him what to do. He was ashamed to let anyone see him look at it. And it offended his dignity to think of himself as a machine. He wanted to be a spirit. I twisted his arm by telling him Big Brother was watching. And Big Brother was. Big Brother was his boss. But inside three months this guy had everyone in the office carrying a card. He even had them pasted on the wall. The reason was simple: It worked. And he postponed the idea of being a spirit until he had to give up the machine.

A friend of mine was faced with going into bankruptcy. He owned a print shop and had been printing up shopping papers for several publishers. Within a single week, they folded their doors one after the other and left him stuck with unpaid printing bills. Without that money, he couldn't meet the demands of his own creditors, and it looked as if he'd be carried under himself. It's often been said that drowning men clutch at straws. That's pretty late for experiment, but most people have to be faced with extremity before they can try something new. What my friend clutched for was the idea of "Fight for it!" He put it on a card and started carrying it around with him. In a few days, he noticed he could take over the ownership of the defunct shopping papers. That night he wrote something else on the card, "You can do it!" He took over the ownership. That's when he noticed that he could manufacture those papers cheaper than other people. That gave him an edge. Then he wrote on the card, "It's a game." He reduced advertising rates, and some of the merchants decided to give him a try. Then he wrote something else on the card, "Solve the marketing problems of your advertisers." That's when he noticed that people liked free items and if they picked them up in a store they usually bought something else. He designed an advertising program built around this. He sold space like hotcakes. He put those shopping papers on their feet, but he didn't stop there. He liked the idea of that card so well that he kept writing things on it. Today he publishes fifteen shopping papers and is the largest independent newspaper publisher in the Pacific Northwest.

He dropped into my office not long ago. He's a millionaire now, but as we stood there chatting he pulled out his card proudly. Don't be ashamed of carrying that card. You're in very good company. Let the people who think someone else is driving go around without one. They'll never have anything anyway, except holes in their pockets.

A MAN FROM MISSOURI

Attitudes on one side, actions on the other, and do them each day, that's how you train the success mechanism into your nervous system. In the navy, they have a thing called the Plan of the Day. It says what's to be done, what time it will start, and who's stuck with doing it. After awhile everybody knows this and does it automatically. But every morning they post the Plan of the Day. They don't want anybody to forget about it. That's how to build habits.

Think of the card with your success mechanism on it as a Plan of the Day. It says what's to be done, what time it will start, and who's stuck with doing it. Even when you get to know that Plan of the Day by heart, keep right on posting it. You don't want to forget it. You want to build success habits.

A guy in a training program decided to have some fun with me. He thought mental rehearsal was a bunch of bunk and bet me ten dollars that he could call on his customers and still sell them while imagining that they wouldn't buy. Everybody in the group wanted a piece of his action because the guy was a top salesman. I could have laid off several hundred but just took the one bet. I should have had more confidence. A week later the guy sent me my ten-spot. He hadn't made a sale all week, and his note was an epic of tragedy. Some people were out, some were too busy, some were in crisis, some were in a bad mood. He'd never seen such a change in people. The test hadn't been fair. He'd run into bad luck. I was reminded of the fifteen-year-old kid who thought his father was stupid. When he got to be twenty-one, he was surprised to find out how much the old man had learned in six short years.

The interesting thing is that guy didn't make any sales the next week either. His boss called me on the carpet. Some program I was running, I'd ruined his top salesman. I had to admit that I'd started his man on failure habits. "But call him in here," I said. "I think we can fix it."

The guy came in glowering. I said, "You lost ten dollars to me. How much did you lose in commissions?" He didn't need a computer to come up with that answer. "Four hundred!" he shouted. I suggested that anyone had to be awfully stubborn to starve to death in a grocery store, then I handed him a card and told him to follow instructions. He glanced at it and walked out without a word. But the next week he made nine sales. What was on the card? "Imagine you'll sell him." He became a believer, but he sure was from Missouri.

HOW A BOSS LEARNED A SUCCESS HABIT

There are other hecklers, of course. One guy pointed out that he was always imagining playing golf but never got to do it because he had to work. That showed that mental rehearsal didn't produce action. I led the whole group out to his car and opened the trunk. Sure enough, there were his golf clubs. And in the pocket of the bag was a green fee stub showing he'd played eighteen holes the previous day. Since that had been a working day and his boss was in the group, it put him in a rather embarrassing position. For the rest of the seminar, he just sat there and listened. His boss learned a good success habit. He no longer hires guys who carry golf clubs in their cars.

What this all adds up to is that anyone who ignores the power of his imagination to influence his actions and perceptions is playing with dynamite. He might as well be striking matches in a powder keg. If he lets his imagination run off into failure patterns, all his aspirations will be blown to bits. Mental rehearsal for success is the alert, watchful disciplining of the imagination to envisage only those attitudes and actions that result in success. You can't be a success envisaging failure. You can't be a failure envisaging success. Sure there are problems in everyone's life. But if you let those problems push your imagination into viewing them as obstacles, that's just what they'll be. Disciplined imagination doesn't dwell on problems. It concentrates on solutions. By thinking of solutions, it thinks of success. That produces the experience that allows successful action. It also produces solutions.

HOW TO TAKE CHARGE OF YOUR WIFE

There's often a. slight problem in using auto-suggestion. A guy falling asleep mumbling, "Fight for it!" occasionally opens his eyes to find he has an interested onlooker—his wife. She's usually hard to convince that he hasn't flipped his wig. If she begins to gather he's serious, he often finds a fight quicker than he bargained for. If he's going to talk to himself all night long, how's she going to get to sleep? This has been known to develop into a brannigan, with things being tossed besides snide remarks. If she moves into another bedroom, he's liable to decide that the price tag for success is somewhat too high. To preserve domestic bliss, it's often necessary to point out that you don't have to speak to make a suggestion, you just have to think it. It comes as a surprise to some people that it's possible to think without talking.

I am reminded of the reason that God doesn't answer prayers. Here's a guy mumbling his Pater Nosters with his mind on the golf course, as if God were a big ear and only words mattered. If you don't listen yourself, why expect anyone else to?

Words aren't important. It's what you think that matters. What you think is auto-suggestion. If you don't believe that, try convincing your girl friend that your intentions are honorable when you invite her to a candle-lit dinner and say you want to be her brother. If you want to be her brother, think it. Then there'll be no candle-lit dinner, that's how she'll know. You don't have to say it.

So you can keep your wife in the same bedroom by closing your mouth and thinking your auto-suggestions. The beauty of this is that she'll never know that you're doing it. When you begin acting masterful, she'll start inspecting the medicine cabinet for bottles of hormones. If she runs true to form, she'll investigate several other interesting clues of this nature. One thing about wives, they've all got Sherlock Holmes beat. Meantime, however, she's keeping herself occupied and isn't busy telling you that you can't do it. This allows you to think that you can. Like Hercules, your strength grows day by day. When you pull on your socks in the morning, you feel like a man. When you sit down at the breakfast table, you act it. This will have a curious effect on your wife. She'll notice she's a woman. When that happens, you've got it made at home and can turn your attention to the office.

SUCCESS CYBERNETICS TRAINING

We write down the attitudes and actions of our success mechanism and carry them around on a card. We train these attitudes and actions into our nervous system by mental rehearsal and autosuggestion. We reinforce them into success habits by their conscientious performance day after day. That's the training program of Success Cybernetics.

·6· HOW TO CONSTANTLY IMPROVE YOUR SKILLS AND ABILITIES

I'M THINKING of the IBM learning machine. How smart will it get? Even now it's consulted by the heads of industry and the best banking brains. I wouldn't be surprised if even the President occasionally drops by for a little chat. Some people are afraid we've created a Frankenstein monster that one day soon will take over the world. Others pooh-pooh this. They say there's nothing to be concerned about because the machine isn't conscious. Frankly, that's exactly what worries me. Seems to me that you have to be conscious before you have conscience. I get the idea that the computer has about as much conscience as a steam roller. Until it develops a little, we ought to be careful where we point it. It might even be encouraging to consider that right now, among the humming wires and transistors of the busy machine, a little consciousness may be in process of forming. A self-conscious computer will be something to see. It will probably get embarrassed if it makes a mistake.

HOW NOT TO ROLL A ROCK UP A MOUNTAIN

Meantime what we can learn from the learning machine is that it continues to improve because it corrects its mistakes. It does this by throwing out the things that don't work, keeping the things that do work, and trying the things that look as if they might. That's a process that normally stops in people when they're twenty. If it didn't, everybody would get smarter than Einstein. That's how you constantly improve your skills and abilities.

There was the Greek god who got in trouble with the brass on Olympus. They made him push a boulder up the mountain. When he got it to the top, it would roll back down, and he'd have to start all over, ad infinitum. Mighty monotonous. He carried the unlikely handle of Sisyphus, and for all I know old Sisyphus is still pushing his rock. They say thunder is caused when it rolls down the mountain, and I occasionally hear thunder. One thing is certain. This guy must be the alter ego of millions of people who keep pushing rocks up mountains just to watch them roll down. You could say this is a bad habit. You could also say these people have stopped learning.

Somebody said, "Habits are first cobwebs, then finally cables." That's a nice way of saying that you can't lose ten pounds because you can't stop eating. It also accounts for the existence of magic. People would rather have magic than try to break a habit. Such an attitude allows you to believe that you can eat all you want and still lose weight. All you have to do is eat one thing more. A pill.

I'm toying with the idea that the reason America is overweight is because of the conditioned reflex established between the TV commercial and the refrigerator door. When I'm watching some show and suddenly a dove flies into Mrs. Gurney's kitchen, it seems to me I can hear millions of chairs being pushed back, millions of feet padding across the floor, millions of refrigerator doors being yanked open, millions of hands rummaging about for salami. By the time the dove turns into a box of soap, I can hear millions of teeth chomping placidly away, just as when Pavlov rang a bell and his dogs' mouths watered. What else could they do? They didn't have a refrigerator.

HOW TO BREAK HABITS

The main reason people stop learning is that they keep practicing their errors. This allows them to become excellent at error. I guess nobody likes to give up anything he does well, even if it's making mistakes. Some people like to make their errors by struggling. They found a guy below a bridge ramp with his car stuck up a tree. It looked like a bird's nest. Somebody asked him how he got into such a mess. He answered, "It wasn't easy." You can make a habit of winding up with your car up a tree. All you have to do is practice it. More than that, you can start other people doing it. That's how society is born.

It comes as a surprise to most people that a success habit can turn into a failure habit. They figure that once you've got a good thing going, you ought to keep doing it, whether it works or not. This accounts for the guy who comes into a new company and keeps doing things the way he did them at the old one. He winds up fired but still maintaining he was right. It also accounts for the guy who murdered eighty-three Germans, all nice and legal because there was a war. When the war was over he kept murdering Germans and was terribly incensed when they gave him the gas chamber. What works in one situation doesn't necessarily work in another. If it doesn't, automatic Ike needs a little reprogramming. He needs to change habits. And in order to change, you have to change.

The reason the learning machine is able to learn is that it breaks its bad habits.

That's what it does when it throws out the things that don't work. It might push the rock up to the top of the mountain a few times, but when it discovers that the rock continually rolls down, it stops pushing it up and looks for a new way to solve the problem. Which may prove that they'll never make a god of the learning machine. At least not one called Sisyphus.

A NEW LOOK AT INTELLIGENCE

Now you can say that this machine is inhuman if you want to, which I would gather to mean that you think it's inhuman to learn, and from which I infer that the human state is stupidity. I grant you that this seems to be the state at the moment, but I am encouraged to believe that humans can learn too, and not just until they're twenty, but as long as they live. Strikes me it's just a matter of breaking bad habits.

Let's ponder for a moment this business of thought. If we give a man an intelligence test and he makes a score of one hundred and seventy, we say he's a genius. Yet maybe he can't make a dime and is drinking himself to death. So what are we measuring? Certainly not his ability to think. He's just a machine that could guide a missile to Mars but is so badly programmed it can't turn on the coffee. What's more, he can't learn to turn on the coffee. He just keeps pushing that rock up the side of the mountain. If thinking is anything it must be the ability to learn, so our genius can't think, he just has the capacity for it. If you're on the same track as I am, you can see a train coming. The ability to think is the ability to break habits.

Anything automatic is certainly not thought. So what are intelligence tests measuring? They're measuring complexity, and the more complex a thing, the easier it's fouled up. One of these days the brain watchers will get around to devising a test that shows the ability to break habits. That will be some kind of measure of a man's ability to think. It will also be some guarantee that he won't be trying to make money by methods that don't produce a dime or trying to find cheerfulness on the inside of a bottle. Success Cybernetics is automatic control that hits a target. If the automatic control misses the target, you change the automatic control. That requires breaking habits. That requires that you think.

I am constantly beset by humanists who recoil in horror at the idea that the human body is a machine. They loudly protest against notions of automatic function. They hold out for spontaneity, doing whatever occurs to them. I've yet to find one who can throw a bowling ball straight or hit a golf ball where he wants to or even make money unless somebody leaves it to him. But they're sure proud of the fact that they're free of all habits. They can't see they've made a habit of not knowing how. What's more, they can't learn. They just keep being spontaneous.

Habits are servants. Like any servant, they can start running the master. When that happens, the master has to think. Steam may shoot out of his ears at this unusual activity, but there's no other way to bring that servant back into line. Sometimes the servant has to be fired. Sometimes he has to be taught to smile and bow. But always and ever he has to know who's the boss. That's the ability to think. Without it, you can't be master of either yourself or your habits. If you don't want to try thinking, buy a bottle of booze. At least you'll be numb to the arrows of fortune.

WHEN NOT TO BE A RIVETER

There used to be a riveter on a General Motors assembly line who riveted three rivets. They were the same three rivets on every chassis that went by, and he did this hour after hour, day after day, for twenty years. Then they changed the assembly line. No more rivets. They gave him a wrench and asked him to tighten a bolt. He had a nervous breakdown. Every time a chassis came by he was after three rivets. By the time he got around to finding the bolt, the chassis had moved down the line. To say he was confused is putting it mildly. You could say he was a nut looking for a bolt but seeing only rivets. The head-shrinkers diagnosed him as having a neurosis. They gave him the ego-id treatment without too much luck. Then somebody got the bright idea of training him to tighten the bolt. Eventually he got the hang of it and built up the habit. It must have straightened out his id too, because he lost his neurosis.

Bad habits can make you sick. Good habits can keep you well. Getting rid of bad habits enables you to learn. That's how you constantly improve your skills and abilities.

The only test of a habit is whether or not it produces success. If you aim to the left and shoot to the right, that's a bad habit. You change it to a good habit by building one that causes you to shoot where you're aiming. If you're looking for rivets when you should be looking for bolts, you have to build a habit of looking for bolts. All this sounds very elementary, I know. Maybe that's why so few people see it. I gave a lecture the other day and afterwards a guy came up to me and said he didn't think people could improve their skills after they were thirty. I asked him what clinic this experiment had been conducted in. It turned out to be inside himself. He'd held the same job ever since he was thirty. But you couldn't convince him his attitude caused it. Oh, no. What he came up with was a universal pronouncement: People can't improve their skills after thirty. He liked those three rivets. He didn't want to change to tightening the bolts.

In order to grow you have to think that you can. If you arrive at thirty and think that you can't, that's where you stop. And it's caused by an attitude that's hardened into a habit.

HOW TO WALK ACROSS A PLANK

I once took my eight-year-old daughter out for a walk. We came upon a ten foot plank that was raised a foot off the ground. It was about twelve inches wide, and I asked her if she could walk across it. "Sure," she replied, and skipped across it like a gazelle. Then I said, "Let's play a game. I want you to imagine that plank lies across a deep canyon. Way down below is a river. See that little trickle of water? That's the river. See that match by the water? That's a log. It's thousands of feet down there. If you fall off the plank, you'll be sure to be killed. Now walk across the plank."

It was a different little girl who stood looking at that plank. The gazelle had deserted her. As she edged herself out, her arms jerked around as if they didn't belong to her. She had taken only three steps when she lost her balance and fell with a scream. She might have died of fright if I hadn't caught her. It was only a foot, but in her mind it was a mile.

You can walk across a plank if you think that you can, but you're certain to fall off if you think that you might. You can continue to grow if you think that you can, but you're certain to stop if you think that you can't. Surely the most important possession a human being can own is the belief that he can. It installs a learning circuit within your human computer, just as they installed a learning circuit in the IBM computer. The rest is just a matter of throwing out the things that don't work, keeping the things that do work, and trying the things that look as if they might work. It's difficult to convince people that they're captive to their attitudes, yet the evidence proliferates all over the landscape. If you don't believe that, check the number of times you hear "I can't" and "It's impossible" in the next twenty-four hours. That puts a lid on the cake all right. All the yeast in the world won't make it rise in the pan.

So you launch yourself on constant improvement by emblazoning "I can" and

"It's possible" on your escutcheon of combat. And to all negations you lend a deaf ear. Plenty of people will tell you can't. That prohibits it for them, but if you don't listen, it can't bother you. This is liable to cut you out of eighty percent of most conversations, but don't worry about it, you won't be missing a thing. When people find reasons why things can't be done, they wind up believing them. This allows them to sleep late in the morning since there's nothing to do.

OPERATION DUCK'S BACK

To combat "You cant's," I launch Operation Duck's Back. You see, it can rain on a duck but a duck doesn't get wet. That's highly useful for a duck when it's caught in the rain. A similar impervious-ness is useful to humans when they're caught in the fallout of negative circumstances and people. They can fly through the fallout without getting poisoned.

I'm pretty good at Operation Duck's Back myself. I have to be. When you ask people to change, they tell you they can't. If I listened to their protests and all of their reasons, I'd wind up believing them. So I never hear what they say. I hear something different. During a seminar, somebody is almost sure to relate how he's tried and tried to do something and has never been able to do it, so that proves he can't. This sounds like good evidence. Without Operation Duck's Back, you'd be almost sure to believe it.

Remember my daughter skipping across the plank like a gazelle? Did she look as if she were trying? Not to me she didn't. She looked like a seagull soaring the sky effortlessly. What happened when she got the idea she might not be able to walk the plank? She tried her little heart out. Five minutes of that kind of effort would have exhausted her. Remember the two hundred pound executive who couldn't get his hands apart? He was trying so hard that if you let him go at it for an hour you'd have to call an ambulance. How hard do you suppose he ordinarily tries when he takes his hands apart? I doubt he's aware of any effort at all. He just takes his hands apart because he has the idea that he can.

If you ask a healthy man to walk up a hill, he gets to the top without drawing a deep breath. But if you put enough weight on his back, he can't take the first step. He can struggle and sweat and try frantically, but the weight keeps him down. Substitute for the weight the idea of "I can't," and you'll see what I'm driving at. Get rid of "I can't" and you skip across the plank like a gazelle.

HOW TO PROTECT A PRECIOUS JEWEL

If a person tries and tries and never can do it, it doesn't mean that he can't, it just means he thinks he can't. In fact, I'd go so far as to say that most evidence of effort is evidence of an inner "I can't." I support this out of my own experience in athletics, business, speaking and writing. The things I've done well I've done easily. The things I've done poorly have required inordinate effort. I even use this today to see if I'm set for success. If I'm moving easily and effortlessly, I'm set on "I can." If I'm moving with effort, I'm set on "I can't." Needless to say I turn all my attention to getting set on "I can."

If you had a precious jewel, you'd put it in a safe place. You have a precious jewel. It's the belief that you can. Operation Duck's Back gives you a safe place to keep it. The reason a duck's feathers never get wet is because they're coated with oil. Water can't penetrate oil. Hence the duck never gets wet. Operation Duck's Back is designed to coat your "I can" with repellent oil to ward off the rain of "You cant's."

Here's how you generate the repellent oil: When you hear a "You can't," you listen "I can."

I've seen enough open mouths when I've issued that statement to realize it must violate some basic rule of reason. But the point is it works and is one of the profound secrets of success. And don't tell me impossible, we've been over that. And don't tell me you can't, because I'm telling you that you can.

Anything that can be demonstrated in a person under hypnosis can be achieved in the waking state by a process of conditioning. Every hypnotist and conditioned reflex psychologist knows this. I once put a man under hypnosis and told him that whenever I said, "You can't" he was to hear, "I can." This guy was a prototype of Charles Atlas' one hundred and thirty pound weakling, but he lifted two hundred pounds over his head when I said, "You can't." He was normally shy and had a slight stutter, but he made a great speech when I said, "You can't." He was a wallflower with the ladies, but he started dragging one off to the bedroom when I said, "You can't." I had to bring him out of the trance so he wouldn't be embarrassed later. She was a little disappointed.

A PROFOUND SUCCESS SECRET

There's no question about it. You can train yourself to listen "I can" when someone says, "You can't." Think of the power generated by Operation Duck's Back. People are always telling you that you can't but you're always hearing them say that you can. You develop into a whirlwind of achievement and improvement, skipping across canyons on twelve inch wide planks. Just like a gazelle, because you think that you can.

Now anybody who pays any attention at all realizes that all successful people have this trait. I've sat across enough wide mahogany desks and listened to enough success stories to know that they all have a common denominator. Somewhere, sometimes, in each successful man's life, someone said "You can't" and he listened "I can." Usually it comes out like this: "I went to work for so and so and he fired me and told me I'd never amount to a hill of beans. I decided to show him." This is hearing "You can't" and listening "I can." In the stormy sea of negatives it's a sure-fire ship to the shores of success.

We have a lot of fun with Operation Duck's Back. As soon as people start consciously turning "you cant's" into "I cans," they find them as plentiful as grains of sand on a beach. The first reaction is a kind of chaos as people begin moving in opposite directions and saying opposite things. There's a kind of initial perverseness as everyone laughs uproariously because he did the thing you said he couldn't do. Then there's the problem of signs. Most of them say "You can't," things like STOP, KEEP OFF THE GRASS, DON'T SPIT ON THE FLOOR. Some of these have to be allowed to filter through the repellent oil or you can wind up in jail. A few people have a fling at treating prohibitive signs in the opposite manner, though I trust no one runs a stop sign, but most are content just to realize they can and then tolerantly put up with these negative evidences of society's orderliness.

Operation Duck's Back is highly successful. I'm sure one of the reasons is that it gives people the same pleasure as stealing a cookie from the pantry jar. Everybody has a whale of a time, and excitement is a powerful ingredient in getting a job done. And you've no idea the magic it works on negative people. When they see that the arrows just make you stronger, they throw away the arrows and have a try at using your armor. Pretty soon they're as good at Operation Duck's Back as anyone else.

HOW TO BECOME A TOP PILOT

Everything we do in Success Cybernetics is aimed at getting control of our minds. We have the success mechanism which consists of the guidance mechanism and the power mechanism, and we have the techniques of mental rehearsal and auto-suggestion. The power mechanism is our idea of what we can do, the guidance mechanism is the actions by which we intend to achieve our goals. Mental rehearsal is the technique of playing success experience in the imagination. Autosuggestion is the technique of prompting ourselves to do the things we intend to do. Operation Pretense reminds us that we turn into the image of the role we assume. Operation Bootstrap reminds us that we have a lever to move ourselves upward in Success Cybernetics. Operation Duck's Back is the technique of reinforcing ourselves with the belief that we can. All these various techniques you may regard as instruments on the control panel of the mind. They allow you to get top performance from your brain and nervous system.

I learned how to fly in a Piper Cub. It had a stick and rudder pedals and a compass and an altimeter and an airspeed indicator and that was it. The most sensitive instrument was the seat of your pants. I took off from Portland to pick up some friends in Beaver-ton. I saw them standing down there and buzzed the field a couple times to show them I was a hot pilot. Then I landed. Much to my surprise, another plane was taking off right at me. I managed to avoid it, scooted off in the brush, and my plane went over on its nose. I had arrived. One of my friends walked up and inquired sarcastically, "If you're trying to scare us, don't you think that's going too far?"

I'd landed into a cross wind according to the windsock, but the field had special rules because it ran a little downhill. I was effectively kept in ignorance because I didn't have a radio. The Civil Aeronautics inspector thought I might have overcome this handicap if I'd used my eyes. I bring up this business because not long ago I was invited into the cockpit of one of Continental Airline's Boeing 707's. I'd addressed their executives at the annual convention and told them that aviation was with us today because somebody said the first airplane wouldn't fly. So on my next trip east they decided to show me the end result of what one man had caused by turning "You can't" into "I can." It was a far cry from the cockpit of my Piper Cub. I've never seen so many dials and switches and gadgets in my life. The guys sitting in the middle of it looked like magicians. I recognized one thing immediately. These boys had control. I felt mighty secure when I went back to my seat, and it started me thinking that one day soon we'll probably have that same kind of control over the mind. The techniques already evolved have taken us well out of the Piper Cub days. You don't have to control your mind by the seat of your pants, or by guess and by God. Your control instruments tell you exactly where you're going and how you're going to get there. Learn how to use them, and you'll become a top pilot.

HOW TO CONDITION YOURSELF FOR SUCCESS

Success Cybernetics-Training is aimed at conditioning the nervous system to the automatic reflexes that produce success. The entire training program is a conditioning program. I'm using conditioning in the sense used by Pavlov. It means training the nervous system to automatically produce a certain response to a certain signal. The bell rings, that's the signal. The dog's mouth waters, that's the response. The dog doesn't try to make his mouth water. It just waters when he hears the bell, and he couldn't stop it if he tried. That's a conditioned reflex. Long before Pavlov, athletes were known to say that they had to get in condition. When they were in condition, they could make skillful responses to signals. There are two kinds of conditioning in the Pavlovian sense. You can take a natural reflex that responds a certain way to a certain signal and condition it to respond a different way. That's classical conditioning. You can take a response that is normally under conscious control and condition it to respond automatically to a signal. That's operant conditioning. The techniques vary according to whether the response you want to condition is a natural reflex or one that started out under conscious control.

A natural reflex may be conditioned without conscious intervention. It's the lowest form of nervous reflex and can get to think a bell is food simply because they are associated together in the same signal. But a response that is under conscious control can't even be made automatic until the guy at the control panel is persuaded that the price is right. In other words, he has to be paid off. He has to have a reward. For example, work habits start off being under conscious control. In order for them to be made automatic, a guy has to see that he's got something to gain. If he works hard and is amply rewarded, he surrenders control and makes hard work a habit. Then he's able to work hard even though there's no immediate gain. He's been operant conditioned to work hard. On the other hand, the digestion and ingestion of the stomach is a natural reflex. The stomach normally digests and ingests strawberries. If you eat putrid strawberries, it regurgitates them and you feel sick. Several experiences of this sort can produce a vomiting reflex at the odor of strawberries. That's classical conditioning. It will be obvious to you that Success Cybernetics works exclusively with operant conditioning.

HOW TO SEE A REWARD

This is not to say that the responses we seek to change are not now automatic. By far the great majority of them are. This is to say that they were originally under conscious control and have become automatic through operant conditioning. Let's say a man avoids people. Today that's his automatic reaction. But at some earlier period in his life, he could seek them out or avoid them as he chose. Then something happened that caused him to find a reward in avoiding them, so he started avoiding them. Repetition created an automatic response. Remember our thirty-year-old salesman who couldn't call on people because they'd given him black eyes when he was five? At five his reward for avoiding them was not getting black eyes. At thirty, he's no longer concerned that they'll give him black eyes, but he still avoids them because it's an automatic response. In order to recondition this response so that he automatically seeks people, the price has to be right. He has to see a reward. That causes him to try it. If he obtains the reward, he'll continue to do it. Repetition will establish a new conditioned response.

You may now begin to see the importance of playing only success experience in the mind. This establishes a reward, and motivates a man to try something he's automatically been avoiding. With a properly designed success mechanism, he'll find that reward waiting for him. Repetition will establish a conditioned response. He'll build success habits. Operation Bootstrap keeps alive the promise of a reward, so do Operation Pretense and Operation Duck's Back. A man who believes that he will be rewarded is a man motivated to grow. Reward is symbolized by the words "I can." They promise pleasure. Punishment is symbolized by the words "I can't." They seek to avoid pain. When a man concentrates his mental activities on the words "I can," he produces a feeling of pleasure about whatever he associates with them. This motivates him to do it. A man constantly improves his talents and abilities by constantly thinking "I can."

HOW TO KEEP PRESSING A LEVER

Brain scientists have actually found reward and punishment centers in the brain. They call them pleasure and pain centers. They have been able to plant a tiny electrode in the pleasure center of a rat's brain and lead it to a lever which the rat could press down. When the rat pressed the lever, it would make him feel good. As soon as he got the hang of it, you've never seen such activity. That rat pressed the lever all day. They couldn't get him to eat, and they couldn't get him to sleep. He just wanted to press the lever. They brought in a female who was in the mood to make love. The rat paid no attention. He was in love with the lever. They finally disconnected the electrode, but the rat kept pressing the lever. When it didn't produce pleasure, he just pressed it faster. That's operant conditioning. Now, of course, if you don't reconnect the electrode, you eventually wind up with a disappointed rat, and he'll quit pressing the lever. Oh, he may occasionally give it a try just in case, but if it doesn't produce pleasure, he'll eventually forget about it.

Operant conditioning is not so simple in people because of their imaginations. They keep pressing the lever when the electrode is disconnected because they imagine it feels good. They can be salesmen and not call on people because they imagine they don't feel well and are in need of some rest. That keeps them pressing the lever. They can be Indians and dance around campfires to bring rain and imagine the rain's coming or actually falling. That keeps them pressing the lever. In order for people to be operant reconditioned, they have to take control of their imaginations. They have to discipline their imaginations in terms of what produces right results. When they learn to do that, they can recondition their own responses. Everything is aimed at controlling the imagination. If you don't learn to control it, it controls you.

WHY PEOPLE CATCH SNIPE AND FLY TO MARS

There's a guy around Los Angeles who says he's flown to Mars. He also reports a trip to Venus and one into the center of the earth. He's talked to the space people and they've told him about the Watchers, a race of humans without souls, created by Lucifer. Seems they're running everything into the ground and the people with souls ought to get rid of them. One day this guy ran into the Head Watcher. He was able to recognize him because the Head Watcher looked evil. He found the Head Watcher's car and saw a box in the back seat. Instantly, he knew it contained the beating heart of Lucifer. He set off for tools to break into that car. If he could destroy Lucifer's heart, the Watchers would be finished. By the time he got back, the car was gone. That was fortunate for him. They would have run him into the pokey for breaking and entering.

Now you might think this guy is a fraud or a science fiction writer. I can tell you with authority, he's dead on the level. Not that he's been to Mars or to Venus or into the center of the earth. Not that there are any watchers. It's just that he imagines them. What we concentrate on seems real.

If that doesn't shake you into taking charge of your imagination, I don't know what will. Picture if you will people looking for flying saucers. They look up into the sky and concentrate on seeing one. If they concentrate hard enough they find what they look for. If they concentrate still harder the whole sky is covered with them. We once left a kid in the woods holding a gunny sack with which to catch snipe. We were supposed to herd them his way. We all went home and fell asleep laughing at that kid in the woods waiting for fictitious snipe. Next morning he was chagrined that he hadn't caught any, but hundreds had flown by, they were just too fast for him. That kid was so convincing that he nearly had us believing the woods were full of snipe.

The laws of the mind are the laws of inner conviction. Remember them well: We are what we concentrate on. What we concentrate on becomes real. What we concentrate on grows. We always find what we look for. These four laws are the key to disciplining your imagination into patterns of growth.

PUTTING THE PROGRAM TO WORK

In order to change, you've got to change. What that means right now is that in order to derive benefit from Success Cybernetics you have to put it to use. That means you must follow its training program. First, you must establish a power mechanism made up of a fighting self-concept. Second, you must design a guidance mechanism made up of the daily actions that will achieve your goals. Third, you must train this success mechanism into your nervous system by writing it down and carrying it with you, mentally rehearsing successful achievement, using auto-suggestion while falling asleep. Fourth, you must condition yourself into thinking "I can" by launching Operation Pretense, Operation Bootstrap, and Operation Duck's Back. And fifth, you must train yourself to constantly improve your performance by throwing out the things that don't work, keeping the things that do work, and trying the things that look as if they might work. These are the five steps on the Cybernetics Success-Training Program.

The next two sections of this book will discuss solving problems and handling people from the standpoint of cybernetics. Special techniques will be laid out for improving skills in both. The final section will return to the development of Cybernetic Success Patterns. But right now you have the essentials of Cybernetics Success-Training. Put them to use.

Recently I was in a corporation office when an outsider called and inquired about Success Cybernetics. The president of the corporation answered with these words: “It works.” Something that works is something that you can use.

·7· HOW TO ROCKET YOUR BRAIN POWER UP INTO ORBIT

EVERYBODY HAS HEARD the story of Aladdin and his lamp, how he rubbed it and smoke poured out and formed into a genie who carried out his every desire. Where is the man or woman who at some time in his life has not wished for such a lamp? Some people even have searched the whole world for it, all in vain. Now we know why they haven't had better luck. For if such a lamp exists, and today modern science indicates that it does, it is not to be found in the outer world, but in the six inch span between our ears.

Do ten and five ever add up to three? If your answer is no, you need to develop the creative attitude, the attitude that investigates possibilities. That ten and five could possibly add up to three seems to outrage reason itself. But in point of fact, you add them that way every day. You add them that way on the face of a clock.

HOW TO GET A JEEP THROUGH A TUNNEL

Today the creative attitude is more in demand in this nation than any other skill or ability. New ideas, new methods, new ways, better products, better services are the constant cry of every organization in this country. Never before in history have we lived in such a period of change. Minds that become standardized, that adhere to the old even for a few years, are quickly relegated to the scrapheap. How shall we keep pace with our changing world? How shall we contribute to its progress? Why, by learning how to investigate possibilities. By breaking our old habits of perception and reaction. By expanding our knowledge and combining it into new forms, new ways, new insights. In short, by developing the creative attitude.

A number of years ago I was traveling with a geologist through the back country of Utah in a jeep station wagon, searching for potential oil lands. We came to a place where the dirt road ran through a tunnel in the rocks, and our station wagon was four inches too high to get through. I was thunderstruck. It was fifty miles back to the nearest town, and I had to get into the back country that day in order to file for oil leases. If I'd had a hack saw, I'd have considered sawing off the top of that station wagon, but I didn't, and my only reaction to solving this problem was to slump down in my seat and grumble, "The wagon's too high. We can't get through."

Then this grizzled old geologist, a guy who'd spent half his life in the wilderness and hadn't got his mind locked in by habit, turned to me and said, "Think of it differently. That extra rise isn't necessarily on top, it's on the bottom too."

Then he got out and let the air out of the tires. Then he drove the jeep through the tunnel.

He had it, didn't he? He had the creative attitude. He knew how to investigate possibilities. He hadn't developed those deadly habits of perception and attitude that make us think we know all about something simply because we know its name and how it worked before. He was a problem solver. And it's problem solvers that this nation needs so badly today.

THE DEMAND FOR PROBLEM SOLVERS

Look what we're faced with: Automation—a revolution in the means of production. A runaway science that has lost communication with the people. Disassociation of mind and spirit due to living and working in masses. The increasing need for education to teach learning skills rather than stuffing the mind with facts. The conflict of cultures and ideologies due to the shrinking of our world. The constant pressure of producing more and better and more efficiently. Who will solve these problems? Then there's space travel, defense production, race integration, world government, religious evolution, advertising, selling, the list is endless. The greatest challenge and the greatest opportunity of today lies in problem solving. Where will these problem solvers come from? Why, they'll have to come from people like you and me. Because we're here now. The reins are in our hands. We can't wait for a new generation. By then the problems will be too big, too complex, too tough even to tackle.

Developing problem solving ability is a matter of assuming a creative attitude, using the imagination to investigate possibilities, relying on the power of intuitive thinking, and developing the brain's capacity through mental exercise.

It's only been recently that we've come to understand the creative attitude. For years we've had our little platitudes. Think big, do big. A winner never quits, a quitter never wins. The magic power of positive thinking. But now cybernetics has demonstrated to us that we can see and hear only the things that our mental apparatus is set to see and hear. It is this "set" that has such tremendous significance in problem solving. Let me give you an example.

A number of years ago a friend of mine called me up with a rather interesting question. "How would you like to make a million dollars?" he asked. I called a quick conference of my board of directors and we kicked it around and decided it wasn't a bad idea, so I told my friend I would like that fine, and asked him if murder was involved.

" Not at all," he said. "It's the commodity market. Specifically, coffee. I've got it nailed to the wall. Come out and see."

HOW NOT TO SOLVE PROBLEMS

He had it nailed to the wall, all right. He had a room twenty by twenty, the walls all covered with charts. He'd charted the price of coffee since its inception on the commodity market. Red, blue, and green lines ran up and down over the years, and then, three weeks into the future, all three lines intersected. He pointed at those intersecting lines. "That's the spot," he said. "Right there the bottom will fall out. Coffee will go to the lowest price in its history. We sell short now, and clean up."

I looked at that mass of charts. "How long did it take you to figure this out?" I asked. "I've been working on it for years," he said.

" And you know me, I never leave a stone unturned."

But that's precisely what I didn't know. The way I had him figured, he would always leave one stone unturned. And that stone was the possibility that the price of coffee might go up. I hadn't got the scoop from cybernetics yet, but it was his "set" I was worried about, what he could see and hear. It occurred to me that for years he had subscribed to Babcock's financial reports which annually predicted a forthcoming depression that the literature scattered around his house had the incessant theme that capitalism couldn't work and pretty soon the bubble would burst. So I began to wonder what he was prepared to see in the charts he had drawn. "Let me think it over," I said.

I thought it over until the three weeks passed and the break in the price of coffee arrived. I didn't become a millionaire, but I did save my nest egg. Coffee went to the highest price in its history.

Oh, he'd drawn the charts all right. He'd taken the figures and plotted them on his graphs just exactly the way they occurred. And he'd found the place where the red, blue, and green lines intersected which gave him the exact date something would happen. But now he had to interpret. Now his attitude came into play. What would happen on that particular day? Why, the price of coffee would go down. He simply couldn't interpret any other way. That was his "set." He was blind to any other solution.

He might as well not have drawn the charts at all. They were just one giant rationalization for a conviction he had before he began his research. His attitude made him closed-minded, incapable of learning, unable to come up with the right answer except by pure coincidence.

OLD WAYS, NEW WAYS, AND BEST WAYS

So now we learn something about attitude, something that's gotten mighty confused with all the emphasis on positive thinking. A negative attitude is any attitude that blinds us to solutions. A positive attitude is any attitude that opens our minds so that we can see them.

In the offices of Ogilvie, Wentworth, and Brown, the planning chief presents a disconsolate face to all those gathered. "We're stumped," he says. "Our experts tell us there's nothing we can do." "Oh, yes there is," says the president. "Get another group of experts!" He didn't become president by accident.

Let somebody say that it can't be done and somebody will immediately do it. The creative attitude says that it can be done, that there's a better way to do it. And the creative attitude is open-minded. It listens first, and judges later.

In the old days, the Pacific Northwest was a country full of Swedes. They worked in the woods and the mills, and they didn't talk much, and they fought a lot, and they had the answer to everything. Biff Larson was Bull of the Woods at the Columbia Sawmill, and you did things his way or you wound up with a black eye, so his way was considered best. One summer when I was working in the loading yard, it occurred to me that it might be easier to snake the cars of lumber into the dry kilns with a wire line from a donkey engine, rather than calling everybody from his job to push them in by hand. I mentioned this to Larson. Two days later, I recovered sufficiently to go back to work.

But while I was healing, I jotted down some figures on paper, and when I returned I walked up to Larson and said, "This proves you can save two hundred dollars a day with a donkey engine and a wire tow line." He fired me. I was paid to pile lumber, he said, not to think. I asked him what he was paid for. "Thinking!" he shouted. I mentioned that he was somewhat overpaid and left with my dignity intact.

Two years later every sawmill on the river was moving lumber with steam-power, but not Larson, and he took his company down with him. He had a way to do it and a way not to do it but never a better way to do it, and the march of progress has put his kind of mind on the shelf where it belongs.

HOW TO BECOME A THINKER

What good is power if it holds back progress? What good is authority if it says nothing better can be done? All over this nation men who would rather be right than discover the truth are being replaced by men who would rather discover the truth than be right. And that's the creative attitude. That's the attitude that leads to human growth and progress.

And something else we've learned about attitude. Most of us didn't deliberately think up ours. They've been conditioned into us by our experience. They've literally been written into our nervous systems and cause immediate reactions to outside signals. They've become habits that stereotype our responses that keep us acting as if today's situation is the same as a situation twenty years ago. This would be a pretty sad commentary on the ability of the human being to keep learning and improving were it not for the fact that cybernetics has found a way to break these mental habits and establish attitudes that produce creative responses. It does this by teaching us how to improve our signal skills through developing and training our symbol skills.

Cybernetics is the science of sending feedback signals from a machine's output to a machine's guidance mechanism in order to zero out performance error. One of the truly remarkable discoveries of this age is that the human nervous system functions in exactly the same manner. We learn to walk, speak, drive, play the piano, and typewrite by developing the ability to respond immediately to a signal without having to think or to wonder what to do. This remarkable facility is carried to astonishing heights by athletes, acrobats, and concert pianists, and it is only when it begins to block out thought, or more accurately, to prevent the growth of thought, that it becomes a liability instead of an asset. For thought is symbol skill—skill in using, interpreting, and reforming symbols. If thought begins to function automatically, always delivering the same response to a symbol, it is thought no longer but a conditioned reflex instead. A signal reaction is immediate, non-critical, operates without logic, simply exists and is triggered by the appropriate signal. If it produces the wrong response, we must retrain it by calling into service our symbol skills. In short, we must think.

HOW TO THINK YOUR WAY OUT OF THE WOODS

What we've learned from rocketry, the computer sciences, the whole field of cybernetics is that we can teach a machine to react, even improve its performance, by giving it highly sophisticated signal skills, but we cannot teach it to think. It simply cannot develop symbol skills. In signal skills, machines already have surpassed man, and shortly will replace him in all kinds of repetitive, routine work. And that leaves wide open the field of symbol skills, the field of creative thought, the most remarkable opportunity of history.

Fundamental in the development of creative thought is the creative attitude, the attitude that says there's a better way to do it, the attitude that says that in every obstacle there is hidden an opportunity.

I remember a seminar for automobile executives. There was one guy who must have weighed three hundred pounds, and all muscles.

During a coffee break, we struck up a conversation, and I remarked on his size. It turned out he had worked in the woods and had once won a log cutting contest in a timber festival. By the size of his arms, he could have beaten Paul Bunyan. I asked him how he ever got out of the woods and into the automobile business. He said he thought his way out.

It seems he was working in a logging camp when a flood hit the river. It jammed things up so badly that the logs couldn't be floated down. There were no roads to truck them out, and the fellow running the camp panicked. He couldn't meet the payroll, so he folded his tent and stole quietly away in the night.

The big guy looked the situation over and decided that in this obstacle there was hidden opportunity. He hustled into town and made a deal with a trucking firm to furnish Caterpillar tractors for cross country log hauling, absolutely free, just to show what those tractors could do. Then he went back to camp and told the crew they'd get fifty percent of what the logs brought when they'd moved them to the mill with the tractors. When the operation was over, he had a nice nest egg. He was about to indulge in some free spending when he was called on by the owner of the trucking company. He was hired to run it. That's how he thought his way out of the woods.

HOW TO BECOME AN EXPERT

Solutions come to the man who is willing to jump off the shore of the known into the sea of the unknown, and by swimming in these strange currents to chart a way to undiscovered shores. Nothing sustains such an adventurer but a leap of faith, an intuitive knowing that if he casts off his old habits and limitations, a new and better way will be revealed to him. It is this aspect of creativity, that it is new and strange and different, that makes it so difficult to accept for some people. It has been said, and rightly so, that there is an element of charlatanry in every creative act, and this is so because the creative individual finds himself alone, propounding a new idea without the support of authority.

There was this guy in Portland who was the last of the great losers. Like Joe Blftspk, he walked around with a rain cloud over his head. He started seven businesses, and each one blew up in his face. But he never lost his smile, and the light burned every night in his room over the corner drugstore. People would ask him what he was doing, and he would answer, "Figuring out my mistakes." The standard reaction was that he'd found a lifetime job. But you know what? This guy became successful. He became a top-flight management consultant. "You name the mistake," he'd say. "I've made it. I'm a mistake-expert. And you want somebody to help prevent yours, don't you?" They did, so they hired him.

Experts are great mistake makers. That's how they become experts. They're mistake makers because they try many things. And they try many things because they're not afraid to fail. Only a man who is unafraid to fail can try something new and unusual, a fundamental aspect of creativity.

The creative attitude is not afraid of sneers or jeers or ridicule. It is willing to cut away from tradition and the things everybody believes to be true. Every great discovery has been made because somebody was willing to try the impossible. And all too often the reward for this kind of effort is the label of charlatan or fool because everybody knows that it can't be done except the man who is doing it.

HOW TO CARRY FOUR TONS IN A TWO TON TRUCK

I wrote the story and screenplay for the movie, *The Charlatans.* It was about Mesmer and Cagliostro. Mesmer had people sit around a tub full of magnets to be healed of disease. Cagliostro melted down minerals over a burner and had people drink this nostrum to get rid of their aches. Both got results. But that didn't make any difference to the people in authority. They thought it couldn't be done. They ran Mesmer and Cagliostro out of France. This bothered Mesmer but not Cagliostro. He took with him a diamond necklace that they're still looking for.

I bring this up because in my considered opinion charlatans are often creative, but they're out in left field so they're targets for sandbags. A charlatan might take you for a couple of bucks, but you're little the worse for it because he's taught you a lesson. It's fanatics who are dangerous. They can't learn, can't change, can't be creative. They're dead sold on the products and often generate a legion of believers. Then everybody winds up in the gas chamber. Witness Hitler.

Whatever is new always looks strange to the people who see it, but that doesn't make it charlatanry. There's a story about a guy driving along a narrow country road behind a big truck. The road was so narrow that he couldn't get by. After a while, the truck stopped, the driver got out, and began to beat the truck all over with a two by four. Then he climbed back in and drove on. Pretty soon, he stopped again and beat the truck all over. When he stopped a third time it was too much for the guy in the car. He got out and walked up to the truck driver.

" Friend," he said. "I've seen you beat that truck with a two by four three times now. What gives?"

The truck driver answered tiredly, "This is a two ton truck, see? And I'm carrying four tons of canaries. I have to keep half of them flying or I'm overloaded."

That's creativity. It always looks ridiculous to the people watching, but it gets the job done.

SIGNAL SKILLS AND SYMBOL SKILLS

Guidance mechanisms and electronic computers are programmed to proper performance by having certain attitudes, responses, and beliefs set into them. Human beings are also programmed by having certain attitudes, responses, and beliefs set into them by their experience. Unfortunately, the experience of the individual often gives him a set of responses that disqualifies him from solving certain problems. Nothing is wrong with the machinery of his brain and nervous system, only with its programming.

Faced with a challenge, for example, he may produce the automatic response, "It can't be done," simply because he failed to solve a similar situation many years before. Faced with the necessity of winning an ally, he may try to do this by attempting to use force, simply because this response worked long ago. He literally may be programmed with dozens of such erroneous attitudes and beliefs that prevent him from solving his problems. If these aren't changed, they can create an even bigger problem. They can cause him to want to talk about them and to pay somebody to listen. This has given rise to a band of professional listeners.

I heard of a guy who paid a visit to one. He was told that his case could be taken care of by two hundred visits at $25.00 each.

" Well," he said, "that solves your problem, Doc. Now how about mine?"

Such listeners proliferate because there are talkers. In order to change, you have to change. That requires action.

Machine cybernetics is concerned only with the development of signal skills. Press a button, you get an automatic response. The more precisely adequate the response to the signal, the better fitted the machine to solve its problems. Success Cybernetics is not only concerned with the development of signal skills, but with the development of symbol skills as well. Signal skills are trained into the brain and nervous system by using the imagination repetitively, rehearsing a desired experience over and over until it becomes a conditioned response. Symbol skills are developed by giving the imagination free rein, allowing it to roam explorative over the whole terrain of a problem, searching for new aspects, new ways, new combinations. Training in signal skills produces the skillful automatic response. Training in symbol skills produces the skillful chosen response.

HOW TO USE YOUR INTUITION

Once I had for gunner's mate on a five inch gun a young Mexican boy who could never get his left hand and right hand straight. During night battle practice, he was supposed to fire star shells off the starboard beam, and he fired them off the port side. Those star shells exploded beautifully. Only they didn't illuminate the target. They floated gracefully down over one of our ships. The only comment came over the radio. "You found me all right," said an acid voice. "Only don't shoot. I'm still friendly."

I didn't exactly get a promotion for that demonstration, but I did learn the difference between signal skills and symbol skills. The captain pointed them out the next day. "Shoot where I tell you," was what he said. He'd use the symbol skills. He wanted me to use the signal skills.

And that brings me to what intuition is not. It's not aiming to the left and shooting to the right. A lot of people tell us what it is. Some of them tell us it's hunch, or luck, or fate. A man was telling me the other day that he's finally discovered that his wife's intuition was really only suspicion. I know another guy who plays the stock-market by sticking a pin into stock lists while he's blindfolded. When he wins, he calls it intuition. When he loses, he calls it bad luck. Needless to say, he has a lot more bad luck than he does intuition. So what is intuition? Here's a definition that seems accurate in the light of cybernetics. Intuition is using the whole brain, including the part that lies out of the sight of consciousness like a giant iceberg. There's nothing mysterious or magical or supernatural about it. Cybernetics has taught us that only a small fraction of the brain's working is available to consciousness. We've learned that the brain is always active, even when we sleep. Everyone has had the experience of working hard on a problem, straining for a solution and getting nowhere, then turning his attention away, and suddenly the solution has come. Cybernetics has taught us that the work that produces this solution has gone on unceasingly, even while attention was elsewhere. Deep in the recesses of the brain, electrical charges in the neurons and synapses were reforming, making new connections, assessing and recombining, then finally the resultant new formulation popped up to the surface of consciousness like a cork on a lake.

HOW TO FIND OIL WHERE OIL IS NOT

There was a guy in the oil business who used to find oil where oil was not. I remember sitting with him on a rig floor in the San Joaquin Valley while he unrolled an electric log under the dim light of a sixty watt bulb. He stuck his finger on the jagged lines and said, "We'll perforate the pipe there."

The engineer screamed, "You must be crazy! There's not a sign of oil at that depth!"

" That's what makes me suspicious," the madman answered, and he perforated the pipe and brought in the well.

There are a million aspects to every situation, and our consciousness traps only a few. But most of those aspects are fed into our minds without our conscious awareness. That computing machine between our ears can give us better answers than our consciousness when we learn how to trust it. That's intuition. That's what the madman had.

Intuition appears to be produced by a sudden leap from one kind of thing to a totally different kind, a leap that logic is incapable of making. And today we know that this leap is not a leap at all but only appears to be, because that's the way it's delivered to consciousness. Actually, the whole process has been taken step by step in a portion of the brain and nervous system that's unavailable to our scrutiny. A marvelous and intricate subconscious computer has worked out all the steps to a completely new solution. It will always do this, provided its subconscious workings are not interfered with. And they are only interfered with by excessive reliance on logic.

Tests at leading universities reveal that there is no correlation between intelligence quotient and creative ability. Similarly they reveal that there is no correlation between IQ and the ability to perform well. So now we are forced into a new definition of intelligence. First there is IQ, which indicates a certain mastery of the tools of thinking and a strong reliance on logic. Then there is PQ, performance quotient, which indicates motivation, how the head and hands are tied together, the degree of action-mindedness, achievement orientation. And then there is CQ, creative quotient, which indicates the ability to let go and allow the mind to make its own formulations free of supervision and dogmatic direction.

A SIMPLE WAY TO GET BRAINS

Intuitive thinking follows a pattern. First, the mind is stuffed with facts. Then a conscious solution is tried for. Then attention is turned elsewhere. Then the answers of the subconscious data processing machine are delivered into consciousness.

Probably you've experience struggling with some apparently unsolvable problem only to have some ignorant cuss immediately put his finger on the solution. "But that's so simple!" you protest. Truth is always simple. The better way is always simpler. A primary aspect of creativity is to clear away the clutter of detail so that the bare bones of a problem can be seen.

Across the street from the Columbia Sawmill was Joe's Fish Diner. A lot of other restaurants tried to open along the street, but they never made it. They served hamburgers, hot dogs, stew, chili, but everybody went to Joe's and ate fish. Aspiring restaurateurs stared at their empty stools and simply couldn't figure it out. Why would anyone put up with a steady diet of fish? It sure wasn't Joe's personality. He would as soon poke you as look at you. It was the sign behind his counter. It said, "Fish make brains. Brains make money. Eat fish. Get rich." Joe must have eaten a lot of fish. He retired at forty-five, a wealthy man.

Nobody admitted he wanted more brains, and nobody admitted he wanted more money, but everybody ate at Joe's because Joe had the creative attitude. He intuitively knew that people seldom say what they want, and he knew how to appeal to what they seldom said.

During the intuitive process, a reforming procedure is going on in the deeper recesses of the brain. Neurons are discharging, synapses reforming, new connection being established between one nerve cell and another. The brain is being changed in this process. Its habits, attitudes, and beliefs are being subtly altered. When the reforming process has been completed and new connections established, the idea, perhaps as a hunch, perhaps as a visualization, perhaps as a feeling, is delivered to the output terminal of consciousness and is immediately seen as the solution to the problem.

HOW TO PUT YOUR IDEAS ACROSS

Michelangelo wrote, "In every block of stone there lurks a perfect form"; the idea that has been delivered to consciousness is not yet perfect. It must be refined and honed, the rough edges chipped away, the perfect form revealed. This is done by critical logic, by reliance on symmetry and esthetics, by concentrating on simplifying and reducing the idea to its most useful form. Finally, the time arrives to settle on it, put it into action.

How do you sell a new idea? Why, you sell it by pointing out how the other guy can be benefited. You sell it by showing how it can make or save him time and money, how it can make his life easier, better, more worthwhile. You sell it the same way you created the idea. You sell it by creating benefits.

I remember an advertising account, a dairy that couldn't sell its eggs. They were good eggs too, grade A, just a trifle higher in price than competing brands. How would you go about selling such eggs?

Why, you'd sell quality, wouldn't you? That's just what the dairy did, but they couldn't sell those eggs. So they tried selling quality harder. The eggs moved off the shelves slower.

" No one wants to buy quality," the president moaned. "Everyone wants to buy price."

" Then why not sell price?" I asked him.

" I can't reduce the price," he hollered. "I'd lose money."

" You don't have to reduce price. You just have to sell price."

" How in the world can I do that?",

" Just headline each ad, 'Cheaper by the Dozen'."

You know what? People began buying those eggs. Sure, they weren't cheaper. But it sounded like it. Everyone had a signal reaction to buying price, and

Cheaper by the Dozen was the right signal to start a buying reaction.

HOW TO MAKE YOUR BRAIN BIGGER

And that brings me to mental exercise, the launching pad that rockets your brain power up into orbit. Einstein is reported to have had one corner of his bookshelves filled with problems and puzzles. It is said that he spent many hours with them. What was he doing? Why he was exercising his mental muscles in order to make them stronger. Today, clinical tests have conclusively demonstrated that mental exercise causes the brain to grow larger. This should come as no surprise. If you lift a weight every day, your muscles get bigger.

The creative attitude accepts every problem as a delightful challenge, whether it's a matter of increasing sales, building a business, fixing a clock, dissolving a traffic jam or straightening out the kids. People who exercise their minds solving little problems never feel they are stumped by big ones. They never have the automatic response, "Oh, that's bad luck. I can't do anything about it." They see in every problem a chance to exercise their mental muscles, and they enter into it with a spirit of adventure.

Demosthenes said, "Small opportunities may be the beginning of great enterprises," and the obvious but seldom recognized truth is that every opportunity is hidden within a problem. Charles Kettering said, "My interest is in the future because that's where I'm going to spend the rest of my life." And the real joy in being a problem solver is that you're advancing, going somewhere, getting better day by day.

Nothing has ever been done quite so perfectly as it should be, and so practically everything needs to be done over, and better. People who exercise their mental muscles grow increasingly fruitful with age. Benjamin Franklin invented bifocals at seventy-eight. Alfred Tennyson wrote Beckett at seventy-five. Christian Pfaff synthesized fumaric acid at seventy-two. Galileo invented the telescope at seventy-three. And Winston Churchill wrote his greatest works in his eighties!

WHY THE SKY IS NOT THE LIMIT

Creativity makes a man a thinker. And the best way to raise your standard of living is to raise your standard of thinking. And something else, a side effect, but perhaps the most important of all. Disciplined exercise of the imagination drives out worry and promotes mental health. In a national symposium, our nation's leaders discussed creativity's main benefits. They listed absorption, intensity of consciousness, peak experience, fulfilling participation, delight, ecstasy, and above all, the joy of creating ideas.

This is the age of creativity. With a reconnaissance missile probing the solar system two hundred million miles into outer space, anyone who still thinks the sky is the limit has no imagination. As a friend of mine so aptly puts it, "Now is the time for all good men to come to!"

Today cybernetics has proven to us that the human brain and nervous system comprise a fantastic creative machine. As we master its controls and uncover its possibilities there will be ushered in an age of human accomplishment far beyond anything dreamed.

A man's mind stretched by a new idea can never go back to its original dimension. Begin stretching your mind today, rocketing your brain power up into orbit. Assume the creative attitude. Use your imagination to investigate possibilities. Rely on your powers of intuitive thought. Build up your brain power by mental exercise.

·8· HOW TO USE THE TECHNIQUE OF IMAGINEERING IDEAS

THERE'S A CURIOUS controversy that rages across the drawing boards of most engineering offices. It has to do with function and design. One set of engineers lines up on the side of function, the other on the side of design. They don't exactly hate each other, but they aren't bosom buddies either. The functioners often don't care if they make something so ugly it horrifies Satan, as long as it does the job. The designers often don't care if they make something that just sits there, as long as it looks good. There once were two children, Pretty and Useful. Each wanted to be the favorite of Mother Attention. They fought and fought and Attention wandered away. You get the idea.

HOW TO SELECT AN IDEA WHEN YOU'RE DROWNING

If you ask me, people are the same way. Some want to be useful. Others want to look good. Some do things for results. Others do things to be admired. Ideas are like that. Some are useful. Others you admire. The only legitimate test is which you use when you're drowning.

Few people will select a pretty idea when they're drowning, but there's something to be said for pretty ideas nonetheless. When something is pretty, it makes you feel good. When you feel good, you're more likely to take action. When you take action, you're more likely to be useful. I've got a sneaking feeling that without Pretty there wouldn't be any Useful. "And the Lord created the first Useful. Then the Lord created the first Pretty. Then Useful and Pretty combined to produce Able." I'm for Able. You can't sell anything unless it is pretty, and you can't keep it sold unless it is useful, and when you can do both, then you are able. I'm not out to rewrite the scriptures. They just have many dimensions. Male and female, power and appearance. There you have it. When you're Imagineering ideas, you have to have both.

Take the first car. Somebody asked himself, "I wonder if I could make a buggy move without a horse?" Right then and there, he identified function. The next question was, "How can I make a buggy move without a horse?" Now he was toying with the idea of design. Notice the lines on the first car. Straight up and down. Box-like. Very good. It was supposed to hold people so they built it like a room. Then the functioners asked, "I wonder if we can make a car go faster?" The designers went to work with this new concept of function, and the lines of the car changed. They began sweeping backward. The car began to look like an arrow. It began to look as if it would go fast. That's just what it did.

You begin to get the notion that design is an integral part of function, and function an integral part of design. You might be able to soup up a 1920 crate to vibrate along at sixty miles per hour, but by that time you've had it. You've reached the functional limit of the design. There's nothing so frustrating as trying to go one hundred miles per hour in a 1920 idea. The design just won't stand for it. And there's nothing so tedious as watching someone persevere at it. You feel like hollering, "Sell it and buy a horse!" At least nobody kids himself about how fast a horse can go. Except people at race tracks.

HOW NOT TO BE A RUBE GOLDBERG

In order to change the function, you have to change the design. In order to get higher performance out of yourself, you have to change your program of instructions. You have to raise your design limit to permit higher function. There's no use raising your sights unless you also design and build into yourself the habits that will enable you to reach this new target. You could say that a goal establishes the function which you wish your inner automobile to perform, that your habits are the design by which that performance will be achieved. To reach changed goals, you need changed habits.

There's a guy of my acquaintance who has a whole basement full of gadgets and lives off royalty checks from his inventions. Somebody who invents things is always a study in contrasts, because he combines within one person both functional engineer and design engineer. This guy is no exception. One moment he's searching the heavens for divine inspiration. The next he's down on his knees screwing a nut on a bolt. I once asked him how he managed to get so many of his gadgets to market. "The answer is simple," he said. I waited for him to go on, but he just sat there and stared at me. Then it dawned on me that he'd given me the answer. Simple.

I had to admit he was a master at it. He had gadgets that looked no more complicated than a pencil that could put out the dog, change the baby, bring in the paper, and cook a steak dinner. No question about it, he had the answer. Simplicity is efficiency. It saves time, space, money, and that old bugaboo, effort.

That's why he got so many of his gadgets to market.

Years ago there was a cartoon hero named Rube Goldberg. He'd invent something to turn out the lights, and the resulting contraption would fill his whole house. He had to sleep in the basement, he couldn't have guests, he didn't have time for anything except checking his apparatus, but by golly he had something that would turn off the lights. The author of that cartoon must have been a great satirist. He could see the human situation, all right. People messing around with complicated ideas that take all their time and attention, just to turn off the lights.

HOW TO KEEP SWINGING A SLEDGEHAMMER

What Rube Goldberg didn't have was simplicity. He had complexity instead. His gadgets had function, but their design made their function not worth the trouble. So nobody wanted them. He couldn't even get back into his house. I'm not arguing against complexity. Anybody who's ever looked inside a television set knows that the picture on the tube didn't get there so simply. I'm arguing for an aim that seeks to reduce complexity. Notice what's happening to the television sets? They're getting smaller and smaller. Fewer knobs and dials. More efficiently designed. Simpler.

But my successful inventor who made things so simple didn't spend all his time on making them simple. He also spent some time looking at the stars. Maybe looking up helped him. He was continually finding that the impossible was possible. That's how he was able to get his ideas for function. That's how he was able to get down to the business of design. But always the first step was looking up at those stars. Making the impossible possible.

From what I've seen, the biggest block to creativity in people is that they continually think that things are impossible. That keeps them from toying with new ideas. I never knew anybody who did anything he thought was impossible. He first had to convince himself that it could be done. The very first step in Imagineering ideas is to make the impossible seem possible. This requires breaking the sound barrier created by the hot air of people who say that it can't be done. It also requires breaking the stone wall of your own inner convictions. You do this with the sledgehammer of "It can be done." One blow won't do it. What is required is that you keep swinging that sledgehammer. And swinging and swinging and swinging.

HOW TO MAKE A SHORT SPEECH

Now, of course, there are plenty of people who have good ideas, but by the time they get through with them they're such a mishmash that nobody can understand them, much less put them to use. They wind up with Rube Goldberg contraptions that move them out of the house and have the only saving grace of inspiring others to laughter. Today we're barraged with such a deluge of words that our problems often seem insurmountable. To test this, next time somebody is making a speech, stop him and ask, "What's your point?" By the expression on his face, you'll know he doesn't have one. That's standard operating practice for most people called experts. They can describe all the trees but they forget the name of the woods. It takes a sharp mind to penetrate a deluge of words. That kind of mind has to think simple.

There's a story about a speaker who was asked to deliver a one hour speech. Later he was asked to cut it to a half hour. Still later, he was asked to cut it to fifteen minutes. Finally he was asked to cut it to five minutes. "Five minutes!" he exploded. "I don't understand the subject that well!" There you have it. Clarity is simplicity and simplicity is utility. The purpose of design is to make functional simplicity. A man sets himself to bring an idea to fruition when he uses as a guideline the following words: "Keep it simple."

So the function of an idea is established by, "It can be done." Design is established by, "Keep it simple." The link between the two is created by somebody taking action. That's you. Your guideline for that is, "I'll do it."

" It can be done." "I'll do it." "Keep it simple." These are the first steps in Imagineering ideas.

Of these three steps, probably the most important is, "It can be done." Without this first one, you can't reach the second. Without reaching the second, you can't reach the third. The magic in thinking that it can be done is that it makes you look for solutions. When you look for solutions, you find them. Nothing demonstrates this better than the fantastic growth of the aerospace industry. These boys solve more problems in a single day than entire civilizations once solved in a century. And they do it by considering all things possible. That makes them look for solutions.

HOW TO PUT UP WITH PEOPLE WHO ARE GENIUSES

I addressed the Management Club of North American Aviation. The president of General Information Systems, a North American subsidiary, was also on the program. When I listened to his address, I changed mine. He cursorily remarked on eight major problems his engineers had solved that very afternoon. I looked into my bag of creative tricks and decided I was a piker. I changed the title of my talk to How to Put Up with People Who are Geniuses. It got a big laugh, and afterward I asked him what was the main characteristic he looked for in a creative engineer. "Imagination," he said. I asked him to give me an example. He said, "We want somebody who thinks it's possible to walk to the moon." I gathered he was out to make the impossible possible. That's why North American rockets ahead.

There's only one way I know of to get rid of a problem, and that's to solve it. Of course, you can pretend it isn't there. That helps in a surprising number of cases, since many problems don't exist outside the mind. I once considered going into business manufacturing a problem solver for that kind of problem. You could say that it's design was the ultimate in simplicity. It consisted of a box about the size that holds cigars, and when you opened the lid, inside there was nothing. That's where you put your problems. You wrote each on a slip of paper, deposited it in the box, closed the lid, and the problem solver went to work.

The beauty of this little machine was that you didn't even have to press a button, just close the lid. At the end of a week, you opened the lid and went through the problems. Those that the problem solver had already solved, you tore up and threw away. If you had any new ones, you deposited them inside. Each week you opened up the problem solver and got rid of the problems it had already solved. The machine was a whiz. It solved ninety percent of people's problems. I was all set to launch a nationwide business when I ran into a snag. I couldn't get a patent. The design was too simple.

There was a supervisor who was having trouble out in the shop. It was just one thing after another. This wouldn't fit, that would break down, this was too low, that was too high. People spent all their time looking puzzled. I asked him what was the first thing he said when he heard there was trouble. He said that he asked, "What's the problem?" I suggested that he change the direction of his question. After that he began asking, "What's the solution?" Pretty soon, there was no more trouble out in the shop. Things still wouldn't fit, would still break down, this was too low, and that was too high. But they were fixed at once, and he never heard about it. People were thinking solutions.

I had a guy bug me about his marital problems. You'd have thought he was married to the original Delilah and she was cutting off more than his hair. He went over and over the same monotonous circle. Finally, I shouted at him, "Don't keep telling me your problems! Tell me your solutions!" The way he gaped, you could tell he hadn't tried any. But it must have got him thinking that solutions were possible. He came up with a few and eventually tried them. He saved his hair and everything else.

There's something about going over and over a problem that sets it in cement. Pretty soon the cement hardens and you have to follow the grooves. Then you can't get out of the rut and you're going in circles. You meet yourself coming back and don't even say hello. This is called worrying. It's never been known to solve anything except sleeping too much. There was this guy who set out to kill the Medusa. The Medusa had snakes on her head, and if you looked at her long enough she turned you to stone. But he took care of all that. He got rid of the problem by looking in the opposite direction. He brought along a mirror and watched her in that. When he got within range, he lopped off her head. Instead of looking at the problem, he looked at the solution.

If we concentrate on a problem, the problem becomes real. It hardens in cement and looks like the Medusa. That turns us to stone, and we can't take action. If we concentrate on a solution, we find what we look for, and lop off the problem's head in the mirror of viewpoint. Problem thinking is negative thinking. Solution thinking is positive thinking. A problem should be looked at only long enough to establish a goal. Once we have a goal, we concentrate on reaching it. We find what we concentrate on.

HOW TO STAMP OUT THE GOONY BIRD

People are always finding insurmountable problems because they keep right on staring at them. They won't turn their eyes to the mirror of solutions. A guy caught in this trap is a sight to behold. He's built a brick wall in his way, and he claws off his fingernails trying to get through it. I know an architect who has a sign posted over his drawing board. It reads, "If you must worry, worry about answers." When you've got your mind on solutions, the brick wall becomes canvas and you've got a sword and can hack your way through.

I once worked with a sales-manager who had a favorite speech. He called it Straight Line Worrying. I heard it one time, and it was a pip. What it said was worry about where you're going, not what's stopping you. This guy knew his onions. When you concentrate on where you're going, you've got your eye on the target. Everybody shoots better that way.

A world full of solution thinkers could build a stairway to heaven, but if one problem thinker remained, he'd find a way not to climb it. As it is, problem thinkers flourish. I guess they have short gestation periods and are prolific breeders, because they abound everywhere that life exists. They point out what's wrong. Typically, they run in packs. Usually they have a leader who says what's wrong the loudest. When somebody says what's right, they say what's wrong with that. They are noted for not taking action, just making noises. The two that they make best are screaming and crying. This keeps the neighbors awake and the towel industry busy. They have excellent hindsight and absolutely no foresight. Like the goony bird, they fly backward, because they don't care where they're going, they just want to see where they've been.

You can change a problem thinker if you've got time and patience. If not, push him off a cliff. He won't mind because it will give him another problem. But if you decide to change him, you have to teach him a new language. This will take time because you'll find that he's stupid. When you say left, he turns right. When you say right, he turns left. You have to be patient. He's not trying to get anything done; he's trying to make it a problem. If you can get his eyes off his problems and onto the solution mirror, he'll finally get the drift. Then you've reduced his ranks by one and added one to our side. So the war progresses.

You are thinking solutions when you think it can be done. You are thinking problems when you think that it can't. To find a solution, think, "It can be done." That's the first step in Imagineering ideas. Now you're left with a question: "Who will do it?" George isn't here. You're stuck with the job. Just hoist up your pants and take a notch in your belt, then say to yourself, "I can do it." With that simple conviction, it's practically done.

HOW NOT TO GET YOUR CAR FIXED

The president of an ad agency was looking for an executive vice president. One after another, his vice presidents were called in, and he threw a campaign before them. "I'd like this gotten out today," he said. Some of them looked at it and said it couldn't be done. Some of them looked at it and said that they'd try. The president didn't want it not done, and he didn't want it just tried. He wanted somebody to do it. Finally, one guy picked up the campaign and said,

"Sure, I can do it." He got out the campaign, and he got the executive vice-presidency. He was the ugliest of the lot, and he parted his hair in the middle.

It's been my observation that the people who say, "I'll try," cause more trouble than the people who say, "I can't." Everybody recognizes the people who say, "I can't," and nobody gives them anything to do. But the people who say, "I'll try," are insidious. Hardly anyone believes they mean what they say. They mean to try it, not do it. When the moment of reckoning comes and they're accused of dereliction, they blandly retort, "Well, I tried, didn't I?" This leaves the guy who gave them the job vaguely frustrated. He feels he's been had, but doesn't know how.

You go into a garage to have your car fixed and ask what time it will be ready. "I'll try to have it ready by three," says the garage-man. Notice how you walk away. You think your car's going to be ready by three. You're back at three, all pink and panting. "Where's my car?" you ask. The garage-man points a thumb. "That's it over there." You look over at a pile of nuts and bolts that will take three weeks to reassemble. You scream, "I thought you said you'd have it ready by three!" "No," says the garage-man, "I said that I'd try." Gives you a funny feeling, doesn't it? You're mad but confused. Mostly you're frustrated. If you question him about whether he can reassemble that pile of nuts and bolts, and he says that he'll try, don't get trapped again. Go buy a new car.

HOW TO BECOME A BRILLIANT IDIOT

" I'll try" is an excuse, the device of a fence straddle. If the job happens to get done, he gets the credit. If it doesn't, nobody will blame him. Since he's got nothing to lose, that's just what he acts like. What difference does it make? He lets the pile of bolts sit on the floor while he has a cup of coffee. The thermostat on your wall doesn't try to turn on the furnace. It just does it automatically because it's trained that it can.

I don't have to tell you never to give a job to a man who says he can't do it. What I'm telling you is never to give a job to a man who says that he'll try. Give your jobs to people who say they can do them. Same thing applies to yourself. You can't Imaginer ideas with the notion that you'll try. You Imaginer ideas with the belief that you can. There's an old saying, "If you want something done, give it to a busy man." The reason he's busy is he thinks he can do it.

I've got a speech called How to Become a Brilliant Idiot. It's about Imagineering ideas. What it says is that you don't have to know nothing', except that you can. Occasionally I deliver it to an erudite group that talks a strange language, like "vector analysis," "refractivity," "quadratic equations," "oscillating currents," "neutrons," "protons," and "infrared coefficients." In order to save time, we talk in my language. It would take me a century to understand theirs. The speech goes on to say that you can know so much that you can't think simple. When you can't think simple, you can't produce an idea. I point out old Einstein who talked their own language. When he decided to change the world, he said, "$E = MC^2$." I don't know what that means, but I know that it's simple. I also happen to know that it changed the whole world.

Remember "Silent Cal" Coolidge? The reason he was silent was that he was making things simple. He attended a two hour sermon in church, and somebody asked him what it was all about. Cal answered, "Sin." Then he was asked what the preacher had to say about it. Old Silent Cal answered, "He was against it." There was a man who thought simple.

SIMPLE

There was a teleplay one time about a Mexican village that was visited by an earthquake. A huge boulder rolled down the mountain and wound up in the center of the street. It was so hard nobody could dent it. It was so heavy nobody could move it. It was so big it blocked all the traffic. Everybody wanted that boulder out of the street, but nobody could figure out how to remove it. The best brains in the town held a council of war. They tried mechanics, explosion, derricks, and tractors. Nothing would move that boulder. They tried more complicated methods. The more complicated they got, the less that boulder moved. One day they were visited by the village idiot. He said he could get rid of the boulder, but he wanted to be paid for it. That lifted the tension, because everybody laughed. The idiot persisted, and just to get rid of him, they promised to pay him. Next morning the boulder was gone from the street. The idiot dug a hole under it, the boulder toppled in the hole, and he covered it with dirt. He carted the rest of the dirt out of the village, and the boulder was gone from the street. The name of the teleplay was Simple. That's how to become a brilliant idiot. Think simple.

A simple solution comes to the man who thinks he can find one. When we clutter things up with complexity, we can't think our way through the debris. I had a guy in a seminar who was losing his hair. That's a problem I sympathize with, because I'm losing mine. He came up to me and asked, "Can I use positive thinking to get a full head of hair?" I said, "Sure, as long as you think you can." He stared at my own balding pate, but he said that he'd do it. After all, anyone knows that teachers can seldom do what they teach. I wrote something on a piece of paper and put it in his pocket. "When you get a full head of hair, look at that paper," I said. I saw him three months later, and he had a full head of hair. "I read the paper," he hollered. "You were right. It's a toupee!" Just think that you can, and you'll find that it's simple.

" It can be done." "I can do it." "Keep it simple." That's the program that determines function and design. What you come up with is something that works. You've imagineered an idea that is useful. Of course, you have to think in order to do this. Thinking is manipulating symbols.

HOW TO EAT AIR AND NOT PUT ON WEIGHT

A symbol is something that stands for something else. It's a name, or a picture, or a ten dollar bill. If you say, "Kitty," to a dog, he looks around for the kitty. If you say, "Kitty," to a man, he gets the idea of a cat. The dog thinks in signals. The man thinks in symbols. If you've got a painting hanging in your living room, it's just a bunch of color to your dog, but you see the ocean. You don't actually see the ocean, you see something that stands for it. The dog doesn't see it, because he can't see symbols. He can't see them because he has no imagination. That's the primary difference between a dog and a man, though men are somewhat better at walking on hind legs.

The nervous system works with signals. The imagination works with symbols. Unfortunately, the imagination sometimes thinks all symbols are signals. That's why it can't get new ideas. If a man thinks he can't do it, that's a symbol. It's an idea inside his own head. But he usually acts as if it were a signal coming from outside him. He looks around for the kitty. If he can't find the kitty, he finds a dog and calls it a kitty. That doesn't change the symbol, but it changes what he sees, and puts him in a rather bad way. He hears a bark and thinks it's a meow. More than that he thinks the meow was outside him. All the time it was just in his head.

Some people go so far as to try to eat symbols. They pick up a plastic grape and crack a bicuspid. Some people go farther than that. One night after a lecture, a guy came up and said he ate air. That's doing away with both symbol and signal. I asked him how he was getting along, and he said he was losing a little weight. I asked him how he accounted for that, and he said he guessed air wasn't fattening. I suggested that he bottle it and sell it for a reducing diet. He said that wouldn't work because air was all over and people could get it free. It startled me that he had a glimmer that something existed outside his head. But his eyes were getting glassy, so I got the hell out of there.

Learning to think is learning to manipulate symbols, and it's no work at all because it's all in your head. When you imagineer ideas, you manipulate symbols. You change them and shift them all over the place. If you had to move the things that the symbols represent, you'd come up with a rupture. Thinking saves time, sweat, and hospital bills. You manipulate symbols until they fit in your mind. Then you manipulate the things that the symbols represent to see if they actually fit. If they do, you've got an idea that works.

TURN EVER SO QUICKLY

People who think that a rose is a rose and that's all there is to it can't manipulate symbols. They can't imagine any new ideas about the rose. With the same old rose in their heads, they see the same old rose in the world. If it turns out to be a rattlesnake, somebody switched it. But anyone who can manipulate symbols can change his ideas about the rose. That allows him to grow one that hasn't been grown.

I wrote a short story called *Turn Ever so Quickly.* It was published in Saturday Evening Post, and later in Houghton Mifflin's anthology, *The Best American Short Stories of 1963.* It was about a fishing trip. Now you might say, "What's so interesting about a fishing trip? Everybody's been on them and knows what they are." Exactly. So you manipulate the fishing trip symbol. You try on a few new meanings for size. What could a fishing trip stand for that it hasn't stood for before? You play around, toy with a few ideas, manipulate symbols. Fishing trips are often conducted on creeks and lakes. There could be a lost lake. Ah, there's a good symbol. The lost lake could stand for something else that's been lost. What do people most often lose? Why, they lose their dreams. The lost lake could stand for someone's lost dream. Who most often gives up his dream? Why, a middle aged man. In whom does a dream burn most brightly? Why, a young boy. Suddenly, there are the people—a man and his son. And there's the story— they set out to find a lost lake. And there's the conflict—the man doesn't think it's there and the boy thinks it is. And there's the resolution—the man doesn't discourage his son because he wants him to keep hoping. And here's what the story says—in order to keep looking you have to keep hoping, and in order to keep hoping, you have to switch viewpoints. How do you switch viewpoints? Why, you *turn ever so quickly.*

What I'm trying to say is that a fishing trip remains just a fishing trip until you manipulate its symbol in your imagination. The moment you begin assigning that symbol other meanings, you open up a whole world of possibilities. Ideas flit by like teal duck over a blind. Some you shoot down. Others you let pass. Some you shoot at and miss. But before the shooting's over, you've taken your limit. Now you stack them together and make them coherent. You pluck them and clean them and have them for dinner.

HOW TO RESURRECT GENIUS

In my experience, there's no such thing as an unimaginative person. There are just certain people who think all symbols are signals. They give something a name and think that's an end to it. They give a name to their house and lose sight of the house and just see the name. If the house burns down, they go to bed in the name. Since they refuse to change symbols, the world seems devoid of possibility. Everything seems like it always was, like it always must be. They stop learning, because they stop thinking. In order to think, you have to manipulate symbols.

Which brings me to *Operation Resurrection.* There was once a youngster who wandered into a village. When people asked him his name, he said he didn't have one. When they tried to give him a name, he said he didn't want one. It put them in a quandary. The only way they could refer to him was by exactly describing him. In order to describe him, they had to keep looking at him. As they continued to look at him, they kept noticing more. What was said about him one day had to be added to the next. Everyone thought he must have been sent from heaven because he seemed so profound and inexhaustible. He grew bigger and brighter and always more remarkable. Finally, they decided to elect him mayor. It didn't seem proper to have a mayor without a name, so they insisted he take one. They called him Genius. It was a relief to everyone because now that they knew what he was, they didn't have to watch him. A strange thing happened to Genius. He stopped changing and growing. People began to complain that he kept doing the same things the same way. They grew bored. They felt they knew all about him, that he'd never change. Finally, they didn't give him so much as a glance. They simply ignored him. That got rid of Genius. He withered and died. Of course, nobody knew it. They kept saying his name as if he were there.

Operation Resurrection brings genius back from the dead. It's launched in my training programs when people are instructed that for the next full hour they must talk all the time but cannot use nouns or names. The first part of these instructions, they don't obey very well. They spend little time talking, but a great deal looking. They look at an ashtray as if they've never seen it before. They touch it and smell it. Some even taste it. When they start trying to describe it without using its name, they're tongue tied at first, then with a sudden rush, they're unlocked from the symbol. They see the ashtray in all its possibilities. It could be a weight or a dish or a weapon or a vase or an upside down home for ants. You could wear it as a hat, hang it on the wall as a decoration, use it as a base in a ball game. It could be a door stop, a window, a receptacle for silverware. Why, its possibilities are endless! How to describe all these things without using names? The moment they start thinking about what something can be used for instead of what it is, the possibilities multiply, over and over. Voices grow excited. People yelp as they discover new possibilities. They look, they see, they imagine, they manipulate the symbols. Genius is brought back from the dead.

GOOD LUCK WITH THE LIONS

Most people are never the same after an experience like this. Henceforth, they walk through life with a knowing smile, because there's always someone who's preaching, "It's only an ashtray." Moreover, they've learned that they can unlock themselves from symbols whenever they want, that they can play with them like toys in an attic, endlessly placing them in different formations, assigning them new meanings, tumbling them about in a joy of discovery. The whole world is changed. It becomes mysterious, exciting, fraught with possibilities. They've discovered a game that can never grow boring. They begin to like their own company. Time to be by themselves becomes precious. They become creators, innovators, problem solvers. And all because they've learned that a name is only in the mind and says very little about the thing that it names.

Now nobody can get along without using names, and nobody can get along without using symbols as signals. If somebody shouts, "Lion!" it's no time to explore the possibilities of the symbol. It's time to regard it as a signal and get the hell out of there. What I'm trying to illustrate is you'll never learn anything about lions if you just happen to think of one and get the hell out of there. Conversely, you'll never learn anything about lions if you happen to be faced with one and decide that you'll think about it. There's a time to use symbols and a time to use signals. A time to think, and a time to act. If I had to pick one single thing that best demonstrates a man's ability to cope with this world, it's knowing when to use symbols and when to use signals. Good luck with the lions.

In using the technique of Imagineering ideas, the sequence of command phrases is as follows: "It can be done." "I can do it." "Manipulate symbols." "Keep it simple." Certain combinations will fascinate you, and you'll give them a try in the outside world. Some of these will work and be very productive. Cut it in the mind, try it in the world— that's Imagineering ideas.

·9· HOW TO FIND INSIDE SOLUTIONS TO UNSOLVABLE PROBLEMS

WHEN A MAN is finally stumped by a problem, he'll sometimes try to give it away. If he can find any takers, he usually feels bet ter. But most people like to hang onto a problem. The longer they've had it, the more it seems like a friend. What keeps them from getting rid of it is some distorted value. If they got rid of the problem, they'd have to change their notions about *Good.* Alongside a man who doesn't want to change his ideas about *Good,* a mule is a piker.

Just because one man can't solve a problem doesn't mean that problem can't be solved. Some other guy with a different set of values pokes his finger in the side and it straightens right out. Which proves that there are no unsolvable problems. Just unsolvable people.

HOW TO SILENCE A BARKING DOG

I once had a dog who had a problem. He barked all the time. To put it more succinctly, it was I who had the problem. The dog was unaware of it. I tried to point it out to him by talking to him gently. He no speaks English. I tried talking louder. He understood there was urgency, but he couldn't pick up the language. I tried coaxing him with goodies. He still kept on barking. I showed him the whip. He barked all through the night. I applied the whip gingerly. He tugged on it playfully. I thought I'd hit on something. He couldn't bark with the thing in his teeth, and his growl was refreshing. But he got tired of playing and went back to barking. I applied the whip vigorously. That changed the tone of his barking, but it sounded better before. The neighbors started to complain to the SPCA. Before, they had just complained to the police. Now I was in real trouble. I looked at that barking dog a long time. He was just the kind of dog I'd always wanted, but I hadn't bargained on barking. Since the barking went with the dog, I guessed I'd have to get rid of the dog to get rid of the barking. That may seem like a simple solution to you, but I thought I was lucky to stumble across it. I pawned off the dog on some unwary friends. They didn't care about the dog, but they liked the way he barked. They never found out that the dog had a problem.

For a while I felt better. I'd gotten rid of an unsolvable problem. But in retrospect, I can see how I could have stopped the barking and kept the dog too. I could have cut out his voice box. It wasn't really his barking I objected to, it was just the noise it made. With his voice box out, he would have been a silent barker. He could have barked all he wanted to, and I wouldn't have minded. Other people wouldn't even know he was a barker. They'd just think he was a nice quiet dog that yawned. No question about it, I could have solved that problem. But even now I don't suppose I could do it. My values would stand in the way.

When they ask a computer to give them an answer, they don't ask the computer if it likes it. They just want the answer. When they launch a guided missile at a military target, they don't ask the missile if it's got anything against killing people. They just want the missile to hit the target. If computers and missiles ever develop likes and dislikes, they may begin giving only those answers and hitting those targets that are in accord with their principles. At that point, people will say that they've developed a conscience. They then will be eligible for membership in Rotary or Kiwanis, but they won't solve many problems.

A SURE WAY TO BLIND YOURSELF

What we've learned from cybernetics is that you set up a program to get a job accomplished by the most efficient means possible. The only judgment of that program is whether it works. If it doesn't, you change it until it does. This is why computers give right answers and guided missiles hit targets. But when you apply cybernetics principles to the human machine, you run smack dab into values. The little man in the skull thinks some things are right and others are wrong, likes some things and dislikes others. This is why he's a member of Rotary instead of out solving problems. He'd rather maintain his values than get a right answer or hit a target. This incapacitates him for any competition with the computer, but it does make him what everybody calls human—subject to sin and error and sickness and disaster. At such hi-jinks a well-programmed computer would laugh.

Now I'm not arguing for the abolition of values. I just think they should be based on what produces results. If not, they're a smoke screen and prevent us from solving our problems. Everyone gets to thinking that something is so, when it's not so at all, just a matter of preference. You prefer Germans to Jews so you burn all the Jews. Half the world goes up in smoke, your country is gutted, but you did what was *good.* Let's not kid ourselves that Hitler was guided by anything but his values. If he hit the target he aimed at, he had mighty bad eyesight. You can get mighty bad eyesight when you're looking through value glasses. They're horn rimmed and concave and four inches thick.

You may notice there are many oculists selling such glasses. They're institutions peddling values at least nine hundred years old. You can see 20-20 before you buy their glasses, but after you wear them you're as blind as a bat. No matter, they didn't sell you those glasses so you could see better. They sold you those glasses because those glasses are *good.* That's why you keep wearing them. You stumble over the furniture and bark your shins and bump your head against the wall, but those glasses are *good.* You even get to imagining that pain feels like pleasure, that it's the normal state of man to be ignorant and blind, and when you can't solve your problems you won't think it's your glasses, you'll think those problems are unsolvable because those glasses are *good.*

HOW TO KILL BLACK MICROBES

I once ran into a guy who was in a pretty bad state. His wife was out to kill him. She'd put strychnine in his coffee, wired his bathtub like an electric chair, cut holes in his tires, and even gone after him with a gun. I suggested that divorce might be in order. He confessed he'd considered it, and had consulted a value expert. The value expert had made him see that divorce was *bad,* so he'd decided to stick it out. In some states they can hang you for killing a person, but not if you're a value expert. They give him a degree. That guy's widow is now doing time in a federal prison. The guy himself is pushing up daisies. Other than that, everything is rosy. Values remain undisturbed. They grow withered and rotted and coated with dust, but not a breath of air stirs them. Meantime, some people notice that things are in a mess.

Unsolvable problems require inside solutions, because unsolvable problems are caused by the values inside somebody's head. Picture a scientist looking for the microbe that causes diphtheria. He's sure it's a black one because he knows black is *bad.* He decides on a black one and launches an attack on black microbes. He wipes them out, but diphtheria spreads. Notice he still doesn't think it could be a white microbe. No, the black microbes have gone underground, and he'll have to dig them out. He poisons a few cities and contaminates crops, but he'll get those black microbes if it's the last thing that he does. Meantime, the white microbes are joined by some friends, and we have, in addition to diphtheria, tuberculosis and cancer. But lances are atilt, banners unfurled, the battle goes on. Black microbes are *bad.*

If this shakes you considerably, there's a glimmer of hope. You might be able to solve an unsolvable problem by getting your inside machinery set to think straight. You might be able to imagine you don't have any values and let the data percolate through and see what comes out. I can guarantee you this: It will be the right answer. That computer of yours won't make a mistake as long as you give it the proper instructions. You might get some answers that you don't like, but you don't have to use them. You can still decide that they're *bad.* At least you've gotten the answer and made a decision, and you haven't even had to visit a value expert. But in one way or another, he's still gotten to you.

HOOLIGAN'S LAW

People stay in marriages that wreck a career and two lives. People walk around broke because they have to be liked. People can't improve because they think it's bad to fight. "Papa catch the fishy with a hook. Mama fry him in the pan. Baby eat him like a man." Only mama and papa aren't there anymore, and baby is a man now acting like a baby. He's hungry, and there's nobody to bring him his fish. Get out and fight for it? Of course not. That's *bad.*

I'm not trying to kick holes in all values. I'm trying to kick holes in the values that don't work. I'm saying that the only way anybody has a reasonable chance to solve his problems is to put his values on the shelf while he lets his data processing machine work out a solution. His values won't go away. He can pick them up again and restore error to his machine without any difficulty at all. But he'll have some interesting answers. I am persuaded that there is enough authenticity to truth for some people to start using it once they have seen it. This is an inevitable result of Hooligan's Law: It's nice to stop barking your shins.

Don't think I'm an exception to this barking shins business. I've barked them plenty and have the scars to show for it. I once wrote a novel, *The Other Jesus.* It began with what I'm still sure was a sterling idea. I got to nosing around and was struck by the thought that the gospel story was based on an old myth. Something just like it used to circulate underground in the secret societies. The idea was that you couldn't be spiritually born until you killed off your *bad* self, the one of you who was always trying to make a buck and get ahead of other people. They'd bury an initiate in the ground and just before he suffocated, they'd dig him up again. If he could still manage to speak, he was all spirit and had left his *bad* self down in the hole. Now he could do what he wanted because he couldn't be evil. He was *good.* This nonsense is still with us today in the shape of the Ku Klux Klan, so you can draw your own conclusions about how good it is.

HOW TO DEVELOP AN IDEA

Anyway, there was a line in the old gospels that struck me as interesting. It was about the robber, Barabbas, whom Pilate set free instead of Jesus. What was interesting was that in this line Barabbas had a first name. His name was Jesus too. Curiously, this first name had been deleted from later editions. But, if I got the picture right, here were two Jews named Jesus, and one was *Bad* and the other was *Good,* so you kill off the bad guy and the good guy becomes a member of the elect, just like the secret societies. Whoa! Then the gospels killed off the wrong guy! They nailed the good guy to the cross. That didn't make sense, then something else struck me. Barabbas was the only one who had a last name. Everybody else was Peter, Mark, Luke, John, and so on. What was he doing with a last name? Then I noticed that if Judas was a son of Jonas, they would refer to him as Judas bar Jonas. Barabbas then was Jesus bar Abbas. I got to wondering who Abbas was.

I consulted the word derivation from the old Aramaic. It meant, "Heavenly Father." The early gospels had literally referred to Barabbas as "Jesus, son of the Heavenly Father!" The one they hung on the cross had been call Jesus, the Christ. Christ was from Greek and meant "Warrior King." So the early gospels had told a story just like the rites in the secret society, with the bad guy destroyed and the good guy set free. Somebody must have filched the proceedings from the secret societies and peddled them to the public. The public had promptly turned symbols to signals, thus making it seem that the story really happened. Then the church got hold of it and switched the principal roles, putting the good guy on the cross and setting the bad guy free and leaving Barabbas without a first name. That certainly put more sell in it. If the good guy died for you, that made you feel guilty, and if the bad guy was loose, there was plenty of sin. All sinners would burn in hellfire except those who got into heaven, and you couldn't get into heaven unless you entered through the church. Then they made the church a tollgate and took in the loot. Those piker secret societies! They could have had a good thing going for them.

HOW TO MURDER AN IDEA

Boy, did I have a story! I sat down at my typewriter and set off with excitement, but I hadn't gone very far when I ran into my values. How was I ever going to say that the bad self had been hung on the cross? Even people who might suspect that there was something symbolic in the gospel story wouldn't go for that. Everybody for thousands of years had figured that whatever hung on that cross, whether man or spirit or symbol, was *good.* And here I was about to say it was *bad.* I shuddered in the face of centuries of value judgment. My typewriter began to stutter. The story strained its seams. It sprung leaks, and I busied myself patching them. In sight of port, my ship was barely afloat. Then I chickened out entirely. I beached her on the shores of conventional value. I put the good guy back up on the cross where he had been for centuries, and brought the story to an end. But I was disgusted with myself. I knew I'd blown it. I hadn't been able to solve the problem because my values had gotten in the way.

The book was turned down by thirty-five publishers. When the thirty-sixth accepted, I almost fainted from shock. It turned out that the first thirty-five hadn't exactly been myopic. The book bombed out at a mere eight hundred copies. Which was as it should be. It said very little, and what it said was confusing. I'd sat on an ostrich egg and hatched out a gnat, all because of my values. One guy liked it though. He liked the part where the Zealots attacked Jerusalem through an underground watercourse. He said it was the best suspense story he ever read. But he didn't like the title. He said he didn't see anything religious in the story.

I could handle that theme now. I've laid the demon of value judgment to rest. I buried him out in a lonely part of the desert, in an unmarked grave that only the wind knows. I didn't even say a prayer. He didn't deserve it.

WHEN TO RUN OVER A DOG

There's nothing so interesting to me as a guy who suddenly cuts loose from a value that has been keeping him from solving his problems all of his life. Maybe it's something like, "It's *bad* to fight for what you want. People should give it to you." Nothing has ever worked out for him. He's tried everything but changing the value. He's consulted oracles, soothsayers, and psychoanalysts. He's boned up on astrology, attended séances, read tea leaves, tried magic. He's genuflected and crawled, entreated and prayed. Nothing has worked. Suddenly, he gets mad. He starts to fight. Much to his amazement, he finds that it works. He solves a couple of problems, gets what he wants. How can this be? The thing he always thought was *bad* turns out to be *good.* Compressed steam shoots out of his ears, and he's off and running like a dervish.

That's about the only time people change their values, when they're so beaten and frustrated that they finally get mad. This sometimes has disastrous consequences for innocent bystanders. If you need an illustration, look at the Watts riots. Old Uncle Tom shuffling along with bowed head suddenly got mad and turned into a tiger. And he'll never be the same. He's learned that you get what you want by fighting for it.

A machine that has no values is a machine that produces correct answers. If you free your machine of value judgments, it will produce answers that solve all your problems. If you keep it programmed with value judgments, you'll get only those answers you already know. That means you'll keep making the same mistakes. That means you'll continually be faced by the same problems. I guess it's just a matter of how much you value your values. If you want to stay in the house with a murderous wife because that's *good,* it's your life, not mine. But don't whine about the fact it's an un-solvable problem. If you surrendered your value judgment, you could solve it at once. I know of a guy who ran his car off a cliff, crippled himself and killed his wife and three kids. He did this because he didn't want to run over a dog. That was *bad.*

OPERATION ALL EARS

The reason most people can't listen is because they're busy defending their values. A sure sign of this is a compulsion to prove yourself right. You can get so busy defending this bastion that you can be driving a horse and buggy while everyone else flies. You'll hardly notice. But if you do, you'll be sure flying is *bad.* If anyone mentions flying, you'll start screaming about your *good* horse and buggy. This could make you an excellent hog caller, if that doesn't offend your values. And you'll notice something else. You'll be keeping steady company with the same old ideas. Someday it may dawn on you that you've had them forty years. That will reassure you that they were right in the first place. You've become unteachable, but it will never occur to you.

Now if I've scared you sufficiently about how value judgments can ruin your mental machinery, let's get down to fixing them so they don't. I assume at this point that you want to solve your problems, especially those that appear unsolvable, which nothing has fixed. It requires a little training, and it's done by a program called Operation All Ears. What this means in essence is that you learn how to listen, which means listening without judgment, without *bad* and *good.* This will have the effect of freeing your thought patterns, so that you are able to think without *bad* and *good.* In turn you will find this will alter your speaking, so that you are able to say things without *bad* and *good.* Finally, this will permit you freedom of action, so that you are able to do things without *bad* and *good.* If you free yourself completely, you'll outstrip the computer, because without *bad* and *good* you've got 200,000 times its capacity.

And it all begins with listening, suspending all judgment, letting the data enter your computer through the input terminals of your ears. Data processing begins at once. Your machine becomes more sophisticated. In short, it has learned something. You have become teachable. A miracle has been accomplished, and all because you substituted a pair of ears for a mouth. Like a deaf man suddenly given a hearing aid, you may realize you've been missing a lot.

HOW TO LOSE TWENTY-FIVE CENTS AND REMAIN IGNORANT

In training programs, I often launch Operation All Ears by asking people to discuss politics, religion, or sex. Everybody starts out listening, but everybody winds up talking. And not just talking, but hollering like hell. If I can manage to restore order, I point out that I asked them to listen without judgment. They seem somewhat incensed that I should expect them to listen to such drivel. "Why?" I ask. "Did you think it was *Bad?"* Then I hang placards around everyone's neck. They all carry the same message: *Twenty-five Cents If You Can Waggle My Tongue.* After that, it grows quieter, but old value judgment still provides a nice kitty. Later on, we use it to obtain some of the liquid that unloosens stuck tongue. At least for those who don't think such liquid is *Bad.*

I don't think I have to point out that Operation All Ears is a lifetime program. To keep your mental machinery working, you have to keep discarding obsolete values, and values have a way of becoming obsolete fast. To prevent obsolescence, you have to keep listening, allowing new data into your mind, weighing the evidence. There's no other way to keep from pulling the train of your life with an old fashioned hand car. You won't pull the train, and you'll just think it's stuck. Listening will give you a modern diesel engine. You can add cars to that train without missing a toot.

Perhaps sometime in the future there will be human beings without value judgments, with their brains aimed at the single goal of how best to get the job done. Imagination staggers at what such men might accomplish. If something didn't work, they'd try something different. When something did work, they wouldn't keep using it after it stopped. They might learn in a day more than most of us learn in a lifetime. Likely, they'd stride across the universe with seven league boots. Such a race of men may even now be aborting in space technological laboratories. All that they think of is how to get out there. Not whether it's *good* or it's *bad*. They're a new breed of problem solvers, with their minds free from enslavement.

SYZYGY TO SERENDIPITY

One night I had a dream and my computer produced an equation. At least it seemed like an equation, for all it made sense. What my computer came up with was "Syzygy to serendipity." They sounded like words, so I ran for a dictionary. Syzygy meant "putting together opposites." Serendipity, "rending things not looked for." I didn't need a stargazer to tell me my computer was producing some answers. "Putting together opposites leads to finding things not looked for." All channels were clear, because you can't put together opposites if you think one is *bad*. Immediately afterwards I noticed a difference in viewpoint. I thought nothing was *bad*. I thought nothing was *good*. I could put together opposites without the slightest hesitation. I found things I never knew existed, and I'm finding them still. If I keep my computer cleared, I'll find them my whole life. What an inexhaustible game! The permutations are endless.

Some people will say that Syzygy to Serendipity came as an intuition. Call it what you will, only don't think it's magic. It wasn't divine revelation, or spirits, or drugs. It wasn't extrasensory perception, or the stars, or plain luck. It was just a machine finally freed to produce answers. Since it was designed to produce answers, that's just what it did. If I'd been attached to an encephalograph you could have seen the change in my brain wave. Electrical currents flowed through new channels in a far different way, just as happens in a computer when its programming is altered. Change the program of a computer, and you change its answers. If those answers are better, your program's improved.

There's a guy who writes books on extrasensory perception. People come to him regularly, and he tells them what's going to happen. If any of it happens, they think he's got a pipeline to the future. If none of it does, they think he wasn't tuned in. Few of them notice that he doesn't know himself what he's going to have for breakfast. What's worse, when he gets there, he can't seem to decide. He reasons that he can tell the future for others but not for himself. That saves him embarrassment when he gets in a wreck, but leaves him in awkward position if anyone's with him.

HOW TO MAKE A LITTLE TEST MORE POPULAR THAN A BIG ONE

Even the colleges have been invaded by extrasensory perception. They decided to give it a clinical test. Apparently they'd forgotten that they'd been conducting a test for years, and the results had been conclusive. No student had ever been able to crib another student's answers without looking at his paper. Duke University hired a professor named Rhine to preside over some tests. He had a PhD and all the credentials. He must have been a gambler at heart because he conducted his tests with dice, then threw in cards too, just for good measure. After fifteen years, he decided that the mind could influence the roll of the dice. More than that, people could tell in advance the number coming up when someone else threw them. They could even guess the card on the top of a deck. He submitted equations from here to Calcutta and said mathematics had proved that people had ESP. But people with ESP couldn't solve the equations. So they called in a computer for that little job. A computer without values doesn't care if it hurts feelings. What it said about ESP can be summed up as "Nuts!" Just the old law of averages functioning as always, just as it had for millions of years.

Over at Las Vegas, gambling house owners breathed a sigh of relief. They wouldn't want to lose old law of averages, it had made them a bundle. I guess they'd forgotten that they'd made a somewhat larger test than Dr. Rhine had. Several million people had lined up at their crap tables and tried to influence the roll of the dice. Several million people had sat around the blackjack tables and tried to guess the card on the top of the deck. Old law of averages hadn't budged an inch. He was surer than death and more accurate than taxes. At least the kind of taxes they paid, which was only on unburied money.

HOW TO WIN AT LAS VEGAS

But Las Vegas gambling house owners are known to protect their interests. Maybe ESP wasn't discovered yet, but somebody might invent it. Then he would try to cut in on the take. They'd have to stamp this thing out before it got started. They'd post guards around the casinos and keep them on the lookout for people with big brains who might upset the dice. Somebody wanted to know how to recognize a guy with a big brain. The answer to that seemed easy enough. A guy with a big brain would have a big head. For some time after that, it was noticeable at the crap table that the largest hat size was 61/2. But even such little brains didn't change the old law of averages. It behaved just the same. One thing of interest occurred, however. A pin-headed guy got into the casino, carrying a big brain under his arm.

Nobody noticed, which was natural enough. Since they were looking for a brain, they expected to find it in somebody's head. The pin-headed guy set his brain down at the roulette wheel, then sat there for hours punching its buttons. All the players walking by glanced at him sadly. They thought he was tabulating fabulous losses. The pit bosses were more pleasant, having arrived at the same conclusion. After eight hours of punching buttons, the pin-headed guy started placing his bets. Twenty hours later, he cleaned out the house.

Somewhere in the midst of this unusual demonstration, it got bandied around that old law of averages was taking a beating. The Watchers for Big Heads rushed inside, sure that one had escaped them. All they could find was a pin-headed guy with an adding machine. Well, old law of averages would soon take care of him. They wandered back outside and continued searching for big heads. When they finally woke up to the fact that a big brain had invaded them, hidden within an adding machine, they'd been hit so hard they had to dig up buried money. Thus had Las Vegas its first brush with the computer. It gave them a dim view of the brain-in-a-ma-chine. The thing stole their money and made them keep changing roulette wheels. It could find the slightest flaw and predict variance from chance. Worst of all, there was no way to kill it. Nowadays, the larger hat sizes are allowed at Las Vegas crap tables. But lookouts are still posted. They keep their eyes peeled for pin-headed guys who carry their brains under their arms.

YOU CAN'T SEE IN THE DARK OR HEAR MUCH WITH NOISE

The computer beat the wheel because it had no pet ideas. It didn't have a value that said there was extrasensory perception. It didn't try to influence the wheel or the rolling of the ball. It didn't try to wish the ball into a number slot. It just tabulated the numbers and found the flaw in the wheel. It was the wheel that put the law of averages out of commission. That's how a computer solves its problems. It finds out what works. What a computer can do, the brain can do better. It just has to get rid of pet theories and values.

A friend of mine dragged me to a séance. The medium was supposed to put us in touch with the dead. Everybody was knocking on ninety, and at first I thought I was already in touch. It turned out that the spirits only came in the dark. How dark that would be I had no idea, but I had an edgy feeling. The doors and windows were being sealed with black tape. The medium explained what would happen. When he turned out the lights, everybody was to sing. When the spirits heard us, they would come to visit us. We must be sure to sing loud, because they might be far away. He put a trumpet on the table and said they would speak through it and not to be disturbed if it floated around the room. We'd be able to see it because there was a fluorescent band around it. When a spirit wanted to speak, it would whisper a first name through the trumpet. If we knew a dead somebody by that name, we were to give his last name. If it turned out to be the right spirit, then we could talk to it. The medium turned out the lights, and everybody began to sing.

I held my hand up before my face and couldn't make out my fingers. That was the blackest black I'd ever seen. I got to thinking it was like the inside of a tomb and began pinching myself to be sure I could feel. Just then the trumpet began floating, and everybody sang louder. Along the walls of the room that trumpet floated, across the ceiling, then began bouncing on the table, then took off in a series of delicate undulations. I got a funny idea that a man waving it could make it do that, but I tried to keep an open mind. Still, I couldn't help listening for footsteps, but everybody was right in the middle of "Oh, Susanna." The din was deafening.

HOW HEAVEN CHANGED HENRY

Then the trumpet stopped waving and poised in mid-air. Everybody stopped singing. The trumpet whispered, "Hazel." Somebody asked, "Green?" and the trumpet whispered, "Yes." That started a conversation. It turned out that Hazel felt fine and liked it where she was and had no aches and pains but couldn't exactly describe heaven. It occurred to me that Hazel sounded something like the medium, but then I thought she could have been a relative. Hazel had to go, and an Indian replaced her. He was very jolly and mischievous. He kept knocking the trumpet to the floor and having a big laugh. He sounded like the medium too. Well, maybe there was Indian blood in the family. After that, somebody talked to a woman named Mary. She felt fine too and liked it where she was and had no aches and pains and couldn't exactly describe heaven. Another of the medium's relatives.

When Mary left, the trumpet whispered, "Henry," and I answered, "Andersen?" because I had a favorite uncle who is with us no more. The trumpet whispered, "Yes," and just like that I was talking to Henry. Good old Hank! The times we used to have together. We'd have a couple drinks and start spouting Norwegian. I blurted out my half of our favorite exchange. "Du skal varre kuna, je skal varre mon. Du skal kogge kaffe, se skal je barre vun."

There was a long period of silence. Pretty soon, the trumpet whispered, "Up here we only speak English."

That sort of killed it with Henry. He went on to say that he liked it where he was and felt fine and had no aches and pains and couldn't exactly describe heaven. But I didn't care if heaven was paved with gold. I didn't like what it had done to Henry. I liked him better when he spoke Norwegian. He went away, but I didn't even bother to say goodbye.

After that, I sort of relaxed, because if I couldn't get a kick out of talking to Henry, who could I get a kick out of talking to? I leaned back in my chair and stuck out my legs. I should have been more careful.

Everybody was singing and the trumpet was floating again, and somebody stumbled over my feet.

Now I don't know much about spirits, but I do know something about conditioned reflexes. I know that if a man does something that is habitually followed by something else, when the first thing happens, the second automatically follows. Such as a man stumbling over your feet. He'll catch himself by bracing a hand on your knee, then he'll say, "Excuse me." That's exactly what the medium did.

HOW TO GET ANSWERS TO UNSOLVABLE PROBLEMS

Reading the stars and the tea leaves, consulting mind readers, believing that some men can see into the future, believing that thought power can influence others, believing that prayer can get what you want, believing that mind power can influence the roll of the dice, believing that spirits return from the dead, believing you have to please mother when you're forty years old and mother is dead—this is the garbage that produces unsolvable problems. And it's not fed you by charlatans, it's fed you by believers. The little old guy walking around waving the trumpet and whispering through it believes a spirit makes him move and a spirit make him whisper. And people who come to listen wind up believing it too, because what we concentrate on becomes real.

Do you think a computer could guide a missile to the moon if it was programmed like that? Not on your life. It would have an unsolvable problem. First it would try to wish itself off the launching pad. When that didn't work, it would consult a psychic. If the psychic told it that it should make the trip later, it would wait until then and wish even harder. When that failed to work, it would start looking around for somebody to blame. But don't get the idea that it would blame the psychic. It would get mad at successful computers and say they weren't spiritual. Such is the power of rationalization to maintain a harmful belief.

When you've got an unsolvable problem it's because your brain is acting on a lie. It has a pet theory or value or habitual idea that makes it produce errors. You don't have to search for this faulty programming. It's not subconscious by a long shot. It's the thing you're always yapping about and defending as *good.* All you have to do is keep your mouth shut and your ears open. That will chase out the garbage and allow some facts in. When facts start entering your computer, it produces right answers. You couldn't stop it if you tried. It's designed to process data, and it just keeps processing data. Maybe you get Syzygy to Serendipity when you're half asleep. Maybe it's an idea for your business while you're standing there shaving. Maybe it's a new tooling process while you're driving to work. The idea pops up like a cork on a lake, but it wasn't sent from heaven or Mars or from a spirit. It just got back to the output terminal when the data processing was done.

To provide inside solutions to unsolvable problems, all you have to do is stop defending your pet ideas and keep your mouth shut. Your ears will pick up the information that solves the problem inside your head. When that one is solved, the outside problem can be solved too. That's the way a computer works.

·10· HOW TO PUSH-BUTTON PEOPLE INTO FAST ACTION

PEOPLE HAVE PUSH-BUTTONS. Words push those buttons. When those buttons are pushed, people respond a certain way. That's because they think words are signals. They don't know words are symbols. They don't think about what you say, they react to what you say. That's too bad for them, because words run them like robots, but it's not up to you to change it, they can only do that themselves. Meantime, if you want to handle people, you have to push their buttons. If you want to handle them well, you have to push the right ones.

HOW TO PUSH-BUTTON YOURSELF

Pushing people-buttons can become a great art. Some devotees become so accomplished that they give a better performance than a long-haired maestro at Carnegie Hall. They usually wind up in offices well equipped with telephones. Over the length of the land and the width of the world they send out the words that push-button people into action, and they don't even get out of their chairs. If you ever run into one of these *guys*, don't bother pushing his buttons. He hasn't got *any*. That's why he's so good at pushing yours.

People who haven't got any buttons are people who think. They have to be persuaded. That's a different art altogether, and we'll deal with it later. But it's not too important. There are few people who think.

I am aware that many people believe that they think. This doesn't make them thinkers. It just gives them the wrong idea about thought. I know of a creativity specialist who's an authority on thinking. He has so many push-buttons he looks like a switchboard. You can sit in a chair and move him all over the room, out the door, down the steps, around the yard and bring him back, just like one of those radio controlled toys, and all you have to do is say a few words. If you say the right ones, he'll even get up and give a little talk on how to be a thinker.

One of the things he discovered when someone pushed a button was that if you could move thought outside your head where you could look at it, it seemed to function better. Now this isn't too surprising, since he'd had no experience of anything happening inside his head. If he could get something out in front of him that gave him some signals, then he began to function. It was only natural to assume this response to be thought, since he was trying to get some ideas. He cut up a lot of cards, two inches by four, and put some words on them. Naturally, these were words he'd been responding to for years. Then he'd shuffle the cards around, and when two or three came together so that they caused a different response, he was absolutely elated because he'd thought of an idea. It never occurred to him that all he'd done was react. His hand had done the shuffling, and his push-buttons had responded to the words. Even when he kept getting the same idea over and over, it still didn't occur to him. It was the only time I ever saw anybody use the pushbutton technique on himself.

AN OUTSIDE-THE-HEAD THINKER

He held a little demonstration for a dozen of us. He said he'd thought up a fictitious candy bar called Heaps, which sounded slightly suspicious of Mounds. Anyway, he wanted all of us to think of advertising slogans by our antique method of moving symbols around inside our heads. At the same time, he'd be thinking up advertising slogans by the more streamlined method of moving cards around on a table. He'd already taken the trouble to jot down a couple dozen ideas on the cards, but after all, there were twelve of us, and that was only fair. We'd play this game for a half hour and see which method produced the best slogan, the inside-the-head method, or the outside-the-head method. An inside-the-head thinker who took shorthand was elected to write down what was said, and the outside-the-head thinker got his cards arranged on the table, crouched in his chair, hollered, "Go!" and everybody was off, thinking like mad, but he was the only one who looked busy.

I couldn't help wondering if he would last the half hour, he was so busy shuffling those cards. I couldn't pay attention to doing my own thinking, I was so fascinated at seeing thought in such furious motion. He kept shuffling away for fully five minutes, then he suddenly barked out, "Heaps Seeps!" The guy with the pencil took it down, but I thought it was an inauspicious start. Meantime, the shorthand taker had to change pencils because my colleagues had given him several hundred slogans.

After that, things went badly for the outside-the-head thinker. A gust of wind came in through the window and blew his cards off the table. He scrambled frantically around on the floor, searching for his brains. They proved difficult to pick up and even more difficult to get back in order. Meantime my colleagues kept up a running fire of ideas, seemingly unaffected by the wind. That was reassuring. I thought it might have whistled through the heads of several of them. At least, it didn't blow any cards away.

WHO'S GOT THE BUTTONS?

After the outside-the-head thinker got his cards back on the table, he somehow didn't seem to have his heart in it. He'd lost his old steam as he shuffled the cards about, and he stared at them morosely. We only heard from him once more, and that was toward the end of the half hour. Then he mumbled, "Heaps are Bigger than Mounds." The shorthand guy looked a little awed, and asked him to repeat it.

When the session ended, the outside-the-head thinker put his cards away and seemed to regain some of his brightness. He pointed out that the outside-the-head method didn't produce quantity but guaranteed quality because it got rid of nonsense. I had to give him credit for plenty of guts, but that was some distance below his head. He asked what we considered the best slogan. The guy with the pencil had seven hundred to choose from, so he naturally chose one of his own. He said, "A Dollar's Worth of Flavor for Only a Dime." I didn't think that was half bad. Everybody likes to save ninety cents. But the outside-the-head thinker hit the ceiling.

" Heaps Seeps!" he shouted. His face got red, and he shouted again, "Heaps Seeps!"

There was no question about it, he thought he had the best slogan. Some of the other guys began edging for the door. The outside-the head thinker seemed absolutely speechless, which was all right with us. We were afraid he might holler, "Heaps Seeps!" We finally got out of there and made for a bar. That's where we decided that his slogan had something. Nobody could forget, "Heaps Seeps!"

When you put words together that rhyme you're only responding to a signal. It was conditioned into you in high school when you had to memorize poetry. Advertising agencies often use it effectively, but the only thinking they do is figuring out the buttons it pushes. The button it pushed on my outside-the-head friend was one of utter conviction. No doubt he would have bought a candy bar that had the slogan, "Heaps Seeps!" But no advertising agency would hire him to figure out slogans. They don't want people who push-button themselves. They want people who can push other people's buttons. You have to sell a lot of candy bars, you can't sell only one. Consequently, they hire people without buttons to figure out who's got what buttons. In short, they hire thinkers.

HOW TO PUSH-BUTTON CONVICTS

The most difficult thing to teach a salesman is that he's not to persuade, he's to push-button. All over the country salesmen are turned loose with the idea that a successful presentation is a matter of winning an argument. They win all the arguments and lose all the sales, and they can't understand it. Their presentations are flawless, their logic superb, their evidence overwhelming. If they were prosecuting attorneys they'd win cinch convictions. The only thing they don't realize is that nobody is listening. There just aren't that many thinkers. When you ask a man to think, he thinks of his golf game or his girl friend. The only way you can get his attention is by pushing his buttons.

When I was on the debate team at Stanford University, we had a brilliant young debater, Sherman Melinkoff, now Dean of the U.C.L.A. Medical School. He taught me that even debate is not an argument. It's a matter of hitting those push-buttons.

We went up to San Quentin to debate a convict team on the constitutionality of the National Recovery Act. The Supreme Court had already outlawed it, and we had been given the tough job of proving that the court had make the wrong decision. I got up and made the opening argument. I could hear the shuffling of feet and knew I lost ground. Our second speaker had the same luck. It was clear that the convicts had already made up their minds to vote for the convict team, and the debate was only a formality. They weren't even listening.

But Melinkoff woke them up. When he opened his rebuttal, he hit the right button. He said, "Gentlemen, this whole thing is about a court's decision. And I know that there are many of you here who realize that a judge can be wrong!"

They laughed and cheered clear back to Cell Block 97. There wasn't a man in the place who didn't know that a judge was always wrong. Melinkoff won agreement, not by case histories, not by logic, not by evidence, but simply by hitting the hot button. I don't even remember what else he said and nobody else does and nobody cared. We won the debate because he hit the hot button. Why, those convicts mobbed him afterwards, hoping he'd turn out to be a lawyer. Whatever it took, they could see that he had it.

FREDDIE THE ROBOT

It's amazing that people are so ignorant about buttons, but I guess it's because they believe that they think. I am reminded of Freddie the Robot, a tin plated creature who responded to signals. He did everything reasonably well. He could mow the lawn, put out the cat, drive a car, watch baseball games, and he was especially good in the office where he answered correspondence with form letters. But despite this well ordered existence, Freddie the Robot was troubled. He wanted to be a man. He thought if he could just be a man, he'd achieve his greatest wish, but he hadn't the vaguest idea how to go about it. One day while reading the newspaper, Freddie chanced upon an ad. It told of a man who taught how burning desire could get you anything you wanted. That sounded just right to Freddie, since he didn't have any desire at all, so he pocketed the ad and went down to see how it was done.

He was surprised to find that the class was full of other robots like himself, and somewhat dismayed when he learned that it would cost him a great deal of money. But he paid it as cheerfully as he could. He sat down by another robot and asked, "What are you here for?" The other robot answered, "I want to be a man." That made them friends from the first.

The man who knew about burning desire came into the room then. He stood up in front and jumped up and down and got very excited. That made the robots excited. They stood up and jumped up and down too. "Now," cried the man, "you've got burning desire. Go out and get what you want!" All the robots rushed for the door. Freddie rushed with them. He could hardly wait to become a man. But when he reached the street, the burning desire left him. So he drove home and went to bed.

At the next class meeting he told the man what happened when he reached the street. The man said that in order to have burning desire you had to have investments and that he happened to know of one, in case Freddie was interested. That sounded good to Freddie, but he didn't like it when the man told him it would cost two thousand dollars. That would take all his savings. But the man kept talking about how rich he'd get and how excited he'd be, and Freddie began to get excited. He gave the man two thousand dollars because he was already getting burning desire. But once again, when he reached the street, the burning desire left him. He 'went home and to bed.

HOT BUTTONS AND LOADED WORDS

The next time Freddie saw the man, the man was jumping up and down and was very excited, and all the robots were jumping up and down and they were excited too, so Freddy didn't get to talk to him much. He finally managed to ask the man about his investment, and the man said he'd talk to him later, but he didn't get a chance to that night.

After that, the man didn't come to the meetings anymore. One of the robots said he was sick, but as the days went by and he never came, everybody said that something awful must have happened to him. It was all very sad. Finally Freddie didn't even go to the meetings. There were just the robots sitting there, and they didn't get excited, and nobody had burning desire. He went back to mowing the lawn and putting out the cat and driving his car and watching baseball games and answering correspondence with form letters. After all, it wasn't so bad being a robot. It was too hard to get burning desire.

People never learn by having their buttons pushed. This is the reason we have to have agencies to protect them from conmen. The same sucker can fall for the same gimmick a dozen times and be not one whit wiser. It isn't that he can't learn, it's just that he won't. It's too hard to get the desire. Learning is a matter of retraining responses to signals. It's also a matter of training in the use of symbols. It's also a matter of cleaning the garbage out of the computer so it can produce right answers. But that's too much work for most people. They'd rather be robots no matter how much they might wish to be men.

You push-button people into fast action when you find their hot buttons and the words that will push them. Some words find hot buttons in nearly everybody. Here are a few: Sex, death, money, failure, love, pain, flag, communist, doctor, cancer, strong, nigger, dogs, kike, mother. They're only chicken tracks on a piece of paper, but they produce such strong signal responses that you can feel yourself churning inside as you ride up and down the waves of their attraction and repulsion. Learning how to use words like these, words that have become signals, in the right combination and with the right timing, is how you push-button people into fast action.

WHEN NOT TO BE AN EDUCATOR

Back in the early days of television, I had for an advertising account a manufacturer of television sets, Tony Holzer, three hundred pounds and a mind like a blade. I used to go on the radio with his commercials and say that everybody ought to have a television set because you could see so many good shows and the kids would enjoy it and it was just like having a movie theatre in the home, and one day Holzer called me into his office, that face of his, big and round as a full moon, now dark as a thundercloud.

" You think I'm running a university?" he hollered. "You think you're a professor?"

I tried to be glib. "You're running the university of hard knocks,"

I said. "I'm the professor of sell."

" You ain't selling nothing!" he hollered. "You're educating! This proves it!" He threw a sales sheet down in front of me. I had to admit that sales sheet didn't look good.

Then he said, "That commercial of yours tells people they ought to want television, doesn't it? When you talk to people who ought to want television, who are you talking to? Why the people who don't want it yet, isn't that right? I got a warehouse full of television sets I'm trying to sell now. And you're talking to people who will maybe buy someday, if you can educate them. You listen! Right now you start being a salesman and stop being an educator. You go on the air and tell people I make a better television set, I sell it cheaper, and they can buy it now. And you stick with that. Push the buttons of the people who will buy now!"

Within four months, Tony Holzer's television sales increased three hundred percent, and I learned first hand that the art of getting people to take fast action is not education but pressing the buttons they already have. In a very literal sense, education builds buttons, but if you want fast action you have to work with the buttons a person has now. Education takes time and may never be absorbed in any case.

THE MOST POWERFUL WORD IN THE WORLD

I once knew a man who made a written insurance presentation that was fifty pages long. It was the most comprehensive work of its kind I ever saw. If you read your way through it, you'd be an expert on insurance. He left it with a prospect to read at his leisure. Six months later, the prospect still hadn't found any leisure, and the magnum opus was gathering dust on his desk. Then some other guy who knew about buttons walked in and sold him in three minutes. All he said was, "I can help you retire at sixty-five with an income of ten thousand dollars." You don't have to speak long when you're pushing buttons. You just have to know where you're aiming.

For my money, the most powerful button pusher in the world is the word, help. Maybe it's because most people feel they're drowning and that's what they're screaming inside. Maybe it's because that's what mother did for us. But if you pay any attention you've probably noticed that nobody turns down any help. When you tell a man you'll help him, you don't even have to know his problem. He's already gotten a tinge of the feeling that the two of you together might solve it. If you opened the window right now and shouted, "I'll help!" you'd have so many visitors you wouldn't know what to do with them. Everybody's got problems or something he wants, and everybody's looking for help. When you push the help button, the door is flung open and you're welcomed inside as a guest.

I once taught a guy to use the word help, much to my sorrow. He was a guy I knew and whose company I liked, but I have to admit he was a bum. He could charm the birds out of the trees and tell stories that would make you hold your sides, but all he wanted to do was hang around the beach and play with the dollies. Now I'm not knocking that kind of action, but you have to work sometime or you wind up flat broke. So it was with my friend. His only visible means of support were the occasional taps he made on his friends. They never amounted to much. He had no stupid friends.

HOW TO MAKE TWENTY THOUSAND DOLLARS AND STAY OUT OF JAIL

Once when he was in a bad way, he called on me for advice. In those days, I sprinkled it around like confetti. Later, I learned that people picked it up and used it so I began to hang onto it better. Anyway, it seems he'd gotten himself behind in the rent and at the grocery store and a few other places and he'd been to all his friends with a hard luck story but none of them would come up with as much as a dime. I started to fear for my own pocketbook, but bravely suggested that he go to work. Oh no, he couldn't do that. He had this big deal coming up and he had to be on it all the time and it had possibilities of making a fortune.

" Then let them in on it," I said.

" Let who in on what?" he wanted to know.

" Listen, you knucklehead," I shouted, "you're always walking in and asking for money, right? And people are running the other way. Hasn't it ever occurred to you that if you walked in and told them you'd help them make money, they'd be glad to see you?"

" How about you?" he asked. "I'd be glad to help you make some money." This kid was quick. But I managed to get him pointed in the other direction and forgot about the whole matter. Not for long.

A month later the phone began ringing. It was his friends. They wanted to know where he was. I couldn't help them. Then they wanted their money back. I couldn't help them on that either. Then they thought I'd better or they'd have the law on me because they knew I was in this wildcat oil well with him. That tore it. I called my lawyer and he began handling the calls.

With the little word help, my beachcomber friend had gotten into his pals for twenty thousand dollars. Then he'd cut out, and nobody's heard from him since. That was the last time I ever gave any free advice. Which proves you can stop being a sucker without burning desire.

I've even thought it might be possible to catch fish with a lure that said, "Here's help." Some wise guy pointed out that fish can't read and spoiled my whole project. Since I like to fish, I investigated the possibility of teaching fish how to read in the hatchery. Nothing complicated, of course. Just the two words, "Here's help." I had a long conversation about it with a hatchery attendant one day, but I couldn't get his attention. He kept gulping tranquilizers.

HOW TO CURE CALLOUSES WITH SNAKE OIL

One long hot summer in St. Johns when the mills were going full blast and log booms jammed the Willamette and there was nothing to do after the sun set but listen to the chirping of the crickets, there came into town a man with a big tent which he set up at the corner of Lombard and Clarendon, with a sign posted in front: THE GREAT MARCEL AND HIS FABULOUS SNAKE SHOW. Then he walked around town and promised help.

He was dapper and slim and wore a stovepipe hat and a cutaway coat and he flashed his eyes so you could see the whites, and he looked exactly like the kind of fellow who would have an especial rapport with snakes. He promised help.

And when the crowds thronged around the tent that night and oil torches flickered their light over a lithe young lady dancing with snakes, and Marcel stood there with his pitchman's chant that told of the wonderful oil extracted from snakes that cured every human ill, he looked like a benevolent Mephistopheles come out of his pits with a magic brew. He promised help. It cured corns, calluses, lumbago, colds, indigestion, made trips to the half moon house more regular, and (as he alluded to the men) was especially potent in dealing with certain private diseases. Best of all, it was only a dollar a bottle. He promised help.

Everybody had to agree it was worth a try, and for years, nobody could open a drugstore in St. Johns, because Marcel's Snake Oil was good for everything and everybody had plenty of it. He promised help. And notice: People who believe that something will help are people who are convinced, and they make the product work with their own conviction. Why in St. Johns, Marcel's Snake Oil has cured more diseases than three generations of hard working doctors. He promised help.

I hope I've got this little word help over to you. It's the most powerful word in the English language. If you never learn another button pushing word, remember this one. I don't care how complicated a switchboard a robot carries in his head. You can play it like a piano and hit every button when you've learned how to use the word, help. If you can't learn the sales manual or you mess up the bookkeeping or lose track of the filing, if you stutter and are shy, fat, bald, and ugly, and can't remember a thing, just keep repeating, "I'll help." You'll wind up with money and clients and plenty of friends, who'll all bring you more, because you help.

HOW THE BUTTONS WORK

There are literally dozens of people buttons: Money, recognition, security, power, prestige, authority, love, health, religion, friendship, capability, self-reliance, sex, hunger, industry, parenthood, death, the list is practically endless. You have to know which button is hot. It's no good offering to help a hungry man find God. He's looking for a loaf of bread. This is the fundamental error committed by the Catholic Church in the war it's losing to communism.

Behind each button are two circuits. One is actuated by hope, the other by fear. You can get about a hundred volts through the hope circuit. You can get a thousand volts through the fear circuit. But the fear circuit burns out if it's kept on too long. It can even kill a man. You can leave the hope circuit on forever. It's never been known to do anything but make a man happy.

If you frustrate a man's hope, he gets angry. That allows him to pull voltage from the fear circuit. Now you've got him moving at eleven hundred volts. Curiously, when both the hope and fear circuits are on at the same time, the fear circuit doesn't burn out. A man can be angry all of his life and never know a day of poor health. He just seems to have ten times the power of everyone else.

It's easier to scare a man than give him hope or make him mad. That's because his buttons were mostly implanted by fear in the first place. When he's scared, you've got him running at nearly full power, and you can do anything you want with him. Fear appears to effectively block out that portion of the brain that is capable of thought. It puts people on automatic response to only the button that's hot. This makes fear the most effective circuit to activate when you're trying to move people to fast action. But you can't waste any time. A man with a hot fear circuit can hold out only for hours or days, then he sinks into depression or lethargy as his circuit burns out. It's human to remember that you can do considerable damage to people with fear. A man in the grip of fear grasps at straws. If you have to keep anybody grasping at straws for more than an hour, you better find a new business. Of course, a man grasping at straws can be sold anything. That's why it's the favorite circuit of all push-button artists.

HOW A MAN BECOMES A BULL THAT TEARS DOWN A WALL

Hope moves slower and with reduced power. People who want to get things done seldom fool with it, but it has the saving grace of keeping everybody happy. Oddly enough, the people who sell hope don't have many followers. Which perhaps proves that few people want to be happy. A hopeful guy doesn't always show up at the meetings, and he's a little stingy about dipping into his pocket, and when the jobs are passed out, he'd as soon let somebody else do them. More than that, he's liable to degenerate into being a wish thinker, expecting heaven or luck or other people to get things done for him. Hellfire and damnation religion activates fear. The revival tents are jammed, people cough up plenty, and volunteer workers abound. Some churches have removed hell from Christian theology and have lost the fear motive. They work just with hope. Their attendance is spotty, people leave only a quarter in the collection box, and are hard to find when something needs to be done. To fill up their churches, they ought to make people mad. Then they'd outdraw the fundamentalists.

It's harder to give a man hope than it is to scare him, and if s hardest of all to make him mad. But when he's mad, he's a bull and can tear down a wall. That makes him tough to handle. It takes a strong leader to dare make people mad, but if he can keep them under control, he's got a powerhouse. I doubt I'm exaggerating when I say that a thousand well led angry men could conquer the world. But most leaders haven't got guts enough to tackle the attendant problems. An angry man lashes out at the closest target, and the leader could be standing right next to him. That keeps most leaders working with fear. About the only time there's an exception is when an angry man becomes a leader. Then watch out. There's a rocket coming.

A man has to have hope before you can make him mad. If he's scared, you can't switch him. You can switch him to hope and then to anger, but once he's scared, it takes coaxing to turn on his hope. Anger is caused by frustrating hope, but it has to be frustrated quickly or it can turn into fear. It can be kept on indefinitely by sending out alternate signals that first activate the hope circuit, the fear circuit, the hope circuit, and so on. When fear and hope mingle, you've got a man angry.

HOW TO USE THE BUTTONS

It's easiest to push-button people into fast action by working only with fear. I know a guy who runs a national organization, and everybody's afraid of him. Personally, he's really quite pleasant, but he wants the fear response. It makes his job easier, and that's what he's after. Once in awhile, just so he doesn't burn out the fear circuit, he throws a big wingding that takes all pressure off. But he still keeps his distance. Mustn't pet the monster, or you won't be afraid of him.

There's only one way to use hope to get strong motivation, but it has to be combined with fear and can easily turn into anger. It's to promise people a fantastic reward, then get them afraid that they'll lose it. This inspires a hurry reaction. You can get a lot done quickly with this one, but if they don't get the reward, they're liable to get mad, and if you made the promise, you're the target. This is the favorite device of the conman, but he knows its dangers and is set up to meet them. He embroils people in such shady schemes that they're ashamed to admit they were involved. This is pretty effective, but occasionally somebody loses his head and doesn't care if he appears stupid or degenerate. At that point, the conman's had it.

Let's get down to a few of the buttons themselves. Money is the most powerful, but it's the hardest to use because everybody has a reasonable idea of what something is worth. The second most powerful is self-esteem. It's also the easiest to work. Strangely, not all people want to be better than others, but nobody wants to be worse. Next comes security. This button seems to grow in importance all the time and usually includes a man's family. After this comes the button of death. In some ways, this may be the most important button of all, simply because few people realize they have it. A typical reaction when you push it is, "Oh, I'm not afraid to die." But the guy's face pales and sweat breaks out on his palms. He's looked in the mirror every morning and has seen something gaining on him.

THE USES OF SEX AND LOVE

An overrated button is sex. Oh, people will go to movies about it and read books about it but mostly they'll just do it. A man will glance at an ad with a half naked woman in it but that won't make him buy the product or even remember who paid for the ad. Sex is a leisure time activity, like golf, though I will agree that most people prefer it to golf. But nobody would think of trying to motivate people by promising them a game of golf. Sex is somewhat the same. You can arrange to have a visiting fireman entertained with it, but that won't make him buy your product. He won't even thank you. Sex is good for telling jokes and entertaining, but that's about the end of it with men. With women it's different. They'll do almost anything to be desired. They figure that gives them power over men. With power over men, they've got a meal ticket.

Love isn't much of a button with a man. His experience with it says that's when he pays the bills. Oh, he'll load up on insurance policies for the wife and kiddies and buy a house and a car and all that. Maybe that's the reason he's disappointed in love. He never got a good look at the price tag. But even with his family and house and car, his self-esteem and security are involved. Don't get these buttons confused with love.

Love is a big button with a woman. What she was after all along was to be boarded and bedded. That means somebody will go out and knock wild boars over the head and bring home the bacon and she can hatch her brood out in security. I've never known a woman who wanted anything else. Lots of them wind up with something else, but it's mostly their fault, as we'll discuss later.

You can get fast action from any of these buttons when they're hot. Just inspire the fear that the desired thing may be lost, then offer to help make it better.

·11· HOW TO PERSUADE PEOPLE TO POINT OF VIEW

A MAN CAN be a thinker and still be somewhat daffy. That's because his symbols have no counterparts in the world.They're symbols for symbols for symbols, and so on. He can manipulate those symbols with the best of them, but if somebody asks him his name, he forgets it. He's not used to looking at symbols as names for things outside him. He looks at them as names for things inside his head. Since this in essence puts the whole world in his head, it has been known to give people a very large head. They can be regularly visited by God, for example, or be given rides to Mars by spacemen who think they're just wonderful.

But if it occurs to a thinker that the symbols in his head are just names for things outside his head, he begins to take them outside to see if they fit. This gives him something of an advantage over the fantasy thinker. One guy builds a rocket to get to the moon. The other guy tries to pray his way up there. When you run into the first guy, you have to persuade him by showing him it works. When you run into the second, all you can do is sing his Hosannas. Even his buttons are inside his head.

HOW TO PERSUADE GENIUSES

There's a club that nobody can get into except geniuses. The entrance exam is an IQ test. Some people think the members have swelled heads. And not without reason. Most of them have the whole world inside. On a recent excursion into a coterie of this group, I was somewhat startled to discover that nobody could drive a car, but everybody knew where God was. It was interesting to me that nobody thought God was in the same place. I suggested we look and see. By the withering stares I received, I knew I was blackballed from membership.

It occurred to me that I was face to face with one of the problems of persuasion that I'd never solved. That was how to persuade thinkers to a new viewpoint when they refused to test their symbols. There seemed like no time like the present, so I launched out at once. I said, "I know where God is and I can show him to you." That piqued their curiosity. And despite the fact that they knew all about God. But some of them protested that they didn't have time for the trip. I thought that was something of a slight to God, but I didn't want to lose any geniuses, so I offered to bring God right here. Now I could see I was really cooking with gas. This was their language and just what they'd been working on. I'd sung my first Hosanna and increased my chances of membership. Besides, what could be sweeter than getting a glimpse of God without having to move out of your chair?

One dissenter suggested that I couldn't do it. I pointed out that Moses had gotten the Red Sea to part. He said I wasn't Moses. I thought for a moment of claiming I was, but decided it was risky. So I said that I didn't have to be Moses, I just had to know what he knew. He inquired as to how that information had been transmitted from Moses to me. I didn't like the trend of the conversation. This guy was acting as if there was a world outside his head. I had to get him back in it. So I gave him both barrels. "God told me," I said. That chased him back. After all, hadn't God told him a few things too? He withdrew his objections, and everybody got himself comfortable and urged me to commence.

A TIBETAN LAMA NAMED EVERREADY

I had to go out to the car for my God-finding flashlight and when I came back the room was a buzz, but everybody was disappointed that I expected to find God with a flashlight. I pointed out that in order to see anything you had to have light, but that didn't create much of a stir. So I fell back on instinct and reported that this special flashlight had been constructed by an old Tibetan lama under divine instructions and passed him his hand to mine in a secret cave in the Himalayas. That was better. That sounded like how to find God.

There was one thing unusual about this flashlight. It had a rheostat on it so you could make the light brighter or dimmer. I suppose that by stretching a point you could say that the guy who invented it had a few instructions from God, but the old Tibetan lama was a guy named Ever Ready, and he wouldn't part with it until I paid him $8.95.

I turned out the lights and shined the flashlight on the wall, rheostat full up. It made a brilliant circle the size of a car wheel. That would make God a little small, so I'd have to work with just his head and shoulders. Somebody in the audience piped up that he didn't see God. I told him just to be patient, it would take God a few minutes to get here. Everybody stared at the circle of light on the wall. God was taking a long time. So I filled in the interval by describing what he looked like. I went on to say that he was an old man with a powerful face and a white beard and glittering eyes and looked just like the painting Michelangelo had made of him on the ceiling of the Sistine Chapel. That was because Michelangelo had seen him too. That's how he was able to make the painting. I told about how when God came he would make the light on the wall grow dimmer. That wasn't because the light was actually dimmer, it was because God had so much radiance he made all light seem dim. We'd know he was getting close when the light started to get dimmer. Everybody stared at that circle of light. I edged my finger onto the rheostat and moved it a little. The light grew dimmer.

" Oh, my God!" cried one of the geniuses. I couldn't tell if he was surprised or if he was praying, but I knew he didn't know anything about rheostats.

HOW TO SELL FLASHLIGHTS

The light grew dimmer and dimmer. Breathing grew louder and louder. You could almost believe that everyone had asthma. I heard the sound of somebody choking. I trusted it was from swallowing his pride. The light was pretty dim now. I had to have a little help or I was out of luck. Suddenly, I got it. Somebody cried, "There he is!" Sure enough, there he was. Everybody saw him at once.

He was an old man with a powerful face and a white beard and glittering eyes and looked just like the painting Michelangelo made of him on the ceiling of the Sistine Chapel. You could have heard a pin drop. Everybody lost his asthma. Nobody breathed. If God hung around much longer, everybody would strangle. So I sent him back to heaven by switching off the flashlight.

The room was dead black and silent as a tomb. Apparently nobody knows what to say after looking at God. Now I had to tear it. I had to switch these fantasy thinkers to my point of view. I had to solve that problem in persuasion that I'd never been able to solve.

I switched the flashlight back on, rheostat full up. There was a bright circle of light, but God wasn't in it. Then I told about the rheostat and the Tibetan lama named Ever Ready. Then I pointed out how God was a symbol in the mind but that symbol couldn't be matched up with anything in the world; therefore it was just a symbol; therefore God was inside you; therefore you couldn't see him, you could just see his symbol; and if you concentrated on that symbol, it seemed to be outside you. I jiggled the rheostat up and down to emphasize my point. I was sure that nobody would believe that God could come and go that fast. Then I switched off the flashlight and turned on the room lights.

The first thing that happened is that somebody wanted to buy my flashlight. That started the bidding. It got up as high as two hundred dollars. I could see right away that I hadn't solved the problem, but I had found a way to make a nice profit on flashlights. In a way, it got my mind off the problem altogether, because I couldn't help dwelling on the possibilities of building a flashlight empire. After all, I'd fired my best guns and all I'd come up with was singing Hosannas. So I parted with the flashlight for two hundred dollars. It was a nice evening's work.

HOW TO GET INTO HEAVEN BY APOLOGIZING

Now if you get the idea that I think there are some people who cannot be persuaded to your point of view, you're absolutely right. There's no means of communication with a man who refuses to test his symbols. When he thinks a table is three feet high, he won't measure the table. The table can be two feet high or four feet high, but as far as he's concerned it remains three feet high. That may cause him some difficulty in placing a cup of coffee on it, but he won't change the height of the table, he'll just change the distance of a foot. To try to persuade people who are hung up in their symbols is like trying to pound sand down a rat-hole. Save your sand. All you can do is sing their Hosannas. That will make you one of them, and you might be able to sell them flashlights. But they won't think they bought flashlights. They'll think they bought God.

The symptom of a thinker who is hung up in his symbols is that everything he thinks and does is a fantasy. He can't get a job done because he can't see how to do it. He usually seems bright, often erudite, and everything he says has the ring of good sense, but when he bends down to tie his shoelace, somehow he can't find it. As a group, fantasy thinkers have a certain usefulness to society. They support such endeavors as Teaching People How to Pray, How to Get Things for Nothing, and How to Get Rich Quick. They give rise to such professions as Listening to Other People's Problems, Regaining Your Health by Taking Pills That Are Poison, and Making Written Agreements That Nobody Understands. They cause the industries of Manufacturing the Useless Because It Is Lucky, Building the Expensive Because It Is Cheaper, and Making the Most from Your Money by Letting Other People Use It.

They enable such political philosophies as How to Become Free by Having More Laws, How to Gain Peace by Killing Off Others, How to Get What You

Want by Letting Somebody Decide for You, and How to Be Equal Despite Being Worse. Then there's How to Get into Heaven by Apologizing. That's not exactly a political philosophy, but I think it's becoming one. It's easy to see that without the presence of fantasy thinkers a lot of people would be thrown out of work. So I don't recommend stamping them out. Just learning how to sing their Hosannas.

THE USES OF MULES AND JACKASSES

The only people you can persuade are the people who think and who test the symbols they think with. You will probably gather that they are about as scarce as the buffalo. But you might like to know how to recognize a buffalo in case you run into one. You can recognize a thinker who tests his symbols by the fact that he gets a lot of things done. Now don't make the mistake of looking for somebody who's busy. You can be awfully busy dancing around camp-fires to make rain. Chances are you'll find this thinker who tests his symbols sitting quietly by himself, thinking. In this case, it's hard to tell him from somebody who's plain lazy, and he's certainly easy to confuse with the thinker who doesn't test his symbols. But if you get him into conversation, you'll find a quick clue. You'll discover immediately that he wants to get something done. He's not interested in why it can't be or why it won't be or how it could be or how to avoid it. He just wants to do it. This may cause you to think that he's half mule and half jackass. In a way, you're right. But even though you can't see it, he's educating his jackass. And if you happen to be around when he swings into action, you'll see both mule and jackass swiftly replaced by a thoroughbred who wins.

When this guy's in action, he always has his hands full. He's got something in one hand and something in the other. There's a frown on his face because he's trying to fit them together. If he gets them together, the frown is replaced by a smile. Then he calls in people to make them and sell them and put them to use. The thing he's put together is always useful. The thing he's put together always works. He knows, because he's tested it.

If he doesn't get the pieces together, he continues to frown, but he doesn't say he can't or it has to be done only that way. He just goes back to being half mule and half jackass. The mule keeps him at it. The jackass acts crazy. He tries to hitch them to the symbol that will get the thing done. Pretty soon, he gets them in harness. That pulls him out of his chair and into the shop. Again, he gets his hands full. Again, he puts pieces together to see if they fit. What he cuts in his mind, he tries in the world. If it works in the world, he uses it. If it doesn't work in the world, he doesn't keep cutting it in his mind. He cuts something else. That's why he's a good thinker. It also happens to be why he gets so many things done.

HOW TO DEVELOP CALLOUSES BY THINKING

You might think this guy would be difficult to persuade. Not at all, he's a patsy. All you have to do is have something that works. He'll see it at once, and he'll buy it. Of course, if what you have doesn't work, he turns into all mule and you wonder what happened to the jackass. Otherwise, you'll find him quite open minded. He just wants to see if it works. He won't buy your symbols but he will buy your things, as soon as you show him they work. Sure, he wants them to be useful, but he's open minded about that too. All you have to do is demonstrate that they are.

You persuade people to your point of view by showing them that you have something that works and is useful. You can't do it with words. You can't do it with pictures. You can't do it by being personable or magnetic or industrious. You can't do it by your record. You can't do it by promises. There's no way to escape it. You just have to demonstrate.

I addressed the Annual Supervisors Convention of the Zenith Radio Corporation in Chicago. A hard-bitten guy by the name of Fred Hedblom was in charge. The calluses on his hands must have been an inch thick, which is somewhat surprising in a vice president. I suspected they might have gotten that way from trying to fit things together, and asked him about it. It turned out I was right. He fitted together twelve thousand television sets a day. I mentioned that must keep him busy. "Not at all," he said. "I just fit together the first one." As we sat there, he told about some symbols he was toying with. I could just see him the next morning out in the shop, fitting some new pieces together. That's why his hands had calluses. It also happens to be why Zenith has quality.

Later on I gave a speech entitled, "People in the People Business." It was about putting people together to see if they fit. I mentioned that Zenith put together good television because it put together good people and good people could be recognized because they had calluses. Old Hedblom just sat there and smiled.

I am reminded of a guy who made a specialty of selling television sets to thinkers who tested their symbols. He was a master of persuasion. He didn't have a sales talk and he didn't advertise and he didn't send out any pictures. He just put a television set in somebody's home and told him to try it and see if he liked it. In a few days, he got the inevitable phone call. How much did it cost? He mentioned the price. He got a check in the mail. To persuade, you demonstrate —that's all that you do.

HOW TO BE CONTENT WITH AN AUTOMATIC WIFE

You can't persuade fantasy thinkers, and you can't persuade people with buttons. You can demonstrate that light dims by means of a rheostat, but the fantasy thinker will still believe it dimmed because of God. He's not interested in changing his symbols to fit the world. He's interested in changing the world to fit his symbols. Demonstration is useless. You can't persuade people with buttons because they're on automatic. They think demonstration is some kind of show. They'll applaud and exclaim over how wonderful it is that somebody else can do it. It seems never to occur to them that they could do it themselves.

I once knew a man with an automatic wife. She didn't know how to drive, and he spent a lot of time taking her places. It occurred to him that it might save him some trouble if he bought her a car. He bought her a beauty and demonstrated how to drive it. She thought it was wonderful that he could drive so well. He spent six months demonstrating. She became even more convinced that he drove very well. She kept getting signals that she wanted to go someplace, and she'd call him at the office and ask him to take her. Oh well, at least he had the choice of two cars.

For people without buttons and people without fantasy, demonstration is convincing. It actually changes things inside their heads. They're not only persuaded to a new point of view, they've been educated as well. You've left them better than you found them. I guess that's why persuasion is so deeply rewarding—it leaves you feeling you've done a little something to make the world better.

SOMETHING TO USE IN CASE THERE'S A WAR

Everybody can be hypnotized. In fact, everybody has been. That's why people behave the way they do. But to hypnotize someone and give him new orders with the idea that he's going to get along better is sheer idiocy. After all, the fact that he's alive is evidence that he's not too far out of touch. You have to keep from driving off cliffs in order to survive. Give a man a new way to do things without his being aware of it and he thinks he's driving the car when somebody else is. Suddenly, there's a cliff. All you've discovered is a method of reducing the world's population.

But there's no doubt that people can be switched to your point of view if you hypnotize them. There is some question, however, about calling this persuasion. Persuasion implies an inner consent. Hypnotism is like hitting a man over the head with a hammer. He gets the point, but it's liable to damage his head. But if it's a matter of survival, blitz tactics are in order. That's when it's good to know about hypnotism.

If I ask you to think of a white elephant and you don't want to think of a white elephant, you don't think of a white elephant. Then if I ask you not to think of a white elephant, what do you do? Why you think of a white elephant, don't you? That's all there is to hypnotism— misdirection and suggestion.

These two principles of hypnosis are used very effectively by many sales forces. You get a call on the telephone and somebody excitedly notifies you that you've just won a prize. Since the last time you won anything was in the third grade and that was a dunce cap for being the worst speller, you're likely to feel somewhat set up at this evidence that old lady luck hasn't completely deserted you. This makes it convenient to forget that you haven't entered any contests for the last twenty years. If you remembered that, you'd have to explain it, and then it would probably turn out that somebody with the same name has this prize coming to him. So you gently inquire as to what prize you have won. Now somebody explains that it is so absolutely thrilling that he wants to bring it right out to you. You remark rather desultorily that there's no sense going to all that trouble, he could mail it to you or ship it to you or if it's a house you could go live in it. "No trouble at all!" is the cheerful reply. "It's a pleasure!" The phone clicks and goes dead, and you pad about preparing yourself to receive your prize, which by now is assuming the proportions of the Taj Mahal.

HOW TO BUY AN HONOR STUDENT FOR A FEW PENNIES A WEEK

When the bell rings, you open the door in a flash and are immediately disappointed to see that the guy standing there isn't carrying anything. Ah, maybe it's parked outside! You invite him in with a flourish.

He seats himself and you rush around bringing him coffee and cigarettes and generally gushing, all the time wondering if it's a Ford or a Chevy, or maybe even a Chrysler. Meantime, the guy is surveying things generally and inquires offhandedly if you have any children. Four, you say. He thinks that's wonderful and inquires about their ages. You tell him. Then he wonders how they're doing in school. Lousy, you say. Then he remarks that it's no wonder, he doesn't see any books in the house. You look around the house. That's right, no books. Maybe if the kids had books . . . But then you catch yourself and get back to the Chevy. Your visitor is now recalling a case where four kids were flunking out of school. Then the father, wise man, bought a set of encyclopedias and after that they got straight A's. "Really?" you ask. "Really," he says. You wonder aloud if that would help those dunces of yours to get better grades. You're assured it will not only do that, but they'll all get straight A's. "Imagine," you breathe. "How much does something like that cost?" When it turns out to be only a few pennies a week, you've found the solution to those bad report cards. Straight A's for a few pennies a week. You make a resolution to get some of those encyclopedias. That's when the man whips out a contract and you learn he just happens to have a connection with an encyclopedia company.

It occurs to you that this is a rather pleasant coincidence, but you might as well take advantage of it. So you scrawl your name on some papers that don't say you're paying a few pennies a week for straight A's. Then the man asks you for a check. You get the checkbook and inquire how much. It turns out to be considerably more than a few pennies. You make this observation. Then you listen to a lot of arithmetic that adds up to a few pennies a week. So you give him fifty dollars in order to start paying it. At the door, you suddenly remember your Chevy. You ask about it. The man hands you something and walks away whistling. You look down at the prize you won in a contest. A book. Oh well, it looks pretty short.

If that guy called you up on the phone and tried to sell you some encyclopedias, you'd have laughed yourself hoarse and hung up in his face. He knew that. So he didn't try to sell them to you. He hypnotized you into buying them. It's not unusual for a guy who's undergone an experience like that to come up to me and announce proudly, "I've got a strong mind. I can't be hypnotized." He's got the door locked, all right, but they're coming in the window.

HOW TO BE DISAPPOINTED IN WILLIE THE WOLF

To hypnotize people, you use legerdemain. That's the technique of misdirection. You get them to watch your right hand while your left hand does the work. Then you use suggestion. You tell them what your left hand has done for someone just like them. That makes them want to see your left hand. But you still keep it hidden. That makes them want to see it even worse. Now they begin to concentrate on what your left hand can do for them. That's when they become hypnotized— they're making it real. Now you promise to bring out your left hand if they do something simple. They want to see your left hand, so they do it. You bring out your left hand, and it looks exactly as they imagined. The mind molds the object into the symbol it looks through. This is one of the reasons that people buy beaten up tables and think they're valuable antiques.

I once knew a guy who sold balloons that people thought were toy animals. He did this by hypnotism. He made a lot of money at it because he extended the range of his voice by radio. He didn't tell about the balloons, he told about the toy animals, and he didn't just tell about that, he told about how happy the kids would be when they had those toy animals. It was a masterpiece of misdirection and suggestion. The only trouble was that in order to keep people hypnotized, you have to keep misdirecting and suggesting. That put him in a precarious position once they'd turned off their radios. When they got the balloons, they came out of the trance.

They were just plain old balloons except they were plastic and you could mold them around into different shapes. There was a little card that showed you the twelve different animals you could make with them. Picture a guy waiting for a big package that contains Willie the Wolf, Oswald the Ox, Terry the Tiger, Chippy the Chipmunk, Henry the Horse, and so on, all in different colors, bright and shiny, and he's going to stick them under the Christmas tree as a big surprise for the kids. The postman knocks on the door and leaves him a little package. He opens it and finds twelve limp little balloons. Those are the animals. Out in the kitchen, his wife suddenly thinks he's broken a leg. Even the neighbors rush to their windows. That's what you call switching the hope circuit fast. To say this guy is enraged is the understatement of all time. When last heard from, our balloon magnet was hiding out in Peru.

HOW TO DODGE BOOMERANGS

Everybody can be hypnotized. People with buttons can be hypnotized, fantasy thinkers can be hypnotized, and even thinkers who test their symbols can be hypnotized. Nobody's an exception, except people in insane asylums and those with their brains scrambled. This leaves a pretty broad market for Madison Avenue. It also leaves a broad market for Hitler and his ilk. The only way you can protect yourself is to watch the hand that isn't being talked about. This will lead you to be very distrustful of hidden hands.

So now we've covered the art of persuasion. It consists of demonstrating to someone that the thing you have works. You can't use it with robots who respond only to buttons. You can't use it with fantasy thinkers who have the whole world in their heads. You can use it only with thinkers who regularly test their symbols. Since most of these guys are rich, they're very hard to reach. But you just may run into one. If you've got something that works, you'll soon be rich too.

You can change people to your point of view by misdirection and suggestion, but unless it's a matter of survival you'll leave this one alone. It's the stock-in-trade of both charlatan and fanatic, and it leaves behind wreckage wherever it's practiced. More than that, it inevitably conies back. You have to be awfully nimble to dodge a boomerang forever.

·12· HOW TO DYNAMITE THE SUCCESS BLOCK BETWEEN PEOPLE'S EARS

DYNAMITING SUCCESS BLOCKS is my business. Like any good powder man, I carry the tools of my trade. They consist of plenty of TNT and the shovels and drills to implant it, plus the wires and fuses to get myself out of the way so I don't explode with it. Any powder-man knows that you have to set the right blast to do the right job. You want to blow up a building but not the whole town. The same thing applies to setting off a blast between a man's ears. A little too much, and you've got his brains squirting.

HOW TO STAMP OUT POETRY AND TOO MUCH LOVE MAKING

First thing to understand is that some things can't be blasted. I once witnessed a guy trying to destroy a block of titanium steel by setting off dynamite. He set off a blast every hour. Thirty days later he ran out of dynamite, but the titanium steel only needed polishing. I report to you in all sincerity that many people have a block of titanium steel between their ears.

You don't have to look around you much to realize that people seldom change. If they changed, you wouldn't recognize them, you'd just think they disappeared. There are consistent reports of this phenomenon, of course, notably by puzzled wives. Their husband up and leaves them, and they wonder what happened to Harry. You've probably noticed that in your life not too many people have just up and disappeared. That gives you a rough idea of the percentage of people who change. I'd be padding it a little to say one out of a hundred. But I'm optimistic it can be improved. Let's say to something like one out of ten. The other nine have their brains set in steel.

Most good monkey wrench psychologists know about the dynamiting technique. They don't use dynamite, they use electricity, but manage to squirt brains just the same. They take a guy who's fighting and hollering and stick him in a medically sanctioned electric chair, turn on the juice, and presto, a vegetable. This apparently pleases vegetarians, but it's starting to give a zombie-like look to the population. However, it does change people. I once knew a woman who had an IQ of 165 changed by this method. The one she wound up with read about 80.

Another interesting discovery of the monkey wrench psychologists is that if you cut something in half you get twice as much. Since this worked with apples, they tried it on brains. Again they changed people. There's a book about some psychologists who decide to cut a guy's brain in half because he writes poetry and makes love to too many women. They strap him on the table, stick a wire through his eye, and scramble his eggs. After he recovers from this ordeal, they discharge him, confident they have manufactured a sane man. But he still writes poetry and makes love to too many women. They can't understand it. Personally, I could have told them. The things you need to make love to women are not in the head, and everybody knows that poetry doesn't come from a brain.

ANOTHER BRUSH WITH HOOLIGAN'S LAW

In a more somber treatment of this same theme, a guy is put in a nut house because he's been enjoying himself. He was lucky at that. In the eyes of some people this should carry the death penalty. Anyway, now that he's inside, he continues to enjoy himself. That makes everybody else enjoy themselves. Picture a bunch of nuts sitting around a table, drinking beer, playing poker, talking about the ball game, and in general having a whale of a time. It makes you wonder if it's worthwhile to be sane. In order to get the nuts back to acting like nuts, it was decided to cut the happy guy's brain in half. That would make him half happy. We never did get to see the outcome of this arithmetic because his pals killed him to keep him all happy. I thought it tailed off a little at the end.

You could gather from the foregoing that most of the efforts at changing people are aimed at making them worse. This is a derivative of Hooligan's Law: Nobody should be as good as I am. Fortunately for most of us, the general run of people-changers don't shoot where they aim. If you're making love to more women than there are, they cut off your brain. Woe betide us if they learn how to shoot.

A guy once called me into his office and showed me a chart. It told about how much everything cost to get a gadget manufactured and sold. It was a nice little business. He'd sold ten million dollars worth of gadgets that year. He'd wound up with a profit of five hundred thousand which was a tidy sum and not overly greedy. Still, he wanted to make that five hundred grand bigger, and he didn't think he could do it by selling more gadgets. So we went over what everything cost him. There were parts and tools and office supplies. That added up to two and a half million. The other seven million was for people. That set me back a bit, but he was already crabbing about unions and shop stewards and coffee breaks and the like. People were costing too much, and there wasn't a thing he could do about it. I asked him if he could improve the performance of his machine tools. Absolutely not, he had the best engineers available. Then I asked him if he'd brought in any engineers to make his people run better. He thought about that for awhile, then he wondered if a psychologist was a people engineer. I said that would be stretching a point. They were good at taking people apart, but most of them had trouble getting them back together, and even if they did, they seldom ran better. He thought he knew what I meant and cited examples of several friends who had their works on the table and nobody could find which wheels fit what. We got along real well.

THE FIRST EXPLOSION

I told him I could make ten percent of his people run better. If ten percent of his people ran better, his total work force would produce ten percent more. That meant that for the same seven million, he'd get eleven million dollars worth of gadgets. Instead of a profit of five hundred thousand, he'd wind up with a profit of a million and a half. His eyes simply glittered at making money that fast. All of a sudden, he was out to improve people. And he didn't care if they got as good as he was. In fact, he was hoping they'd be better. It's always nice to find someone who's got the interest of others at heart. He hired me to engineer his people to better performance.

When he found out I was using dynamite, he grew a little alarmed. I set off an explosion in one of the rooms that rattled his golf trophies, and he sent runners to investigate. They carried back the horrible news. Two of his nice workers were in a fist fight, and I was sitting in my chair applauding. This was more than the gadget maker had bargained for, and within three minutes I found myself explaining that you couldn't improve people without making them want to and when they wanted to they started to fight. He wanted to know how I planned to get rid of the blood. I suggested we install drains in each room. He said there was still the matter of the noise. I said we could solve that by sound proofing the walls. He said that would be rather expensive. I said we could take care of that by selling tickets, everybody liked to see a good fight. By this time, he was gathering that I was dead on the level, so he found my contract and suggested we call it quits. I reminded him of the million and a half dollar profit. He pondered that awhile and decided that maybe a little blood wasn't so bad, he could always hire another janitor to help mop it up. I said I could get the janitors fighting too, then they'd mop up more blood and he wouldn't have to hire another janitor. He looked at me kind of funny and said not to carry things too far. I told him I didn't intend to carry them beyond the extra million profit. That settled him down nicely, and he finally gave me carte blanche. Only I wasn't to murder his wife. But I think I could have moved him off that if I'd raised the ante a little.

HOW TO GET A MAN MAD

So I went back to setting off my explosions. Nice little robots began fighting with each other. They'd show the other guy they could do it better. Foremen started coming to work with cotton in their ears. Sometimes the noise was deafening. I got the foremen fighting too, and they took out the cotton. They didn't want to miss an insult. Departments began competing with each other to prove they were better. Teams formed up. Plans of attack were laid. This was war, and people were trying to win. You could hardly believe that these were robots, they acted so alive. They got so engrossed they even forgot to remember that they didn't like their jobs. They got so excited you could almost believe they were enjoying themselves. And there wasn't much blood. It hardly kept the janitors busy, they were so interested in seeing who could mop up the most.

I didn't deliver the gadget maker his extra million. What I came up with was three hundred thousand. He was a little disappointed, so I had to resort to arithmetic. I pointed out that he had paid me ten thousand dollars. Ten thousand from three hundred thousand left two hundred and ninety thousand. That worked out to be a profit of 2900%. He seemed somewhat surprised to find out how smart he was at making investments. So I shook his hand and bid him goodbye. Last I heard, his people were still fighting and profits improving. And he doesn't even have to buy a ticket to the fights.

You may get the idea that my dynamite charges are aimed at doing something to the circuits behind people's buttons. I want to scramble things around so that the hope circuit and the fear circuit come on at the same time. When this is successful, it's easy to spot. A man gets mad. He becomes a bull that could tear down a wall. He doesn't worry about whether mother loved him or how best to get along with his wife or whether the kids need a little more love or if the supervisor has it in for him or how he'll pay the rent if he loses his job. He just takes off charging, out to beat everybody. This has been known to cure ulcers and stuttering and heart palpitations, head colds and asthma, arthritis and impotence. Check this out for yourself. When's the last time you saw a sick man who was mad? That only happens to people who are nice. And they think God's made some mistake by punishing the *good.*

HOW TO GET INTO FIGHTS WITH NO HANDS

I recall sitting in the mess-room of a merchant ship in the harbor of Naples. I was drinking my coffee and watching a quiet little guy at the end of the table. I'd seen him around, and he didn't seem to fit with this crew of tough sailors. He was like a mouse—eyes on the deck. Everybody pushed him around, and he was very unhappy. He had nothing else to do, so he read books of poetry. He had one in front of him now, but he wasn't very absorbed. He kept flicking little glances at me as if my presence bothered him.

Then the Bo' sun came into the mess-room, roaring drunk. He'd been on the beach and had a whale of time. He sang a bawdy song and danced a little jig and told about the Italian women in the most glowing terms. Then he spotted the quiet guy, and he staggered up to him and said he knew about Shakespeare. The quiet guy allowed as to how that was fine. "I'm as smart as you are!" claimed the Bo' sun. He tapped his head. That seemed to give him reassurance. "I'm twice as smart as you are!" he shouted. Now that he knew his head was there, he doubled its worth.

The quiet guy sat quietly. "Wanna bet!" the Bo' sun screamed. The quiet guy shook his head. He didn't want to bet. I was hoping he would and that I could get in on it. I didn't think much of the Bo' sun's chances. "Besides that," announced the Bo' sun, "I could lick you with one hand." He showed the quiet guy the hand. The quiet guy was impressed. The Bo' sun grew bolder. "I can lick you with no hands!" he screamed. The quiet guy didn't dispute this, but the prospect appealed to the Bo' sun. He staggered over to me and ordered me to tie his hands behind his back. I don't ordinarily become a party to slaughter, but I wanted to see how much the quiet guy would take. So I obligingly tied the Bo' sun's hands behind his back. He went back to the quiet guy and offered opportunity. "Go ahead, hit me!" he bellowed. The quiet guy just sat there, but he had closed the book of poetry. He seemed to be calculating.

HOW TO GET INTO FIGHTS WITH NO FEET

But now the Bo' sun had become engrossed in the problem, which as far as he was concerned was to get himself smacked. "I can lick you with my feet tied too," he announced, and he staggered back to me, and I bound up his ankles. Now that I had him all trussed up, I considered taking a poke at him myself. I didn't care for him much, but he was a big guy with muscles like mountains, and I'd never pressed the point. I decided to give the quiet guy first crack at him. If he didn't want him, I'd try to please the Bo' sun.

Now that he was all bound up, he seemed to get mad, as if the quiet guy had done it to him. He hopped across the mess-room like a Billy goat, and butted the quiet guy right off his chair. The quiet guy picked himself up. The Bo' sun butted him down again. The quiet guy picked himself up. The Bo' sun butted him down again. It looked like a piece of film that kept running over and over. Finally the quiet guy stuck out his hand. The Bo' sun ran into it. "You hit me!" he screamed and tried to pick up a chair. I guess he hadn't counted on his hands being tied. He was a smart one.

The quiet guy looked at the Bo' sun standing there trying to get his hands loose. That must have been the first time it dawned on him that the Bo' sun's hands were really tied. A funny look crossed his face, then his eyes got all wild. He let loose a roundhouse swing that caught the Bo' sun smack on the jaw. Down went the Bo' sun. Then all hell broke loose.

I'd hate to have seen that Bo' sun with his hands and feet untied. As it was it looked as if they'd been tied all his life and he'd developed his head into a deadly weapon. He got up off the deck and gave the quiet guy a butt that sent him reeling across the mess-room and crashing into the bulkhead. The quiet guy bounced off the bulkhead like a steel spring and decked the Bo' sun again. This time the punch had some zing in it, and it split open the Bo' sun's lip. Blood began trickling. The Bo' sun stuck out his tongue and had a little taste. It turned his eyes the same color. He staggered to his feet, lowered his head, and looked around for the cape. The quiet guy waved it. The Bo' sun charged. The quiet guy exchanged the cape for a solid right hand, and the Bo' sun ran into it. He sank to his knees. The quiet guy began grinning. The Bo' sun licked his blood, then he grinned too. He got to his feet and went after the quiet guy. It was a sight to see as they bloodied each other, both of them grinning.

HOW TO CLOBBER THE BO' SUN

They smashed all the dishes, broke two of the tables, left not a chair fit to sit on. They smeared up the bulkheads, covered the deck with coffee, littered silverware all round the room. They grunted and wheezed and laughed and shouted and beat hell out of each other. Nobody won. I left them sitting on the deck in the midst of the debris. I'd untied the Bo' sun's hands, and they had their arms around each other.

After that, the quiet guy disappeared from the ship. Nobody knew where he went. He was just suddenly replaced by a feisty little rooster who wouldn't take anything off anybody and later got to be Bo' sun.

You may begin to guess what a success block is. It's not being able to get mad. It's taking the guff that the world dishes out and thinking you only deserve it. It's walking around praying and trying to be pleasant when everybody steps on your toes. It's assigning your problems to the mechanics of chance when they're all really caused by your refusal to fight.

How do you break a success block? You explode the charges that make people mad. But first they have to see that there's some chance of winning. They have to see the Bo' sun standing there with his hands and feet tied. Now mind you, his hands and feet don't really have to be tied. They just have to think they are. It may come as a surprise to them that the Bo' sun can hit back, but once you've started them fighting, they begin to enjoy it. I've got a speech about this too. It's called How to Clobber the Bo' sun. I once gave it in a longshoreman's hall, and the next week there wasn't a Bo' sun on the waterfront fit to work.

THE GUY WITH A CROSS AND THE GUY IN A FIGHT

The main task of a guy whose profession is dynamiting success block is to convince people that the Bo' sun's hands and feet are tied. Once they've gotten the idea that they might be able to get away with taking a poke at him, all you have to do is plant the charge and set off the explosion. But always remember titanium steel. Some people you just can't make mad.

I once explored the possibility of launching nuclear explosions against titanium success blocks. I knew they would probably squirt a man's brains, but I was becoming convinced that in the race for success brains were often a handicap, all you really needed was fight. So one time I talked to a guy who said he was a nuclear physicist, and he scribbled some equations on the back of a cocktail napkin to prove it. I asked him what happened to titanium steel in a nuclear explosion. He said, "It melts." I asked, "Completely?" He said, "You can't even find it." That ruled out nuclear explosion. People have to have bodies in order to be successful.

I got into this work because I was curious about people. The longer I looked at the show, the sadder it got. It made me sad too. I began acting as if I had the world on my shoulders, praying and whining and not fighting back. Finally I got mad and made some things happen. It occurred to me that with this profound discovery, I might get into the show and lighten it up a bit. In order to do this, I had to find out how. That's why I studied cybernetics. It was the long way around the barn, but it gave me some answers.

Old Nietzsche saw the picture many years ago. They thought he was nuts so they put him in the bughouse. He said everything was a matter of whether you wanted to hang on a cross or get down and take charge. He offered as examples Dionysus and Christ. He recommended Dionysus. Since Christ had more followers, Nietzsche had trouble. Into the bughouse he went.

Dionysus didn't promise heaven. He said it was here. And hell was too, depending on how you looked at it. He said that's all there is to it. It depends how you look at it. They're still trying to decipher him. They're still trying to decipher Christ too, because you have to find a pretty good reason for wanting to hang on a cross.

BACK TO THE BALLOONS

Remember the guy who ordered all the toy animals and opened the box and found out they were balloons? He could have lifted a whole city. That's how you break a success block. You have to make people realize they've been swindled. They already know they've been promised toy animals. All you have to do is show those balloons. They'll chase the guy who sold them clear to Peru.

The biggest bill of goods that's ever been sold people is that they can get things without fighting. Turn the other cheek so you can get clobbered again. If you get beat up badly enough here, you'll find a better place afterwards. Trade in your fists for wings. You won't be able to fly, but you'll look like an angel. Apologize. . . stand in line . . . wait your turn, and the Lord will take care of you. The only high priest of sanity runs around on wheels. People only become sane when they get in a car. Then they cut in front of you and snarl at you and tell you to get out of the way. They enjoy themselves and feel better about life, but it never occurs to them that they could behave the same way when they step out of the car. They've bought the bill of goods, lock, stock, and barrel.

There's nothing so touching as watching a man trying to solve his problems by waiting for God to. This puts him in for a very long wait. But after all, isn't patience a virtue? And doesn't the Lord try his sinners to temper their mettle? What he means is that after God gets through kicking the stuffing out of him, he'll probably get a lollipop. I bring some bad news—there's a shortage of lollipops.

I remember a guy who was raised in my neighborhood. He was half the size of the other kids, but he could lick everybody. I thought he might turn out to be President. When I saw him twenty years later, he was sitting on the doorstep out of a job. I poked him in the ribs, and he looked at me soulfully. I glanced at the address to be sure I had the right house. Then he told me about the great change that had come over him since he'd discovered the truth. I didn't need a microscope to see that he'd changed, but I wondered what he'd bought instead of the truth. It turned out to be that you shouldn't win. The way he said it, it sounded a little different. There was something about loving everybody and regarding him as a brother and always letting him be first so you wouldn't offend him. I could see immediately that with that kind of premise it would be hard to win. I pointed this out to him. It didn't bother him a bit. It wasn't winning he wanted, it was just to be loved. I left him sitting there out of a job, but I couldn't help noticing that nobody was around, so maybe he wasn't being loved so much either. Some truth!

WHO SOLD YOU THE BALLOONS?

Let me ask you a question. Who sells the idea that we shouldn't fight? You may think it's some bloated plutocrat trying to protect his empire, but you couldn't be farther off the target. He didn't get where he is by not fighting. And he has no respect for the people who won't fight. If you punch him in the jaw, he begins to respect you and would like to have a guy like you on his side. So what's he got to gain by selling not fighting? He sits at his desk as bewildered as anyone and watches the nicely-nice boys parade past his door. Since so many of them believe it, he may come to believe it himself. Poof goes his empire.

You have to turn the screws way down to find the founders of the cult of passivity. You have to turn them down so far that they chatter your bones. You have to remember the first time you were told not to fight. Who told you? That's right, the Queen of the Nursery. Doesn't that shake you? The reason you can't see this is because mother is *good.* The reason you listened is because mother is *good.* The reason you don't dispute it is because mother is *good.* Only problem is that mother was a woman. Now she's made you like her.

You see, when you've got an organization composed of half the world's people, you've got a big organization. All they have to do is win a percentage point and they control the whole works. If they're got a common purpose, this bands them together. If they get a little fanatic about it, they're hard to oppose. If they tell you that fighting is *bad*, it makes it difficult to fight them. If they're smaller than you are, it makes it even worse. If you need them for service, you don't like to lose them. If they stay in the background, you don't notice they run things. Even while you're breaking your back to pay off the mortgage and listening to complaints that the washer won't work and moonlighting and scrambling to make the money to fix it and noticing the bridge club and the hairdresser and the well read copies of love story magazines, even while you can't get ahead at the office because you won't push the guy ahead of you out of the way, even while you stand patiently in line and ponder life's meaninglessness, even while you're chauffeuring your kids around and they treat you with contempt, even when you take your little darling to dinner and buy her a corsage of flowers and blow your last buck and she complains that her feet hurt—it never occurs to you that you're losing a war. Oh, you know something is wrong, all right. Your gut aches and you have indigestion and you drink too much and you're developing an ulcer and even in the hay things just won't work right and you'd rather play golf than spend time at home. But it couldn't be *her— she's* mother. And mother is *good.*

That's the swindle, boys. The world isn't like what the women say it is. It's like it's always been. You have to fight to survive. You bought some toy animals. Now take a good look. Those are balloons.

HOW TO HANDLE WOMEN

I have to confess that I've had a few guys go home and beat up their wives. I see nothing bad that's come out of this. Just better wives. Guys who go home and murder their spouses just blow a fuse from being pecked by a chicken, and they think they have no recourse but to get rid of the chicken. That's because they think they're a chicken. Roosters don't get rid of their chickens. They just keep them in line. They do that by pecking them, and making damned sure that they're not pecked in turn.

Some guys go home and whale the hell out of the kids. That doesn't kill the kids. That makes better kids. Those among them who happen to be male will get some idea of how a male should act. It will also impress the females. It will make them notice that bulls are better when they're not taught to eat flowers. They will expect men to fight. That will cause them to walk a few steps to the rear so they don't get hit by punches. That will cause them to do what they're told and not complain about it. Don't worry, they'll get to like it. They can't get married if they can't find a man.

I had one nifty looking broad visit me for reprisals. Seems her husband had grown impossible and she knew it was my fault. She had on white gloves that came up to her elbows, a dress out of Saks and a mink coat to boot. I figured she had a pretty good stake in the gadget who'd bought this, so I decided on a frontal line of attack. I asked her specifically what made her husband impossible. It turned out that he wouldn't take her to visit her mother and had spoken harshly to the children. I began to wonder if I was up against titanium steel again. All he'd come up with was not visiting his mother-in-law and saying something harsh to the kids. I tried to recall whether he was too fat to get furious. But a skinny guy came to my mind instead, so that couldn't have been the problem. I decided the problem was inside the dress out of Saks.

HOW TO BREATHE HARD THROUGH YOUR MOUTH AND MAKE YOUR EYES GLASSY

" Do you know I'm a hypnotist?" I asked her. She admitted she didn't, but the thought seemed to intrigue her. "More than that," I went on, "I don't care much about people. When I get someone under my spell, I teach him to kill when he's crossed." That prompted her to wonder if I'd done that with her husband. "You've seen the signs," I said. "Judge for yourself." She was able to equate not visiting a mother in-law with an oncoming murder, and she began to edge out of her chair as if she were heading for the cops. "Wait a minute," I said. "You look like a nice chick, and I wouldn't want you killed. Let me tell you how to recognize the signs when he's about to flip his wig." That stopped her for a minute. After all, if he was hypnotized, the cops wouldn't be able to do anything except put me in jail. That wouldn't help her. She'd better know about those signs.

" He'll start breathing hard through his mouth," I said. "And his eyes will get glassy." She closed her own eyes and gave a little shudder. "Now beat it," I said. She flounced out of there, wiggling her fanny. It must be an instinct.

She didn't go to the cops. She went to the skinny guy's boss. He called me on the phone and wanted to know what it was all about. I told him. He put the skinny guy on. "Listen," I said, "if she gives you any trouble, all you have to do is breathe hard through your mouth and make your eyes glassy." I had to repeat this several times because he didn't quite follow me. Finally he agreed to give it a try. He said he was willing to try anything, he was so very unhappy.

I got some sketchy flashes on the subsequent skirmish as the skinny guy's boss made intermittent reports. Seems the very first night she lit into him about me. She wanted him to talk his boss into firing me. I was an evil influence on the men. That guy couldn't talk his boss into having a cup of coffee, that's how much she knew about how to get things done. So naturally he just sat there. After awhile, the noise began to hurt his ears and he remembered what I'd told him. So he began to breathe hard through his mouth and make his eyes glassy. She ran out of there and hid in the bedroom. He read a book. First book he'd read in years.

FOR ALL MEN BORN OF WOMEN

After that, things got better and better. When he started to get some static, he'd just breathe hard through his mouth and make his eyes glassy. She'd run and hide, and he could do what he wanted. It even started to work with the kids, because naturally she told them about daddy's peculiar condition. The guy really blossomed. He sprouted the tail feathers of a rooster. He even started demanding pay raises from his boss, all the time breathing hard through his mouth and making his eyes glassy. His boss didn't mind about the pay raises, but he couldn't stand the skinny guy breathing hard through his mouth and making his eyes glassy. He called me and told me to put a stop to it. So I did. By that time the skinny guy had the situation at home well in hand.

You dynamite the success block between a man's ears by teaching him to fight. You set off the explosion by showing him that he's been swindled. You let him know who swindled him. Then all you have to do is point him and pull the trigger. The ensuing explosion is sure to jar you. You might try this technique on yourself.

·13· HOW TO QUICK-SHIFT ADVERSITY INTO ACHIEVEMENT

L ET'S GET BACK to carrying the card with the success mechanism on it, back to mental rehearsal that plays only success, back to au to-suggestion that tells us who to fight, how to fight, and what to fight for. Then let's refresh our minds with the swindle we've fallen for and how mad we are about it. You can see where we're heading. We're heading for turning adversity into achievement. Even a bull can knock down a wall. He just has to get mad enough and learn some fundamental things like lowering his head.

HOW TO TOUGHEN UP YOUR MUSCLES

You already know you've got a bigger brain than a computer. You already know your brain works the same way. But you can't produce anything that you think that you can't. A computer can't do it, and neither can you. When a computer thinks it can't, that's an end of it. You can change to thinking you can, and that makes you one up. And you can imagine, there's another advantage. And you can get mad, that's the biggest of all. You can fire up your horsepower one thousand percent. A computer is stuck with what somebody gave it.

Learning how to fight well is first learning what your goal is, then drawing the shortest line between two points, then setting off with the resolve to get there, then battering down everything that gets in your way. You don't have to batter with your head, like the Bo' sun. You can use it to think with. It batters better that way.

A friend of mine got a job in the mines. They gave him a hat with a light on it and handed him a pickaxe. They took him down into a hole that was black as a pit and pointed his head at a wall. That made the light shine on it. "Cut through it," he was told, and they left him swinging his pickaxe. Somewhere toward noon, he got to wondering what was on the other side of the wall. So he went back up into the daylight and asked the foreman what was on the other side of the wall. The foreman said, "Nothing." My friend handed him the pickaxe and the cap with the light on it. He didn't even say goodbye. He decided to find his own walls, with something on the other side.

They had an earthquake up in Alaska. Whole villages were wiped out, with nothing left but debris. The newsreel camera picked up a battered guy with mud all over him and one half of his coat gone. They asked him what he thought about it. "It's not so bad," he said. "We didn't come up here to take things easy. This will toughen us up." If he'd been running for President, I would have voted for him twice.

HOW NOT TO BUILD A HOME

What this means is that you don't keep battering at walls unless you know what's on the other side and you know that you want it. What this means is the longer you batter, the tougher you get. When you know what you're after and what you have to do to get it, you can batter away for all that you're worth. And if you get some guy to batter with you and make it a game to beat him, you'll hardly notice the work.

I heard of an interesting session with a psychic. This rich widow went to visit one and asked how long she'd live. "You'll die when you've finished building your house," she was told. That made things a matter of the moment, since with about ten more bricks the house was all set. Not being quite ready to join the departed, this cagey old widow arrived at a solution. She decided not to finish building the house. She began building more rooms. What had started out as a three room bungalow now took on somewhat larger dimensions. She started spreading the house out all over the grounds and adding little goodies, like stairways that went no place. By the time she had it spread out over three acres, she checked on the time. Five years had passed. She had old man death up the apple tree, and there was no way for him to get down as long as she kept building that house. She bought more land and spread it out farther. She built rooms on top of rooms, rooms inside rooms, another house on top of the house. Forty years passed. She was carried off by a stroke while hammering a nail.

Now I'd like to point out that there's sure to be somebody who reads this who will think the old widow lived longer by building her house. I honestly can't help that. I just haven't yet solved the titanium problem, but if someone gives me that answer to my face, you can rely on the fact I'll try nuclear explosion.

You can see that house up around San Jose. They charge you admission. Don't bother. You can see plenty of such monstrosities for free, all built by people who didn't bother to check what was on the other side of the wall. That's what brains are for. They're for allowing you to pick out useful goals. If you start building houses because a witch doctor tells you that the goblins will get you if you don't, you forget what houses are for. When you forget what they're for, you can't make them right. When you can't make them right, they're useless. That's "a wall. And there's no way to get through it because it's in your own mind.

HOW TO FIX A FURNACE

Here's another guy coping with a wall. His furnace is out, and he's trying to fix it. He's got wrenches and pliers and hammers and saws. He's got axes and drills and torches, and a gun, just in case. He's got plenty of band-aids, and they're all on his fingers. He took the insides out to see if any were broken. He put the insides back to see if they fit. He turned on the switch, and the furnace stayed out. He's mad as all hell and considers an attack with the axe. He could tear down a wall, all right, only he doesn't know how. Finally he calls the furnace man, a chastening experience. Then he sits down on the steps and makes his pipe puff like a train.

In comes the furnace man, gay as can be. "Got a little trouble here?" he sings like a song. The guy reports with a growl that the trouble ain't little. The furnace man peers into the sick furnace, still humming away. He gives a little, "Tsk, tsk," and pulls out a hammer. He makes a tap on a gadget. The furnace comes on.

There is a very amazed man sitting on the steps. Even his pipe has gone out. What was once a wall that resisted all the tools ever invented has suddenly disappeared with a tap on a gadget. He stumbles over to the furnace and listens intently. He holds out his hand and feels the heat. He turns to the furnace man and stares at him suspiciously. The furnace man keeps singing, he hasn't missed a note. The guy shakes his head and feels in his pocket for a quarter. As he holds it out, he remembers to ask, "How much?" "Ten dollars," says the furnace man. He doesn't take the quarter, and he doesn't stop singing. The guy joins him now, at the top of his voice. "Ten dollars! For a tap with a hammer?" "That's only a dollar," the furnace man says. That sounds more like it, and the guy reaches for his wallet, but when he holds out the dollar, the furnace man repeats, "Ten dollars." At this repulsive figure the guy screams again, "I thought you said a dollar!" Now he's befuddled by both furnaces and figures, and he wouldn't be surprised if he got tapped with a hammer. "The dollar's for the tap," the furnace man says. Now the guy puts his head down and begins to look dangerous. "So what's the other nine for?" he asks tonelessly. "Knowing where to tap," the furnace man says. He removes the wallet from the guy's nerveless hand, makes a selection of bills, and carols into the night.

Most walls are broken down just in that manner. I'll have to admit that know-how beats force. But power impels the furnace man to learn how to make the proper tap with the hammer. What we're after is both know-how and force. That allows you to get to the place where you can make the right tap.

HOW TO MAKE A DIAMOND BIGGER

I ran a seminar for disjointed people. I mean by this that I picked them up off the streets. I also mean that they were disjointed. CBS sent a guy over to broadcast it, being somewhat interested in success. The announcer was cynical. He glanced around and doubted these people would make it. From what happened next, he must have achieved utter conviction. He decided to ask them their ideas on success. The first guy he picked was a corker. He said he had a little diamond in his head. The way he described it was interesting. He could make the diamond bigger by smoking marijuana. With four or five reefers, he could make it so big it filled the whole inside of his head. I began to worry that we might be raided and sent somebody outside to watch out for the cops. Meanwhile, the guy with the expanding diamond was describing further ideas.

The way he had it figured, the diamond was God. When the diamond was little, you were out of touch with heaven. When it filled up your head, you walked streets of gold. I gathered some escalator ran up marijuana stalks. I had no idea how many people were listening, but I had a grim vision of a gigantic pot party brewing. Everybody puffing his way up streets of gold. I was surprised they hadn't cut the announcer off the air, but he kept babbling away delightedly. Personally, I didn't like it one bit. I heard my name mentioned all too frequently. It gave me a squeamish premonition about front and side views, fingerprints, and a blotter. Then the guy with the diamond shifted to broads and went immediately to describing some unusual sexual experiences. That ended the broadcast. Dope . . . Sex . . . All we'd missed was a murder.

I didn't do much good with the guy with the diamond because I couldn't get him to decide what he wanted. I suggested all sorts of nice jobs, but he turned them all down. I even set off my charges, but he just kept babbling about the diamond. I finally told him a place he could go to. He left at once, taking the diamond. I hope it melts.

HOW TO MAKE A WALL

Later on, I dropped around to CBS with the idea of interesting them in a training program for their people. I gave a secretary my card, and she went into a private office. Ten seconds later, she spewed out of there like she'd been shot from a gun. She grabbed at a telephone and knocked it off the desk. She fumbled around for it, glancing at me apprehensively. Her finger trembled, and she couldn't get it in the dial. I gathered she was calling for either cops or strait-jackets. I strolled out calmly, looking for the washroom. I hid there an hour. Sometimes you break walls, sometimes you make them.

There was another development from that particular seminar. There was a rich divorcee who wandered in by mistake. Everybody wore rags. She wore full length mink. But she still thought it was a meeting of the Marching and Chowder Society. When it dragged on for three days, it began to disturb her. She asked when we were going to eat. I said the seminar was concerned with thinking not eating. She said she was interested in that too, but first she'd like to eat. I asked her if she had any goals. She said yes, she'd like to eat. So I took her to lunch. You can get worn out by determined people.

It turned out she was a dancer. I couldn't help but reflect that if she ate so much, she'd soon be a fat one. I asked her what kind of dances she did. She said they were Spanish. I said I liked that, with the castanets and all, and maybe sometime I could see her. She said she'd call me, she often had friends over. Just before we finished lunch, she mentioned that she'd fallen out a window and landed on her head, that's how she'd been in a mental hospital. That sort of ended things on an ominous note, and I decided that on second thought I didn't care much for castanets. But when I got back to the office after nearly selling CBS, here was this phone call from her, so I decided to go over and see how she was making out.

HOW TO GET DOWN OFF A WALL

She was making out fine. She lived in a classy bungalow in the best section of Beverly Hills, and when I walked into the living room I was knee deep in carpets. Everything was all set. She was going to dance for me. She got me settled with a cocktail and turned on the music and disappeared from the room. I sat there enjoying myself and reflecting that she seemed perfectly okay despite the fall on the head and maybe the seminar had helped her. Then she burst into the room and leaped over some furniture. She was absolutely naked.

That gal could really jump. She jumped over the phonograph. She jumped over the couch. She must have set a record when she jumped over the dining room table. Everything was flying every which way. Then she began to climb walls. It was unbelievable. She climbed right up the wall. I put my drink on the table and glanced out the window. The drapes were all open and some of the neighbors were looking. I finally managed to sneak out the back door. If the drapes had been closed, I'd have had a different problem. How to get her down off the wall.

Since that's the last place I left her, you can see how I think of her, perched on that wall, naked as a jaybird, all pink and panting and no one to talk to. It's become kind of a symbol. Whenever I think of walls, there's this broad, spread out like a butterfly, stuck there forever. People hung on crosses and people stuck on walls. How do you get them down when they can't seem to listen? Some hack at titanium with tiny hammers. Some scratch their fingernails down to the quick. Some fall in love with walls and embrace them forever. Some stamp their feet and tell them to go away. Some sprinkle incense and call on the supernatural. Some don't even see the wall and keep walking into it. There you have it. Crosses and walls. One you have to climb down from, the other you have to get through. Both actions require that you see the world as it is. You'd think this would best be accomplished by people with eyes, but a blind man taught me how to do it.

HOW TO FIND A DOOR

He came into a lecture one night accompanied by a dog. The dog had eyes, but the blind man didn't need them. It just gave him an excuse for hauling his dog around. He sat down in the front row and looked me right in the eye. I thought he could see, and asked him to take his dog out. That's when he said he was blind.

Now if there's one thing I've learned it's that you don't abuse blind men and dogs in front of an audience. So I let him sit there and keep his old dog. But I thought he was a fraud. He waited after the lecture, and I finally got to talk to him. He said, "You were talking about symbols and how people use them wrong." I allowed as how that had been my topic. He said he knew why people didn't use symbols right. I mentioned I would appreciate any enlightenment in this area. He said, "They think flat."

Since I knew a lot of flat thinkers, I had to agree with him, but I gathered there was more to it than that. I asked him to explain. He said, "I think deep." I thought he meant profound. I said I didn't think that had anything to do with it, there was old Schopenhauer who was plenty profound, but he couldn't punch his way out of a paper bag. "I don't mean profound," the blind man said. "I think in three dimensions." That really grabbed me.

He went on to say that he'd been blinded in an accident and had learned how to use his mind in a different way in order to get around. He felt things with his hands. That gave him a better idea of their dimensions than his eyes had given him. He noticed at once that he began to think of them differently. Before, when he imagined things, he imagined them as he saw them. From one side, or the top, or the bottom.

Now when he imagined them, he saw all sides at once.

That really gave me goose pimples. Here was a guy who surrounded everything. Every viewpoint, instantaneous. How could a wall be an obstacle to him? He was on both sides of it at once, on top of it for that matter. I couldn't help thinking there was some clue here about how to get through walls. So I went right to the point. I asked him what he did when he came up to a wall.

He said, "I look for the door."

If he could have seen me, he would have thought I'd had a stroke. I'd gotten so interested in walls, I'd forgotten about doors. I managed to ask how he knew there was a door.

He said, "There's always a door. All walls have doors."

That's it, of course. All walls have doors. When you want to get through a wall, you look for the door. Just like the boulder was removed from the Mexican street. Just like the furnace was fixed with a tap from a hammer. Simple.

HOW TO GET INSIDE A TREE

During the ensuing three days, I almost had a brain convulsion trying to see all sides of things at the same time. I finally got so I could do it. It gave me an eerie feeling. I was no longer looking at things in my mind, they were suspended there, and I was all round them. I knew at once that they were better symbols and matched more exactly the things in the world. More than that, I wouldn't be trying to break through a wall now that I was seeing all sides of it. I would look for the door. Such earthshaking discoveries always inspire me to prose. Now I've got a speech entitled, How to Break Through a Wall by Finding the Door. If a blind man can do it, so can I.

Since I'd managed to construct better symbols by making them show all sides of a thing at the same time, I was piqued by a further possibility. What about getting right inside the thing itself? Then you'd really have it made. You'd not only be looking at it from all sides, but looking out from it too. This gave me an odd feeling that I might find myself staring back at myself, but I brushed it aside and got on with the work. As it happened, my research was considerably accelerated by running into a guy who took dope. He went on to say that he was inside things all the time. I suspected he meant jails, but he insisted he could get into other things too. Then I ran through a list of things like houses, cars, theatres, buildings, and he grew very impatient. He said he meant solid objects. With that revelation, I knew I'd found my man. I asked him how he got in there.

It turned out there were several entrances and each had a name.

One was called Peyote, then there was Mescaline, and finally Lysergic Acid. This last sounded ominous. Acid was something you needed bicarbonate of soda for. I mentioned this to him. He told me to think of it as LSD. I did. It's funny how a name can change things.

Now that we'd reduced the ominous lysergic acid to a nice name, I found it holding my attention. I wanted to know how you could use it as a door to get through the wall of something that was solid, like a tree. He said you just put it in your mouth and swallowed it. The rest was automatic.

HOW TO MAKE MORE TREES

I don't like to be suspicious, but I think you'll agree that swallowing a pill to get inside a tree has the general ring of a diamond in the head that turns into God. But when you run into a man who says that he's been there, you ask him what he discovered. It turned out to be a discovery of some magnitude. He discovered he was the tree.

I mentioned the fact that he looked relatively normal, no branches or leaves or anything like that. This seemed to aggravate him. He said that it wasn't that he actually was the tree, any idiot could see that. It was just that he thought he was. I didn't regard that as such an unusual experience, and I mentioned that I'd once run into a guy in a mental institution who posed in the lobby all day and thought he was a cypress. And he didn't take LSD.

Something in that turned on his hope and fear circuits at the same time, and he got up off his stool and towered above me. I could see I'd been wrong. He was a tree, all right. He must have been a hundred feet tall. It's one of the few times I've ever seen a mad tree. Since we'd reached the end of discursive conversation, I agreed he was right, one hundred percent. That placated him, and I departed the premises, leaving behind a tree that drank scotch.

I spent the next day pondering how to get inside a tree without turning into the tree, and I happened to notice in the paper where some guy had been run out of the state for slipping LSD pills to people and making them turn into trees. I couldn't help reflecting that this was a little shortsighted. Deforestation was a California problem, and here was the solution—turn people into trees. But you can't expect politicians to see anything so obvious. At this point I began to feel that I needed the company of people who weren't trees, so I called up a friend and asked him what he was doing. He said he was taking LSD. I couldn't escape my fate. I asked him if it turned him into a tree. He said no, it turned him into a Grieg concerto. That sounded more interesting, so I went over to see him.

HOW TO BECOME E ABOVE HIGH C

He had the music turned up so high that the room shook. He was lying back in his chair with his mouth open and looked like he was swallowing Grieg. I shook him, and he mumbled sleepily, "I'm E above high C." That was pretty high, so I suggested he come down an octave. He paid no attention, just kept up there as high as you please. I wanted to talk to him, so I hauled him off to the bathroom and stuck him under the shower. That didn't bring him down a bit, just made him wet. I flung him on the bed without bothering to dry him. Whoever heard of an E above high C catching cold?

I went back to the living room and pondered the problem. When people turned into trees or music, you couldn't talk to them. There was a bottle of scotch sitting on the table, so I pulled the cork and settled down to some drinking. As time passed, my mind became clearer and clearer. I began to see many answers that had escaped me. I got the idea I was sitting up in the clouds and could solve the world's problems. I became a little dizzy from the height and had to brace myself to keep from falling. Of course I'd managed such experiences before with the aid of some scotch, but this time it had an interesting outcome. I'd forgotten to turn off the music, and sometime before midnight I turned into E above high C.

I had a pretty bad headache the next day, but it wasn't so bad I didn't get the point. When you put poison in the blood stream, the brain doesn't work so good. The pictures you get are kind of mixed up, but they're your pictures, so you think they're real. When you turn into a tree or E above high C by taking a pill, that's a wall. And you can't find the door, because the wall's in your mind.

People must look at insanity like a pot of gold. They just have to have it. Its pursuit must be the world's most popular pastime. Everybody tries to say the world isn't here because he likes the one better he makes in his head. You can get awfully bloody in such a state of affairs because your body keeps running into the world as it is. This makes you an excellent prospect for an ambulance. In my considered opinion, sanity is a matter of seeing the world as it is and that's a matter of making symbols that match it.

HOW TO SEE TWO YOU'S AND BE INSIDE BOTH

To get back to the business of getting inside a tree. You might think I'd be pretty discouraged. On the contrary. Now that I'd found out you only turned into the tree when you were sick or poisoned, I'd lost one of the hazards of making the trip. All I had to do was get in the tree in good health and without taking poison. You'll begin to see that you can overcome discouragement by looking on the bright side. But in order to look on the bright side, you have to shift around a little, attack the problem from a different angle.

Here I was able to think of a wall from all sides at the same time, no mean feat in itself, because that gave me a better symbol for what was a wall. Thus I was enabled to know that in a wall was a door, and I could spend my time looking for the door instead of hacking away at the wall. It seemed to me that I'd made some progress in turning a great deal of adversity into achievement, but there was still the matter of finding the door. What if I ran into a long wall? I might start off in the wrong direction looking for the door. That would waste a lot of time. It struck me that if I could just get inside that wall I would know what the wall knew. And one of the things it would be sure to know was where its door was. I began thinking of walls from all sides and at the same time trying to think of them from the inside. Mostly, it just gave me a headache. Once I thought I had something. I could see myself. That meant I was looking at myself from either outside the wall or from inside the wall. But there was no way to tell. I would look like me in either case, and even if I was seeing myself from inside the wall I hadn't made a better symbol because then I wasn't seeing the outside of the wall. There seemed no other alternative than trying to see two me's and be inside both. It struck me that I was getting a little far afield at this point and that maybe by comparison being E above high C was relatively innocuous. I went out to get a breath of fresh air so I could renew my acquaintance with the outside of walls. I had a speaking engagement before the Society of Architects and Engineers, and that's what they were apt to be concerned with.

WHERE TO PUT A DOOR

It was a pleasant evening, with the inevitable fried chicken, and when my turn came, I chattered away. There was a guy sitting next to me at the head table who looked as if his corns hurt. I'd asked him about it, and he said that they didn't, and that was as far as our conversation had gotten. As my speech went on, I occasionally glanced at him, and I could see that if his corns hadn't been hurting before, they were really bothering him now. Such an expression of pain I have seldom seen. It occurred to me that I might stop my speech and suggest that he remove his shoes, but he'd been a little churlish before, and I didn't want to risk offending him. I probably should have. Because he just sat there with those aching corns, and by the time I'd finished, he was in agony. He even got up and started hopping around.

When the applause subsided, he kept right on hopping, and now I could hear that he was hollering something. "What's it for?" he kept shouting. "What's it for?"

I thought he was giving us a riddle and wanted us to guess what his hopping was for, so I shouted right out, "Your corns ache!" I could see by his expression that wasn't the answer. That stumped me for a minute, then I got the idea he might be trying to jump over something. I glanced quickly around and spotted a cream pitcher in the shape of a cow. Making a quick association between cows and moons, I hollered, "You're trying to jump over the moon!" The minute it slipped out, I knew it wasn't right, but it did have the effect of stopping his hopping; He came up to me and looked me in the eye. If anything, he seemed more churlish than ever.

" I build walls," he said. "I put doors in them. I know where to put the door."

That startled me for a minute because I hadn't realized I'd made a speech about walls and doors, I'd been so concerned about this poor fellow's corns. But I found myself deeply interested, so I asked, "How do you know where to put the door?"

" I ask myself what the wall is for!" he shouted. Then he put on his hat and left me standing there with my napkin.

HOW TO GET SUNK BY A DESTROYER

Next day, I went out and talked to a guy who was building a house. I found a nice blank wall and asked him if he was going to put a door in it. He said that he was. I asked him where he was going to put it. He turned and hollered to a guy carrying a hammer, "Hey, Joe, what's this wall for?" You could have knocked me over with a feather.

Joe said the wall was for the dining room. The guy I was talking to said we were in the living room. That meant the door had to go right here. He showed me. I asked, "You mean you know where a door goes because you know what the wall's for?" He said, "Any idiot knows that." I'd graduated to idiot. I couldn't have been happier.

After that, I quit trying to get inside walls because I could learn what they knew without being in there. All I had to do was see them from all sides, then ask myself what they were for. What they were for told me where the door was. It gave a nice new dimension to the symbols I played with. I just started matching them to all the sides and what the wall was for. I started stumbling less, found answers sooner, and best of all saved a headache. I stopped trying to see two me's from inside both.

I once wrote a novel, *The Smoldering Sea.* It was about a guy who got cashiered out of the navy for wrecking his ship, then he took command of a freighter during the war, but he couldn't get rid of the idea of being in the navy so he used that freighter to attack some Japanese destroyers. He didn't get through the wall. He didn't even come close to it.

I got to thinking about that captain because when you write a novel you wind up on pretty intimate terms with the main character, and I was wondering why he never asked himself what that freighter was for. He saw them put cargo in it. He walked around it and saw it didn't have any guns to speak of. When he was on the bridge, he asked for top speed and got eight knots. He saw those merchant seamen slouching around. They didn't look like gunner's mates. But when it came right down to it, he acted like that freighter was for fighting destroyers.

Thinking about old Ransel, that was his name, now gone these many years to the bottom of the Pacific, it suddenly struck me that the reason he didn't see what that freighter was for was because he didn't care what it was for. It was going to be for what he wanted it to be for, and that was that. That didn't change the freighter, but it did change where he thought the door was. He gathered full steam and charged at the door. The door turned out to be part of the wall. That ended the story. There was nobody to talk about.

HOW TO AVOID SNIPERS

There was a guy on television not long ago. He was being questioned by an interviewer who was cutting him up. He'd written a book on positive thinking, and one of the things he thought you could do with it was to keep from being shot by a sniper. The interviewer drew the obvious conclusion that John F. Kennedy must have been a negative thinker. The guy could only agree. Everyone must have been shocked to learn that our President had been so careless with his life as to think an assassin into an abandoned building and think a high powered rifle with a telescopic sight into his hands and think him into the right timing to be there and think him into the skill to hit a small moving target and think the assassin's hand steady and think his own brains blown out. Believing that, you should write a book called, *The Power of Negative Thinking*. *That's power.*

I was somewhat startled during the course of the interview to discover that this author who had learned so many new uses for positive thinking had been launched on his enterprise of writing the book through having come across another book that inspired him, one written by U. S. Andersen. Naturally that made me the same as this guy, so I was target in absentia for several minutes. Ah well, the world is full of labels, and sometimes you wind up with a few you don't fully deserve.

What this author apparently had never asked himself is what positive thinking is for. If he had, he might have gotten the rather obvious answer that positive thinking is for making you think positively. Now that you've found out what the wall's for, you can find the door. The door happens to be that when you think positively you begin to try to get something done. This has a beneficial effect on the outcome of most enterprises. But in my experience it is no protection against snipers.

You turn adversity into achievement by knowing where you're going and what steps will take you there, by generating the steam to get the job done, and by knowing that when you've run into adversity you've run into a wall. To get through a wall, you look for a door. To find the door, you ask what the wall's for.

·14· HOW TO MAKE YOURSELF INTO AN OPPORTUNITY MAGNET

A GREAT DEAL of my experience has been with people who think they are magnets. One guy I knew was so hipped on the idea that he sat around in an armchair for forty years, trying to attract a million bucks. Though there were often reports of money moving mysteriously, none of it made its way in his direction. He did accomplish one thing, however. He became very good at crossword puzzles. I once asked him how he accounted for that. He said he guessed it was because he'd done so many. I didn't say a word for fully five minutes, just stared at him. But it still didn't dawn on him. He went right on trying to attract money.

HOW TO LOOK INTO AN OPPORTUNITY SACK

Funny thing is, people really are magnets, only they don't attract things, they attract people. In order to attract people, however, it is necessary to leave your room. Once you get the hang of that, the rest is easy. You just can't avoid running into them. They seem to be everywhere. Even a magnet made out of metal can't attract any metal that's out of its range. It has to get close enough to exert some influence. Same thing applies to magnets made out of people. They have to get close enough to other people to exert some influence. Once you exert some influence on a few people, you learn a surprising thing. It is they who have money. All you have to do is part them from some of it, and you've turned into a magnet that attracts money.

About this same time, you'll learn something further. People have other things too. They have opportunities, for example. They carry sacks of opportunities, and all you have to do is ask if you can look. They'll open their sacks in a flash. They'll lay their opportunities out on the ground and tell you their names and all of their virtues. They'll ask you to feel them and smell them and weigh them and count them and measure them and look at them through glasses. If you aren't wearing any of your own, they'll give you a pair . . . rose colored.

If you go around asking people if you can look in their opportunity sacks, you'll make an interesting discovery. There are plenty of opportunities. In fact, it may even occur to you that there are too many. They may simply bewilder you. You'd like to take them all, but you don't know which ones. There's a key to that too. It's learning how to attract the people who have the best opportunities. You can tell them easily. They're the best people. Once you've learned to get out of the house and get your magnet within range of people, all you have to do is set it to attract the best people. Then you've become an opportunity magnet.

HOW TO SPREAD SUNSHINE AND CHOLERA

One company called me in to find out if I could help about accidents. Their insurance rates were skyrocketing because they carried on the payroll a few people who caused disasters. Here's a guy walking over a nice dry floor in an air-conditioned room, music piped in to make everything lovely, walls all soundproofed to keep out the noise, safety guards over all the machinery, fire extinguishers propped up in all the corners, even patrolmen patrolling to protect everyone from disaster. He hiccups and sticks his hand in a lathe. The hand comes out in the shape of a cam. This surprises him so much that his cigarette drops from his mouth. It catches his clothes on fire. This flaming torch runs around the room waving a hand that looks like a cam. He catches other people on fire, even some of the machinery. The patrolmen try to put out these blazing objects. They catch fire too. Everybody runs around catching everything on fire. It gets hotter and hotter and noisier and noisier. When the music stops, there's nothing but ashes.

This kind of thing can make a company's insurance rates go up. If it happens several times, they just have to forget insurance. Since everybody likes somebody else to take the risk, companies like to keep their insurance. Therefore they like to get rid of guys who stick their hands in lathes and set buildings on fire.

It's not hard to spot disaster-prone people. One accident is an accident. Two accidents is a coincidence. Three accidents is no accident.

And the guy with three accidents is job hunting again. He'll have three accidents there too, and move on once more, happily spreading sunshine and cholera. If you ask him how things are going, he says he's having bad luck. That's usually apparent. He's so swathed in bandages you couldn't tell him from a mummy.

Spotting disaster prone people is an accurate science. Only trouble is, it exercises its judgment after people have accidents. That makes it useless to the people who have them and not very helpful to the people who want to stop them, since you have to have three of them before they can act.

WHY TO FIRE A FOREMAN

So here we are in this guy's office and he tells me his problem. All the accidents are in one department. It's got so many safety devices, it looks like a rescue ship. He pulls out some papers all covered with figures. Now he's going to recite disasters. I say, "Fire the foreman." But he's right in the middle of his statistics, so he doesn't hear me. I say a little louder, "Fire the foreman." Now he looks up and thinks I'm mad at the foreman. He doesn't want me to be mad because he likes the foreman. I say, "He's causing the accidents." He goes back to his statistics and reports that the foreman has never had an accident. I point out that I didn't say he did, I just said he caused them. He goes back to more statistics and reports that the foreman has the highest marks in safety inspection. I say that's nice, but he's still causing the accidents. Finally the master of statistics thinks to ask, "How?" and I say, "By attracting the people who have accidents." He still can't believe it, but anything is worth a try, so he gives the foreman six months vacation and brings in another guy and lets him hire his own crew. This guy happens to get very poor marks in safety inspection. But his department has no accidents. He just attracts people who don't have any.

You can cure people of being accident prone too. You just have to teach them to match their symbols to the things they keep walking into. This requires more time and most companies won't stand for it. It's easier and cheaper to fire the foreman. But the foreman himself can be taught not to hire accident prone people, just by teaching him to match his symbols to people. Nothing magic about it. We look through our symbols. If our symbols are poor, we can't see what we look at. We stick our hand in the lathe and it comes out a cam. Or we hire people who do because we think that they won't.

HOW TO LEARN ABOUT DOGS WITHOUT BEING BITTEN

People attract certain kinds of people, and the people they attract give them the opportunities they get. I first got to noticing this by observing dogs. I had a place on the Oregon coast with an extensive dog population, and when I wandered outside I had to fight my way through them. I don't know where they came from, but it wasn't from people. There was nobody around for fifteen miles. I suspected it might be because it rained cats and dogs, but I never ran into any cats.

Anyway, we'd all frolic down to the beach together, me in the midst of a hundred and fifty canines. There were terriers and shepherds and collies and spaniels and dachshunds and beagles and bassets and Danes. They jumped over me and past me and under my legs. They licked me and sniffed me and some other things too. They bayed and whined and barked and growled. The noise was deafening. I finally decided I'd select a few friends and tell the rest to cut out. First I decided on the kind of dog I wanted to be friends with. Then I decided on a method of selection. Then I went into action. I threw rocks at all of them.

By the time I exhausted my ammunition, there were only two left. They looked like Mutt and Jeff. One was a dachshund that looked like a salami. The other was a Doberman that looked like the Hound of the Baskervilles. But they had one thing in common. I didn't scare them.

I guess you could say we became friends. They'd pick me up at the house every morning and we'd walk on the beach and chat about things, especially about the other dogs skulking in the distance. I'd make a remark about some little group, and the Doberman would report, "That's the bunch that likes to play." Then the dachshund would point out the bunch that liked to whine, and the Doberman would point out the bunch that liked to eat, and the dachshund would point out the bunch that liked to bark, and the Doberman would point out the bunch that liked to sleep, and the dachshund would point out the bunch that liked to tremble. These all had their tails pointed down. I learned a lot from the Doberman and dachshund. We never loved each other or anything like that. We just sort of respected each other. It's possible I may have respected the Doberman more than he respected me. He had teeth like daggers.

HOW TO FIND LINES THAT ARE CLICKS

When I finally lit out for the city, I made for a physics laboratory. I had a theory I wanted to investigate. What got me started on it was the dogs hanging around in bunches. None of them could get out of his bunch. One dog might be with the whiners and want to be a barker, but if he started to bark, he only got in trouble with the whiners. I thought I remembered that magnetism held things in bunches, and I got to thinking that maybe these dogs were held in their bunches by some kind of magnet.

The guy I talked to wore glasses that were held on his nose by a clip. I told him I'd like to see some iron filings thrown on a magnetic plate. He got out a plate, shot the juice to it, and tossed on the iron filings. Sure enough, they congregated in bunches. I pointed out to him that they were just like dogs. He didn't quite follow me, so I explained more carefully. "These are the whiners," I said. I pointed them out. "These are the barkers. Here are the growlers. Here are the tremblers. They congregate in bunches." He took his glasses off and rubbed them, then clipped them back on his nose. He looked at the plate carefully.

I asked him to turn off the magnetism and throw the filings back on the plate. He did. None of the filings congregated in bunches. That got me pretty excited, because I could see that it proved my theory. I grabbed the guy by the lapels and told him about it. "Whiners aren't whiners, they're held together by magnets!" I shouted. His glasses came undipped and fell on the floor. He tried to reach for them, but I wanted his attention. "Barkers aren't barkers!" I yelled. "They're magnets too!" He sagged a little, and I couldn't hold him, so I let him go after his glasses. Next thing was to get a magnetometer and test this on people. The minute I got out the door, I heard the lock click behind me.

I guess they closed early.

I rented a magnetometer. It was about the size of an adding machine, but didn't look like much. The man said it made clicks when you walked over magnetic lines. I asked him if you could see the lines. He said no, you just had to listen to the clicks. I asked him what was the use in having lines if you couldn't see them, why not just call them clicks? He insisted they were lines, and I couldn't change him, so I set off looking for lines that were clicks.

HOW TO HIDE BEHIND A DRAPE

This friend of mine was having a party, and I brought my magnetometer. I had a hard time getting it into the house because he took a dim view of my intentions. He could hear it clicking and insisted it was some kind of bomb. He made me take it back out to the car, but after the party got going real well, I sneaked out and brought it in through a side window.

Everybody was standing around in bunches, just like dogs and iron filings. There were barkers and growlers and whiners and tremblers. I thought if I could just get one of the whiners over with barkers and watch what happened to the clicks, I'd be able to tell why the barkers didn't like him. That would give me some clue about changing his magnets. I had to keep my magnetometer out of sight, so I decided I'd move around behind the drapes. There was a big drapery along one wall, and I could see that the barkers were standing at one end of it and the whiners at the other. It was a pretty nifty setup, and I was quick to take advantage of it.

First I checked the whiners. I got little clicks, very slow. Then I edged along behind the drapery toward the barkers. I bumped into a woman who was a growler, but when she saw I was just a drapery, she growled at a guy with her. When he didn't growl back, I thought of stopping for a minute. He must have been a trembler in with the growlers. But I had no means of checking this so I went ahead with my plan.

The barkers were barking about the same thing the whiners had been whining about, which was lucky for me because I got a good test. The clicks were big, very fast. Now all I had to do was get a whiner to mix with the barkers. Then if I got a little slow click in with the big fast ones I'd know that all I had to do to make a whiner into a barker was to give him a big fast click. I started edging back behind the drape after a whiner and bumped into the same woman again. This time she didn't sound like a growler, she sounded like a trembler. She whispered, "I think there's somebody behind the drape." Nobody answered. She must have been with a sleeper.

HOW TO GIVE A WHINER BIGGER CLICKS

When I got back to the whiners, there was a guy with horned rimmed glasses leaning against the drape, so I pulled him inside and told him I was conducting an experiment. He didn't even look at me, he just looked at the magnetometer, and his glasses fogged up and he began to sweat a lot. I dragged him back along the inside of the drape, and when we got to the place where the woman was, I heard her whisper, "There he is again," and somebody hit the guy with the horned rimmed glasses over the head, right through the drape. That rendered him unconscious, so I continued without him.

By the time I got back to the barkers, there was only one left. All the rest were down barking at the unconscious whiner. I came out from behind the drape and handed the magnetometer to the barker and told him to follow me. He started right off barking, so I had to drag him with me. I got him down there alongside the unconscious whiner, and sure enough, there were little slow clicks mixed with the big fast ones. Now all I had to do was figure out how to give the whiner a big fast click. I didn't have to wait long.

He opened his eyes and felt his head, then he caught sight of the magnetometer, then he looked up into the face of the barker who was holding it, then he got mad and the little slow clicks disappeared. He began to make bigger clicks than the barker. He got up and hit the barker. I had to catch the magnetometer. Then the barker began making bigger clicks too. They both began hitting each other, back and forth, making bigger clicks all the time. The clicks got so big that the magnetometer began to smoke. Somebody hollered, "Bomb!" and everybody left except the barker and the whiner and me and the magnetometer.

After the barker and the whiner got exhausted, I put them in chairs and handed each a drink. They introduced themselves and discovered they were from the same home town. The barker invited the whiner to play a game of golf. When they left together, they were making the same size clicks. The whiner joined the barker's club and became a barker too. But I lost my magnetometer. Somebody put it in the bathtub and covered it with water. It cost me two hundred bucks to learn how to give a whiner bigger clicks. Naturally I wrote a speech about it, so I wound up making a profit.

HOW TO BECOME A MILLIONAIRE

You may get the idea that I'm a little long on research. It's because people don't understand symbols, they only understand things. I once had a guy try for three days to climb a greased flagpole. He ruined forty dollars' worth of clothes and never got off the ground. I let him sleep while I took the grease off the flagpole. When he woke up, I talked him into trying again. He went right up to the top, and I asked him how he made it. He said it was because I'd taken the grease off the flagpole. Then I asked him if he'd been using grease to climb higher in his business. He rubbed the grease off his talk, and now he's made it to the top.

If you talk greasy, you wind up running around with greasy people, and you can't get out of the bunch. People are magnets for people. Greasy people have greasy opportunities. They slip right through your fingers.

In order to become an opportunity magnet, you first have to find people who have the kind of opportunity you want. Then you have to measure their clicks. Then you have to click like they do. That makes you one of the bunch. They open their opportunity bags and offer you your choice.

I've been pretty successful at changing people's clicks. I once had a guy in a training program who crabbed all the time about not making enough money. He hung around with the clerks, and as you might have guessed, he was a clerk. I explained that you had to click like a millionaire in order to get to be one. He got the idea right off and went down to Palm Springs and hired a Rolls Royce. That's really clicking. He drove the Rolls Royce out to a ritzy golf club. They wanted to know who he was. He showed them the Rolls Royce. They put him in a golf game with several other people who owned Rolls Royce's. The Rolls Royce bunch played for five hundred dollars a side.

The clerk won three thousand dollars. He was a scratch golfer, and the Rolls Royce bunch played pretty bad golf.

That kept him around Palm Springs for some time. He kept putting the money he won from the Rolls Royce bunch into the opportunities of the Rolls Royce bunch. They were fine opportunities. Now he takes care of his oil wells and real estate during the week and only plays golf on Sundays.

SOME OPPORTUNITIES OFFERED BY BUNCHES

I've seen several people given smaller clicks, but am happy to report I had nothing to do with it. Usually people are given smaller clicks by their wives. Wives make a specialty of handing out smaller clicks. I heard of a guy whose clicks got so small that even the whiners wouldn't have him. He finally found a bunch called the escapers. Their opportunities weren't so hot, but he selected one called How to Buy a Bottle of Wine for Twenty Nine Cents. They finally had to open him up to find out what was wrong. Now he has a very small liver. Another escaper tried a different opportunity. This one was called How to Get High by Mainlining Heroin. Now people find employment scraping him off walls. He's also incoherent. He's got his own bunch, but is always babbling about finding a new connection.

I was acquainted with a guy who thought you could get along better if you didn't have any clicks. Then nobody would notice you, and you could sneak into the bunch. He thought the best way to do this was to love everybody. He had a credential that qualified him. It said he was a psychologist. He came down to the Oregon coast when I had all those dogs, and went outside to pet them. They almost tore his leg off. But this psychologist was challenged. He was determined to love those dogs. He'd walk outside in the morning with his arms open to embrace them, and five seconds later he'd disappear under a snarling heap. I'd run out and rescue him and get him bandaged up and try to talk him into throwing rocks at the dogs, but he wouldn't listen, he wanted to love them. It got so bad that I finally had to send him back to practicing on people. The dogs wouldn't eat. They liked the taste of psychologist.

HOW TO LOVE PEOPLE WITHOUT EVEN HALF KILLING THEM

Later on, I got him to clicking. I invited him to a meeting to hear what people had to say about psychologists. He came right over and seemed very interested. People started saying they didn't like psychologists, which must have surprised him, since he loved them so much. But he didn't let on he was a psychologist, he just sat there and loved them. After awhile I thought I smelled something burning and got up to investigate. When I got back, I discovered it was the psychologist. I thought of calling the fire department. He was jumping up and down and waving his arms, and fire was coming out of his nose. Like a tall blowtorch. I forgot the fire department and sat down and marveled. Now that he was finally burned up, it looked as if he'd make it to ashes.

He made a speech about how smart he was. He knew how the world was run, who made it, why it was made, and what it was. To get as smart as he was, you had to love everybody. He kept waving his arms and jumping up and down, and fire kept coming out of his nose. Then he lost his balance and stumbled over an onlooker. They immediately began swinging at each other. The psychologist had his nose fire put out by a sudden rush of what looked like his blood.

After that, he calmed down, and I led him to the bathroom and wiped off his blood. He told me that he wanted to go home. I hated to lose him. Now that we'd got his bloody nose stopped, I thought we could relight its fire. He told me he hated me. I told him he'd feel differently in the morning. He insisted he wouldn't and would hate me forever. I put him in the car and watched him depart. He ran into a telephone pole and spent the night in a hospital. Altogether, I'm not sure he enjoyed himself. Later on, he sent runners with messages. They said he forgave me and still loved me. So I guess he got back in the rut.

I'd always been curious why people who loved everybody seldom ran around in a bunch. Mostly, I'd find them alone, loving everybody. This seemed to defy the law of magnets. People should collect people like them. But as I got to thinking of the psychologist jumping up and down and waving his arms and getting in a fist fight, I could see that he really wasn't a people lover, he was just a growler who didn't know it. That's why he couldn't find his bunch. With this new clue, I started out to get people-lovers back in their bunch.

HOW TO GET PEOPLE-LOVERS BACK IN THEIR BUNCH

Right off I discovered that people lovers never knew the bunch they belonged to. Some were growlers, others whiners, some barkers, some players, others sleepers, some eaters, but most of all, they were tremblers. This last point raised a problem in ethics. Should I lead a people-lover back to his bunch even if that bunch turned out to be tremblers? I consulted Mammon about ethics. I asked a guy if he would pay me to make tremblers out of people-lovers. He said no. After that, I never led people-lovers back to their bunch unless it was growlers or barkers.

I also made a study of opportunities, so I could point out the bunch that had the best ones. The results were conclusive. The only bunches that had good opportunities were the growlers and barkers. None of the rest had any good ones at all. The whiners and tremblers didn't even carry bags. This simplified my work considerably. To become an opportunity magnet, you had to become a barker or growler. That got you in with the right bunch. Then you could dip into their opportunity bags.

I once wrote a novel called *Hard and Fast.* It was about a private detective who couldn't solve murders. He learned things like fingerprinting and how to follow people, then he would politely ask if they did it. They said no. He could never get the right answer. He tried to learn how the cops got the right answer, but they wouldn't let him into the bunch. But he noticed they barked and growled. He decided to bark and growl too. The cops let him into the bunch, and he began to solve murders by approaching people differently. He just growled out that they did it, and some of them began saying yes.

I had trouble with one guy who said he was a people lover. He ran a big business and had me mixed up because I thought you couldn't run a big business and be a people lover. I never was so happy in my life when I found out he was really a growler and had just been pretending. He used to amuse himself with such pastimes as moving matches by mind power. He'd get some matches floating in a goldfish bowl and gather some people around it. Then he'd tell everybody to concentrate and move the matches by mind power. That would show they were brothers and ought to love each other. He had carbide on the heads of the matches, and the water made it smolder, and the matches began to move. Everybody was convinced they were brothers and ought to love each other.

That allowed him to kick them around. That's how he built his business.

HOW TO DRINK BEER AND EAT A LITTLE CHICKEN

I probably never would have gotten wise if he hadn't invited me to dinner. He started bragging about how he never ate meat because he wouldn't hurt a fly. I must say he served up a lousy dinner. It looked like somebody had already eaten it. There were little globules all pasted together in the same consistency as I'd sometimes seen on a bathroom floor. I didn't eat much and neither did he. He talked about how wonderful it was to be a vegetarian. I stared at the globules. When he finally left to go to the kitchen, I wolfed down thirty-seven crackers in rapid succession. After that, there was nothing left but the globules, so I decided to see what was taking him so long. I eased open the kitchen door, and there he was, attacking a chicken leg. He reminded me of the Doberman. I could hear the bones crunch.

He knew he'd been discovered, but he didn't miss a bite. He just pointed to the refrigerator and said, "Help yourself." I got out some chicken legs and opened up a beer. He opened a beer too, and we really enjoyed ourselves. But I pointed out that we were enemies. He was trying to keep people asleep, and I was trying to wake them up. He said that was true, but it shouldn't keep us from having an occasional beer and eating a little chicken together.

I once ran a training program for a finance company. They help people spend money by giving it to them when they haven't got it and trying to get it back afterwards. This requires two different bunches. A bunch of barkers to give it away, and a bunch of growlers to get it back. You have to be careful in picking both. If you happen to hire a barker who turns out to be a whiner, he gives money to whiners, then the growlers have trouble getting it back. And if you happen to hire a growler who turns out to be a trembler, you're in real trouble. He never gets any money back at all. They'd already put their finger on the whiners and tremblers, and all they wanted me to do was to make them barkers and growlers. They gave me two days. God got seven, and had one day to rest.

THE TROJAN HORSE CAPER

Emergency measures were in order, so I tried nitroglycerine. I told the whiners and tremblers that they were all fired. That started them whining and trembling. Then I told them a lot of nasty things the boss had said about them. They whined and trembled ever more. Then I told them that the boss had spread the word that they weren't to be hired by anybody else. They were locked out. Now they were really whining and trembling. Then I told them the story about the city of Troy and how some guys who were locked out got inside with a horse. That quieted them a bit. I told them that I thought that with a little organization they could get back in with a horse too. They stopped whining and trembling and wanted to know how. I said all they had to do was put a horse in the boss's office. Nobody seemed to understand, so I had to explain. I said the boss was mad at them because they didn't solve problems. All they had to do was show him they could solve problems, and he'd hire them right back. I said the boss knew about the Trojan horse. He knew that was the biggest bit of problem solving anybody had ever pulled off. Once they'd put a horse in his office, he'd know they knew how to solve problems. That would make him happy to hire them back.

I had to repeat this line of reasoning and point out its merits a few times, but it was finally decided to adopt it. Anything was better than being locked out of the city. I found a horse that had seen better days and prepared him for promotion to the boss's office. Everybody got busy and lettered signs which they hung all over him. They said, TROJAN HORSE. Nobody wanted to take a chance on the boss missing the point. Now came the problem of timing. I suggested that the best thing to do would be to sneak the horse into the boss's office right after he went home. Then when he came back in the morning, he'd have a big surprise. Somebody thought that we ought to take the horse in when the boss was there, but I said no if you really wanted to impress somebody you had to surprise him. So it was decided to take the horse into the boss's office right after he left for home.

As soon as we got the horse in the building, we started running into problems. He didn't like it. He kept jumping around, and his hooves would slip on the tile, and he finally fell down. Nobody could pick him up. We just had to wait until he felt like it. Then we couldn't get him in the elevator. Everything would go in except the part that held his tail. We pushed on that, but the horse began kicking, so we decided we'd have to take him up the stairs. I've never seen such a lousy stair climber. It took us an hour and thirty minutes to get him up three flights, and by then everybody was pretty well exhausted, including the horse. But it was nicer in the boss's office.

It had deep rugs and soft-looking furniture and carried a nice feeling. The horse liked it too. He lay down on the floor and started taking a nap. That started some comment about how he wouldn't look very much like a Trojan horse if the boss came in and found him sleeping like that. I said not to worry, the horse was just tired because he was hungry. After he'd had something to eat and drink, he'd feel better. That set everybody scurrying around for alfalfa and water and pails. We set everything up right by the horse so he'd be sure to eat and drink as soon as he woke up. Then we all left and turned out the lights so the horse wouldn't be disturbed.

A HORSE OF A DIFFERENT COLOR

I got down to the office early the next morning and started hanging around waiting for the boss. The whiners and tremblers showed up too, and I instructed them that when the boss found the horse, we were all to yell, "Surprise!" They were all excited and looked forward to yelling it.

The boss came in with a cheery hello and went immediately to the door of his office. When he opened it, he was struck by a very strong odor. He glanced around for the source. What he saw was the horse. He rubbed his eyes and choked a little. My eyes were watering, and I was choking too. The odor was real strong.

The boss turned around and looked at us thoughtfully. "There's a horse in my office," he said. Everybody yelled, "Surprise!"

" There's a horse in my office!" shouted the boss. Everybody yelled, "Surprise!"

The boss roared, "There's a horse in my office!" Everybody shouted, "Surprise!"

There was a whiner standing next to him, and the boss knocked him down. Then he knocked down a trembler. Then he knocked down another whiner. Then a trembler. He was knocking them over like pins in an alley. By the time he had a dozen on the floor, the first one got to his feet and jumped on the boss's back, hollering, "Giddap!" This caused the boss to buck around like a horse. An-other whiner jumped on. This prompted a trembler to join the fun. So many people began jumping on the boss's back that the boss couldn't carry them. He went down under the whiners and tremblers who strangely enough were acting like players. I never did get to see how it all came out. I decided to talk to the boss later.

He never would pay me. Most of his whiners and tremblers became barkers and growlers, but he said that I'd gone too far. Maybe so, but what can you expect when you ask a man to do seven days work in two?

People are magnets that attract other people. That clusters them in bunches. The bunches who have the best opportunities are the barkers and growlers. To get into those bunches you have to bark and growl too. Then they open their opportunity bags and let you dig in. That's how to make of yourself an opportunity magnet.

·15· HOW TO USE A GREAT SECRET THAT BRINGS LASTING HAPPINESS

IF YOU PUT a rat in front of some tunnels and a piece of cheese at the end of one, the rat will search all the tunnels until he finds the piece of cheese. After that, he'd go down the right tunnel. If he keeps finding the cheese, he'll keep going down that tunnel. But if it stops being there, he'll try the other tunnels again. That's where rats have it over people. People will keep going down the same tunnel whether the cheese is there or not.

HOW TO FIND CHEESE IN A TUNNEL

This doesn't necessarily make rats smarter than people. It just makes them better at finding cheese. People are interested in other things. Whether the particular tunnel where the cheese is supposed to be is *good* or *bad*, for example. This gives them a chance to write books about ethics. Then they're also interested in how the tunnel got there. This gives them a chance to write books about philosophy. Then they're also interested in making the cheese move up the tunnel to them. This gives them the chance to write books about religion. Then they're also interested in pretending that the cheese is in the tunnel that doesn't have any cheese. This gives them the chance to write books about psychology.

All this makes people very poor cheese finders. Some of them starve to death happily because they'd rather have the tunnel than they would have the cheese. If you begin to feel sorry for them and try to point out that the cheese is in another tunnel, you'll find out what keeps them in the tunnel where they are. They make reasons.

I've never met a man who didn't have his reasons. Here's a guy pouring some kerosene on a building. He strikes a match to it, and when the people run out he mows them down with a machine gun. Ask him why he did this and he says he wants to make the world a better place to live in. It just never dawns on him that that kind of activity continued indefinitely would produce a world without anybody to live in it.

What keeps things so simple for the rat is that he doesn't make reasons. The cheese is either there or it isn't. If it is, he nibbles it happily. If it isn't, he looks someplace else. People say that rats are stupid, that they'll go after cheese even if it's in a trap. I must point out that people sometimes do this too. What's worse, they stay in tunnels even when there is no cheese. More than that, the reasons they give you for not finding cheese and staying in tunnels and getting caught in occasional traps are all sound, sane, and logical.

The rat has an efficient nervous system because he keeps doing only the things that work. The human being has an inefficient nervous system because he keeps on doing what doesn't work. He keeps on doing what doesn't work because of his imagination. It gives him reasons. He tells those reasons to other people. They become laws. Then it becomes mandatory for people to go around doing what doesn't work. This has been known to produce considerable frustration. It also gives rise to a number of buildings to house the people who can't stand it, like hospitals and insane asylums.

People love their reasons. Their reasons make them feel smarter than a rat. They sit around and talk about their reasons all day. It never dawns on them that reasons are excuses. The cheese is either there or it isn't. If it isn't, you have to look in a different tunnel.

HOW TO SIT UNDER A BO TREE

Here's a guy looking for cheese in a tunnel. He can't find it so he imagines a reason: Cheese can't be found. If he gets a report that somebody else found it, he imagines another reason: He himself isn't capable of finding it. Now that he has these good reasons, he sits down and starves. You can see that imagination is not always so handy.

Yet people multiply faster than rats, so imagination must have survival value. In order to discover this, you have to see it used by somebody who finds cheese. When the rat starts looking, he picks just any old tunnel. The guy using his imagination picks the one that looks best. If the cheese isn't in any of the tunnels, the rat just starts over. The guy using his imagination starts wondering where else it might be. The end result is that he finds more cheese than the rat, and bigger and better cheese too, and pretty soon he can even build a trap to snuff out the rat. This guy has kept his mind on the cheese and not on the tunnel. He's kept his mind on how he can find cheese instead of on why he can't. He's used his imagination as a tool to get something done. This makes him not only king of the cheese finders, but the master of all those who are caught in the tunnel.

The key to Cybernetics Success-Training is to keep your mind on the cheese. That disciplines the imagination to work for you instead of against you. That trains the success mechanism into your nervous system. That keeps you matching your symbols to things and making better symbols so you can handle things better. But everything begins with the imagination. You just have to keep thinking about finding that cheese.

I had a guy in a training program who wanted to find himself. I led him over to a mirror and pointed. "There you are," I said. He said that's not what he meant, he wanted to find his real self. I asked him what made him think he had any other self than the one who looked back at him from the mirror. He said Buddha said so. I asked him what Buddha did. He said Buddha sat around under a Bo tree. I asked him if he wanted to sit around under a Bo tree. He said of course not, he wanted to sell insurance. Then I told him not to pay any attention to what Buddha said, just to what he did. He sat around under Bo trees. The rest was his reasons.

I seldom persuade people by such demonstrations because most everybody thinks there's something more than results. Time after time some guy comes around and starts giving me his reasons. I cut him right off and say, "Don't give me your reasons, tell me what happened." What happened was that he missed the target. "Okay," I say. "Aim different next time." He just can't believe that settles it. He still wants to give his reasons. He's thought about them and thought about them, and they would make a book. I know that. I don't want to read books about reasons. I want to read books about what happened.

HOW TO FIND YOURSELF IN CASE YOU GET LOST

People who have to make reasons let their imaginations run away with them. They forget about the cheese and concentrate on reasons. They keep finding more reasons. Pretty soon there seems to be nothing but reasons. They don't even remember that there used to be cheese.

There was an old Chinese guy who got fed up and decided to leave the country. He never talked much, so everybody got to thinking that he knew more than he said. When he tried to cross the border, they wouldn't let him pass until he wrote a book about all the things he knew. This was a pretty tough job for a guy who'd learned only a half dozen things in his lifetime, but he wanted to get out of the country, so he settled himself down to his task. He put down the half dozen things he knew and padded the space between them to give the book some length. Still, he could only manage twenty-five pages which read like this: "When people are hard to govern, it's because they're full of fight. Hobldygook, horanung, matsercall swent. If someone sticks his finger in your eye, you'll find he's not a friend. Piff, tiffle, gooligan, prend."

The guards took the little book and let the old guy through, then they settled down for some reading. They immediately discerned that some parts were very profound. But they couldn't figure out the meaning of these parts, so they took the little book to a philosopher who wrote a long book explaining the meaning of the parts that had no meaning. Since this also was difficult to understand, other philosophers wrote long books explaining the meaning of the long book which explained the meaning of the parts that had no meaning. Then a lot of people began writing explanations explaining the explanations of the parts that had no meaning.

It turned out that there was a wonderful valley hidden away somewhere and anybody who managed to get into it would live forever. In this valley was a lake, and anybody who bathed in it would stay young forever. Everybody went on describing where the valley was and what the lake looked like, but nobody could find it, and the little book of twenty five pages grew longer than a library. It became known as Tao, which is Chinese for How to Find Yourself in Case You Get Lost. That's what Buddha was doing when he was sitting under the Bo tree. He and the old guy started a lot of people doing it. It makes a handy reason for not doing anything, which seems a popular pastime. But up to now, it's never found anything that wasn't here in the first place.

HOW TO SELL A MODEL T THAT HAS A MAGNETO

I've never seen anybody sitting around who was happy. Most people are happy when they're busy doing something that makes them forget themselves. That makes them aware. When you feel aware, you feel lucky to be alive and are pretty happy about things. When you sit around doing nothing, you begin to feel numb, and life doesn't seem such a bargain. That makes you start thinking about what it's like to be dead. Then you start hoping there's a little valley where you can live forever. What do you want to live forever for, when you're tired of it already?

Anybody can be happy, and he can be happy his whole life. It depends how you look at it.

There used to be a wheeler-dealer in the automobile business in St. Johns. In those days, the cars weren't so hot, but he'd line up the Model T's on the sidewalk and collect a crowd, and he could really sell cars. One day he ran into a guy who gave him a special problem. It was about the magneto. You started the Model T on the battery, but after it was going, you could run it on the magneto. The guy was worried about that. It gave him something to think about, so naturally he didn't like it. He wanted to buy a car without a magneto. That would show it had a good battery. This kind of reasoning might exasperate a lot of people, but not the wheeler-dealer. That's why he was a wheeler-dealer. He said that the magneto was there only as a decoration and just to forget it. That didn't satisfy the guy because he couldn't imagine anybody putting a magneto in a car just for decoration. The wheeler-dealer said, "It depends how you look at it." Then he asked the guy if men had babies. The guy was quick there. He said no. Then the wheeler-dealer asked the guy if there was anything about men that might make him think they ever would have babies. The guy thought about that for awhile and then he said he couldn't think of a thing. "Aha!" cried the wheeler-dealer. "They have nipples on their breasts! It depends how you look at it!" He sold a Model T that had a magneto.

HOW TO MAKE LIFE A GAME

Everything depends how you look at it. That's what makes you feel what you feel and do what you do. You can't feel unhappy when your symbols are happy. To become happy, all you have to do is make happy symbols. You can't feel unhappy when you think of something happy. You can't feel happy when you think of something sad. When you make happy symbols, you make lasting happiness.

It may occur to you that you can make yourself happy without getting anything done. You can sit under a Bo tree and make believe you're in a valley where you will live forever and everything is sweetness and light. To an onlooker, you may look like a bum, but you're in your little valley and you are completely happy. Your happiness could be destroyed, of course. A coconut could fall off the tree and hit you in the head. In that case you might start complaining that something nasty is destroying your happiness. If you complain long enough, they'll take you away and put you in a place where nothing can hurt you. Then you can be real happy. For people whose only aim in life is happiness, I recommend this procedure. You won't even have to feed yourself.

Anybody can be happy. He can be happy his whole life. He just has to concentrate on the things that make him happy. It's simple. Anybody can do it. You don't even have to be able to tie your shoe to do it.

But for people who want to get things done and be happy too, the problem becomes more complex. If they don't happen to get things done, they tend to become unhappy. Since it looks as if the world is causing their unhappiness, they feel they can't become happy. They become easy marks for people who sell distant valleys with magic lakes where everybody is ecstatic. They trade in the idea of getting things done for the idea of being happy, someday, maybe.

When you get things done, you're happy—anybody knows that. But there's also a way to be trying to get things done and not doing so well and be happy despite it. That's to make life a game, a crazy, hilarious, exciting, fun-provoking game, played by strange bipeds who are still learning the rules. You pay two bucks to go to a theatre and laugh at a comedy. Save your money. You don't have to go to the theatre, just look around you. It's the comedy-drama of all time. The belly laughs are enormous. And you're one of the clowns. Just don't forget that. When you can laugh as hard at yourself as at anybody else, you're happy.

HOW TO CLIMB THE GOLDEN GATE BRIDGE

I once wrote a book that ended with the statement that each man is God. Five hundred years ago they would have used me for kindling, but now they managed a little chuckle. Not very big mind you and not very jolly, but still, a chuckle. So I got by with it, which was small consolation, because hardly anybody knew what I meant. I meant that each of us creates his own world. It takes us considerably longer than seven days and we don't get any days off and we never get it finished, but every stick, stone, tree, and river we put there ourselves. We put it there because it's all in our heads. It depends how you look at it.

Maybe you won't get around to putting horses in offices, but you can have fun. You can have fun by killing the spirit of seriousness. The most joyful guy I ever knew used to dive off buildings and walk away smiling. He was a fraternity brother. He used to stand on the top of the three story fraternity house and wave at the girls to get their attention, then he'd dive off the building. They'd run screaming for ambulances, and he'd pick himself out of the hedge and wait to tell how he landed on his head and it didn't bother him at all. He had fun. He played football, and he had fun with that too. One time an alumnus was buying him some drinks and telling him what a fine fellow he was for bringing glory to the old school, and when the alumnus wasn't watching, he urinated in his drink. That seemed to pep the old boy up. He got brighter and brighter. You may have noticed that's what happens to everybody who swallows that stuff.

I like to think of myself as the guy who climbed the towers of the Golden Gate Bridge. It reminds me of how to be happy. And I did too, before it was even finished. I climbed up there in the dead of the night with a buddy of mine, all the way up on a slippery cable, seven hundred feet above the water below. Nothing serious. We enjoyed it. The best part was when we got to the top where there was a platform and a guy came out of a little shack that was built on it. You know something? He looked up. He thought we came from heaven.

HOW TO GRADUATE OUT OF SEASON

There are other things too. Like the night a bunch of us held our own graduation exercises in the memorial amphitheatre. We prepared for the exercises by first mixing a batch of well-spiked punch and stirring it with a bone from a skeleton that one of the participants had stolen from the physiology lab. The rest of the skeleton we hung on the wall so he could watch. After we were well punched, we drove over to the amphitheater and ran a Model A Ford down onto the platform. Everybody climbed over the top of the Ford and got his diploma. Somebody impersonated the president and somebody the dean and the rest of us drank beer and clapped. Everybody didn't graduate however, because the cops came and said graduating was out of season. The next day, Ray Lyman Wilbur, a tall guy with a big Adam's apple, who always dressed like a funeral director and just happened to be president of Stanford, was showing some visitors around and stumbled across the Amphitheatre. There was the Model A Ford, and acres of beer cans. It didn't look very neat. I always liked the picture of that big Adam's apple moving up and down, very slowly.

There was another guy who had a lot of fun. His name was Doodles Weaver. He had a big picture of Our Savior over his bed. It was personally autographed, "To my good friend, Doodles, from J.C." Later, he made a living telling jokes, so other people could have some fun too. That's how you get to be happy.

If you look back over your own life, you'll probably notice that the times you were happiest were the times when you weren't so serious. Then it may dawn on you that the way to be happy any time at all is not to be so serious. Let me tell you how you do this. You don't look in, you look out.

The reason why people who try to find themselves are so unhappy is because they look in. They've got their eyeballs turned backward. They can have their eyeballs rolled back for thirty years and not find a thing but plenty of gloom. But that doesn't mean a thing to them. As soon as they find themselves, then they'll be happy. Meantime they stumble over the furniture and have to be led around by people who can see.

Pay no attention to you, just to what you see. Pay no attention to reasons, just to results. Pay no attention to seriousness, only to comedy. Pay no attention to any other world than the one that you're in. That's how to be happy. That's also how to get things done.

And don't give me any static about how you're searching for the meaning of life. Why do you have to have reasons for something that is? The truth of life is the fact that it exists. The truth of you is the fact that you exist. The comedy of life is trying to learn how. The drama of life is getting things done. That's meaning enough for anyone who lives. It's a hell of a show, and you're in it. And let me tell you something else. Even if there's a guy with a broad, powerful face and a white beard and glittering eyes who looks just the way Michelangelo painted him on the ceiling of the Sistine Chapel, it isn't going to be the people with their eyes rolled backward who find him. It's going to be the people with their eyes pointed where they should be. And they'll find him with spaceships or something they built. They'll find him by getting things done.

HOW TO BECOME A GERMAN SUBMARINE COMMANDER

I once sailed on a freighter with a chief engineer who knew about things other than engines. He was the only guy I could talk to because everybody else talked about reasons. He just wanted to do something. Some of the things he wanted to do took a lot of imagination. I guess that's why I liked him, he got me excited. He had the idea that if he shaved off my hair I would look like a German submarine commander. He got so obsessed with the idea that I finally let him do it. In those days, I had a little more hair, but it still wasn't much of a job. Then he stood me in front of the mirror. No question about it, I looked like a German submarine commander. That got him thinking of how he could cover himself with a little glory. He wanted to handcuff me to him and take me ashore so that everybody could see what he'd captured. I don't know how I let him talk me into it, but I guess I was feeling sorry for him. He spent all his tune down in the bottom of the ship with his engines and hardly got any credit at all. We pieced together an outfit that was half storm trooper and half burger Meister, but the bald head topped it off with splendid effect. Then we found some handcuffs and bound ourselves together and set off for the beach to impress the natives.

We happened to be in Suez, and Rommel was shooting up the other end of Egypt, so the natives weren't too friendly toward Germans. I hadn't counted on this, and after we collected a crowd, some of them began throwing rocks at me. The chief told them he had everything under control, but they weren't too sure, so they kept throwing rocks. After he got hit himself, he decided the fun was gone from it, so we ducked into the closest building. It turned out to be the Officer's Club of the British Navy. They were somewhat surprised to find a German in their midst, and several drew pistols. The chief told them that I was his prisoner and that I was an officer and a gentleman and had given my solemn word to be nice. Pistols were put away, and everyone sat down and had a few drinks.

The chief told how he had captured a German submarine singlehanded. Somebody wanted to know how he did it. He said that he'd developed a special device for capturing submarines, but he couldn't say anything about it because it was top secret. "Isn't that right, Fritz?" he asked, and dug an elbow into my ribs. I answered, "Ja." He'd coached me in German. The other word I knew was "Nein." Since I wasn't going to be talking much, I concentrated on drinking. Meantime, the chief was getting to be a hero. Everybody crowded around and everybody bought drinks. It wasn't costing us a penny. Leave it to the chief. He had good ideas.

HOW TO KNIFE AN ARAB

Pretty soon, I noticed this girl. She was sitting at a table with an Arab, and I decided to go over and talk to her. I mentioned this to the chief, but he wouldn't go. I tried to talk him into it, but he was obstinate, so I finally had to drag him over with me. Pistols came out again, but when the British Navy saw my objective, they wished they'd thought of it themselves.

It turned out that the girl was French and danced at the Chez Paris, which I gathered was a nightclub somewhere in Suez. The Arab scowled at me for several minutes, then disappeared. I sat down in his chair, and the chief sat on the floor. He kept peeking over the edge of the table pretending he was interpreting what the French girl said. All of a sudden, she began spouting German, and the cat was out of the bag. Anyway, it was nice to finally be able to talk to her, and I told her my hair would be black and curly when it grew out and asked her if she would keep our secret. She said I'd look nice with black curly hair, and she promised she wouldn't tell anybody. With that, the chief unhandcuffed me and went back to his bragging and told everybody that I'd promised not to escape.

Pretty soon, the French girl said she had to go and do her dancing, and I thought it might be a good idea if we all went and watched her, then maybe I could see her after she was finished. I got hold of the chief and mentioned this to him and he got everybody together and pretty soon we were all bouncing along toward the Chez Paris, packed in a land rover. The French girl sat on my lap, and it was hard to understand why the French and Germans were fighting all the time.

The Chez Paris was a joint. It had bare wooden floors and rickety chairs and an oil lamp hanging from the ceiling, and somebody walked around serving drinks that were poison. Four guys plunked away on some little instruments with strings. It didn't sound like music at all, more like somebody tuning a violin. The place was smoky and stank of hashish and everybody was an Arab or Hindu. But it wasn't so bad when the French girl started dancing. She wore a few beads which swished all around, and she was the color of toffee. I was really enjoying it, when suddenly an Arab ran out on the floor and tried to dance with her. Then another Arab ran out and stuck a knife in the first Arab's back. Then the lamp went out.

I lit out for the nearest exit, stumbling over bodies. When I got outside, I kept running because I thought one of those Arabs with knives might be behind me. I finally ran out of breath and stopped to listen. Not a sound. I breathed a sigh of relief and took my bearings.

HOW TO HIDE IN A SEWER

The nearest I could figure it, I was somewhere in Suez. That meant that the waterfront had to be east. I caught sight of the Big Dipper and started navigating myself back to the ship. Suddenly a bright light glared out of the darkness. "Halt!" somebody cried. I answered gaily, "It's all right. I'm an American." There was an orange flash, a loud noise, and something ugly thudded into the wall over my head. Then I remembered I was a German.

What happened next was kind of a blur, but whoever was behind that light must have had a machine gun. I started out for Germany as fast as I could, with the air full of hornets. They kept buzzing around my head and bothering my concentration. Finally, I saw what looked like a ditch and dived in. It wasn't a ditch. It was a sewer.

I didn't have time to worry about my mistake because of the thunder of approaching cavalry. I just kept my nose above the goo and stayed very still. People flashed by on horseback and in trucks and after them came several tanks. It was an impressive show of military power. The thunder rolled along the street and finally faded into the distance.

I climbed out of the sewer, slightly shaken. A warm sickening odor rose up all around me. It gave me an almost overpowering desire to get rid of myself. Well, at least there was a bright side. No one would mistake me for a German submarine commander. Not unless German submarines were patrolling some very unusual places.

I took a bath in the Suez Canal and walked back to the waterfront in my shorts. There was the chief sitting on a piling, whistling a tune. He told me I shouldn't be walking around like that, I might catch cold. Then he sniffed a little and asked me if I'd been sick or something. Just then the shore-boat came, and we climbed aboard and started back to the ship. Over the noise of the motors, he hollered that he'd taken the French girl home and she'd been very nice. I asked him what happened to the Arab with the knife. The chief explained that he'd had an accident with a chair. That chief had guts. He'd tackle a buzz saw.

It was when we were coming up alongside the ship that this thing happened I wanted to tell you about. I got off the shore-boat onto the landing of the ladder, and then the boat drifted away. There was the chief, ten feet away from the ladder, and he stepped right off the side of the boat and into the drink. He couldn't swim a stroke and went down like a rock so I went in after him. I finally dragged him back to the ship and got him pulled up on the landing of the ladder. The shore-boat left, and we just lay there together, listening to the sounds of the waves slapping against the side of the hull. Overhead, the stars were out and it was nice and quiet, about four in the morning. It was one of those times when everything seems just right, just as it should be. Finally, I asked thoughtfully, "Chief, why didn't you wait for the boat to get closer?" The chief was silent for awhile, then he said, "If you want to go somewhere, you have to take the first step."

HOW TO TAKE THE FIRST STEP

Remember the saint who said, "If you want to change, you have to change"? He and the chief would have been very good friends. Don't wait until the boat gets closer, step off right now, even if you get wet. There's a long list of tomorrows. Something to be done tomorrow never gets done. If you want to change, you have to change. You have to take the first step.

So now you've learned about Success Cybernetics. Let's review what it is so you can take the first step. Things get accomplished because of guidance and power. Guidance is provided by work habits, power by scrappy attitudes. Put them together and you have a success mechanism.

It's futile to have good work habits if you're not generating the power to get the job done. It's useless to generate power if you don't have the work habits to guide you to a target.

You develop good work habits by doing the things each day that will eventually reach your target. You develop the power to propel you by keeping your imagination centered on these attitudes: "Fight for it!" "It can be done." "I can do it." "I'll prove I can do it." "It's an exciting game." "Keep it simple." "I like me."

You train the success mechanism into your nervous system by mentally reviewing your goals and work habits, by keeping your imagination concentrated on the power-attitudes that will propel you to your target.

You develop your signal skills by training yourself to make automatic responses in performance situations.

You develop your symbol skills by playing with symbols in your mind and giving them different combinations and meanings.

You produce workable ideas by cutting them in the mind and trying them in the world.

You solve unsolvable problems by getting rid of false values that blind you to solutions.

You start people into fast action by using loaded words that hit their hot buttons.

You persuade people by demonstrating that something works.

You dynamite a success block by making a man mad.

You turn adversity into achievement by asking what the adversity is for, then finding the door that leads through it.

You attract opportunity by associating with people who have opportunities.

You achieve lasting happiness by keeping your imagination concentrated on attitudes of action and excitement, then playing life like a game, laughing at yourself and the other clowns too.